LOGICAL STRUCTURE AND LINGUISTIC STRUCTURE

Studies in Linguistics and Philosophy

Volume 40

The titles published in this series are listed at the end of this volume.

LOGICAL STRUCTURE AND
LINGUISTIC STRUCTURE

Cross-Linguistic Perspectives

Edited by

C.-T. JAMES HUANG AND ROBERT MAY

*Department of Linguistics, University of California,
Irvine, California, U.S.A.*

KLUWER ACADEMIC PUBLISHERS
DORDRECHT / BOSTON / LONDON

Library of Congress Cataloging-in-Publication Data

```
Logical structure and linguistic  structure : cross-linguistic
  perspectives / edited by C.T. James Huang, Robert May.
      p.   cm. -- (Studies in linguistics & philosophy ; v. 40)
  Includes index.
  ISBN 0-7923-0914-6 (alk. paper)
  1. Language and logic.  2. Grammar, Comparative and general.
I. Huang, C. T. James.  II. May, Robert, 1951-   . III. Series:
Studies in linguistics and philosophy ; v. 40.
P39.L597   1990
415--dc20                                                    90-5153
```

ISBN 0-7923-0914-6

Published by Kluwer Academic Publishers,
P.O. Box 17, 3300 AA Dordrecht, The Netherlands

Kluwer Academic Publishers incorporates the publishing programmes of
D. Reidel, Martinus Nijhoff, Dr W. Junk and MTP Press.

Sold and distributed in the U.S.A. and Canada
by Kluwer Academic Publishers,
101 Philip Drive, Norwell, MA 02061, U.S.A.

In all other countries, sold and distributed
by Kluwer Academic Publishers Group,
P.O. Box 322, 3300 AH Dordrecht, The Netherlands

Printed on acid-free paper

Printed in The Netherlands

TABLE OF CONTENTS

C.-T. JAMES HUANG AND ROBERT MAY

INTRODUCTION

In comparative syntax a general approach has been pursued over the past decade predicated on the notion that Universal Grammar allows of open parameters, and that part of the job of linguistic theory is to specify what values these parameters may have, and how they may be set, given primary linguistic data, to determine the grammars of particular languages. The papers presented in this volume are also concerned with language variation understood in this way. Their goals, however, do not strictly fall under the rubric of comparative syntax, but form part of what is more properly thought of as a *comparative semantics*. Semantics, in its broadest sense, is concerned with how linguistic structures are associated with their truth-conditions. A comparative semantics, therefore, is concerned with whether this association can vary from language to language, and if so, what is the cause of this variation. Taking comparative semantics in this way places certain inherent limitations on the search for the sources of variability. This is because the semantic notion of truth is universal, and does not vary from language to language: Sentences either do or do not accurately characterize what they purport to describe.[1] The source of semantic variability, therefore, must be somehow located in the way a language is structured. The structure of language which is relevant to its interpretation can be roughly broken down into two parts: Its *compositional structure*, concerned with the proper integration of argument structure, and its *logical structure*, concerned with the proper application of the truth-clauses for the logical terms. In the latter case, the application of the semantic rules which effect the association of this structure with its interpretation is based on the recognition of certain syntactic properties of their input. These properties constitute what we think of as the *logical form* of language. The nature of logical form, therefore, is an aspect of the more general syntactic structure of the language. As such, we may expect languages to vary in the class of logical forms they represent, but only as a function of the variation allowed, by Universal Grammar, in their syntactic structure. In this regard, comparative semantics forms a branch of comparative syntax.

The common thread among the papers collected in this volume is their concern with these issues in the relation between syntactic structure and logical form, as this is placed in the more general question of how syntactic structure determines semantic interpretation. Concern with this issue dates back, within the generative literature, to the early 1970's, for instance, in the work of Bach (1970), McCawley (1971) and Lakoff (1971) and others. What ties together the papers here in approaching this issue is the underlying assumption that the syntax of natural language represents logical form of incorporating a level of Logical Form (LF). Historically, this research stems from the appearance of Noam Chomsky's "Conditions on Rules of Grammar" in 1976 and Robert May's dissertation *The Grammar of Quantifiction* in 1977, and over the past decade and a half an extensive literature has emerged exploring the idea that the interface of syntax and semantics is mediated by this level. The assumptions underlying this work are now well-known: That LF is transformationally derived from S-Structure; that among these rules is QR, which leads to a representation of quantificational scope at LF; that conditions on anaphora, particularly bound variable anaphora, are defined over structural configurations at this level. Because this level is conceived as a structural interface with an interpretive component of the grammar, we can distinguish two sorts of constraints on LF, "extrinsic" and "intrinsic" (May (1991)). By extrinsic conditions, we mean those imposed by the need to recognize at this level the formal properties required for the application of semantic rules. For instance, the proper application of the semantic clauses for quantifiers requires that open sentences can be discerned from closed sentences, and this in turn requires that a syntactic notion of binding be well-defined. Focus on such extrinsic conditions will reveal the semantic side of LF; focus on intrinsic conditions will reveal its syntactic side. By intrinsic conditions, we mean those structural conditions which determine the well-formedness of representations at LF. Thus, it has been a persistent theme in research on LF that the rules mapping onto this level are transformational, and as such they are subject to well-formedness constraints generally applicable to movement rules. From this perspective, a central comparative issue which arises concerns the sensitivity of grammatical conditions, as they are applicable to LF, to language particular parameterizations. In the papers collected here this issue is broached, relative to empirical matters such as quantifier scope, question interpretation, and anaphora and variable binding, cross-linguistically in languages as diverse as

Spanish, Italian, Chinese, Japanese, Toba Batak, Navajo, Hungarian and Arabic. In doing so, their goal is to broaden our perspective on the nature of logical form in natural language, as well as our understanding of the extension of grammatical conditions and constraints.

One sort of variation that has been observed relative to LF is that languages differ in the derivations which apply in directly mapping onto this level from S-Structure. For example, languages can vary in the class of phrases subject to LF-movement. While in English this class includes some occurrences of *wh*-phrases, in other languages all occurrences of such phrases are involved. It was suggested in Huang (1982) that differences between Chinese and English are attributable to whether *wh*-movement is taken to apply in the mapping onto S-Structure, or in the mapping from S-Structure onto LF. Katalin Kiss, in her paper "Logical Structure in Syntactic Structure: The Case of Hungarian," shows that comparable variation also occurs with quantified phrases. While in English QR effects (essentially) all such phrases, in Hungarian only some are effected by LF-movement. Thus, Hungarian allows not only for the preposing of *wh*-phrases at S-Structure, but of quantifier phrases more generally. In a sense, for QR, Hungarian stands to English as English stands to Chinese for *wh*-movement: In Chinese *wh*-movement applies solely in the mapping from S-Structure to LF; in Hungarian, QR can apply in the mapping from D-Structure onto S-Structure.

In showing that QR is applicable in the mapping onto S-Structure, Kiss bases her discussion on her previous work on Hungarian syntactic structure (Kiss (1987)), in which she showed that Hungarian has three base-generated positions which can serve as the locus of preposing: COMP, a TOPIC position, which is a daughter of S and a FOCUS position, which is a daughter of VP. Thus, possible are structures such as the following:

(1)   [$_S$ János [$_{VP}$ 'Marit [$_{V'}$ kisérte *e e*]]]
        John-nom   Mary-acc   escorted home

        'As for John, it was Mary who he escorted home'

Distinguishing topicalization from focus in Hungarian, Kiss turns to the central thesis of her paper: That in Hungarian QR applies not only in the mapping from S-Structure onto LF, but also in the mapping from D-Structure to S-Structure. Structurally, Kiss argues that QR in Hungarian, which she refers to as Q-raising to distinguish it from the standard LF-based formulation, adjoins quantified phrases to VP, in a position below the TOPIC and above the FOCUS. Thus, we can have multiply quantified sentences as in (2), with the structure indicated:

(2) $[_S$ János$_i$ $[_{VP}$ többször is$_j$ $[_{VP}$ mindent$_k$
        John-*nom*   several-times   everything-*acc*

    $[_{VP}$ villàgosan $[_{VP}$ el   magyarázott e_i e_j $e_k]]]]]$
    clearly   *pref.* explained

'As for John, on several occasions he explained everything clearly'

What is of particular interest is Kiss' observation that the scope interpretation of the moved quantifiers in (2) follows their surface order. Different orderings from Q-raising give different scope orders:

(3) $[_S$ János$_i$ $[_{VP}$ mindent$_k$ $[_{VP}$ többször is$_j$ $[_{VP}$
        John-*nom*   everything-*acc*   several-times

    vilàgosan $[_{VP}$ el   magyarázott e_i e_j $e_k]]]]]$
    clearly   *pref.* explained

'As for John, everything was several times explained by him clearly'

(4) $[_S$ $[_{VP}$többször is$_j$ $[_{VP}$ mindent$_k$ $[_{VP}$ János$_i$
        several-times   everything-*acc*   John-*nom*

    $[_{VP}$ magyarázott el   vilàgosan e_i e_j $e_k]]]]]$
    explained   *pref.* clearly

'On several occasions, it was true of everything that it was John who explained it clearly'

In (3), the universal quantifier has broader scope; in (4) it has narrower scope, although (4) also differs from (3) in that 'several times' is the topic. The interest of Hungarian, therefore, is that it, so to speak, wears in logical form on its sleeve. That is, where preposing of quantifier phrases occurs overtly, then their scope order is determined by their overt order. But where quantifier phrases are moved "covertly," that is, in mapping onto LF, then scope is undetermined by overt order, as in English, for unmoved quantifier phrases in Hungarian.

An underlying assumption regarding LF is that the syntax of quantificational and non-quantificational elements is distinct at this level. This is because the former elements are subject to movement to Ā-positions, from which they bind a trace, interpreted as both a syntactic and logical variable. In turn, pronouns can be bound by such elements, and they too will be interpreted as variables, as opposed to those pronouns which are anaphoric (bound) to non-quantificational elements, with which they are coreferential. While this is a common picture, it has been an issue in discussions of anaphoric occurrences of pronouns, that is, those whose construal depends on a linguistic antecedent, whether a unified treatment is possible, either by assimilating all occurrences of pronouns to variables, or all occurrences to (co-)referring expressions.[2] The difficulty with such unifications, however, is that there appear to be systematic differences in the behavior of the two types of pronouns which indicate that the grammar must incorporate a basic distinction between coreference and bound variable anaphora. Perhaps the most often cited argument that bound variable pronouns are subject to additional conditions is weak crossover, the observation that while an anaphoric connection is perfectly possible in *His mother saw John*, it is not in *Who did his mother see* or in *His mother saw everyone*. Here, constraints are hypothesized to come into play which limit the direct local binding of a pronoun by an operator expression, constraints whose effects are masked when the pronoun binds the trace of the moved operator. Thus, in this latter case we have the strong crossover paradigm, in which *He saw John*, *Who did he see* and *He saw everyone* are anaphorically indistinguishable.[3]

Joseph Aoun and Norbert Hornstein join this issue in their paper "Bound and Referential Pronouns," arguing for distinguishing pronominal types on the basis of observations from Japanese, Chinese and English. Their statement of the issue is based on the observation that at LF the position of quantificational and non-quantificational elements is distinct. Whereas the former appear in Ā-positions, because of having been moved by QR, the latter are to be found in A-positions. Because of this, pronouns bound by quantificational NPs are subject both to constraints on A-binding, in virtue of the position of the variable bound by quantifier, and constraints on Ā-binding, in virtue of the position of the quantifier itself. Non-quantificational NPs, on the other hand, are subject only to the former constraints on A-binding. Aoun and Hornstein highlight the sensitivity of anaphora to whether there is A and/or Ā-binding through discussion of cases in which a quantifier Ā-binds (c-commands) its trace, which in turn A-binds the pronoun that are acceptable in English but are not Japanese and Chinese. In Japanese, they argue, the pronoun *kare* must be Ā-free, but can be A-bound, as shown by the contrast between (5) and (6), from Saito and Hoji (1983)):

(5)   John-ga   [kare-ga atamaga ii to]   omotteiru
        John-*nom* he-*nom* be-smart   COMP   think

        'John thinks he is smart'

(6)   *Daremo-ga   [kare-ga atamaga ii to]   omotteiru
        everyone-*nom* he-*nom* be-smart   COMP   think

        'Everyone thinks he is smart'

(5) is well-formed, as *kare* is only A-bound, as opposed to (6), in which it is Ā-bound, at LF. In Chinese, Aoun and Hornstein point to contrasts such as in (7) versus (8), and (9) as opposed to (10):

(7)   Zhangsan$_i$ shuo Lisi taoyan ta$_i$
        Zhangsan   said Lisi hates him

(8)   Meiren$_i$ shuo Lisi taoyan ta$_i$
        No one   said Lisi hates him

(9)   Zhangsan$_i$ shuo ta$_i$ yao   lai
        Zhangsan   said he   would come

(10)   *Meiren$_i$ shuo ta$_i$ yao   lai
        No one   said he   would come

Since here there are occurrences of the same pronoun in all of the cases, matters cannot be stated as simply as in Japanese. Aoun and Hornstein argue that what is involved here is a difference in the domains of A and Ā-binding:

(11)   A pronoun has to be A-free in the least Complete Functional Complex containing this pronoun and its governor.

        A pronoun has to be Ā-free in the least Complete Functional Complex containing this pronoun, its governor and a c-commanding SUBJECT.

Since in Chinese there is no agreement, SUBJECT will reduce to the standard grammatical subject. From (11) it now follows that we will find in Chinese classical specified subject condition effects, but only with respect to bound variable anaphora. Ā-binding, Aoun and Hornstein thus argue, is subject to more exacting constraints than A-binding.

In the previous discussion we have been speaking of "bound variable" and "coreference" anaphora. We must be careful in our use, however, because we do not wish to be saying that such notions are syntactical notions. Rather, their relevance to the overall theory of anaphora only comes into play when we consider the *interpretation* of anaphora. The syntax is concerned with the distribution of binding, to wit, coindexing, as this is formally determined by binding principles. In his paper, "Towards a Modular Theory of Coreference," Robin Clark reminds us of this distinction, and sets out to show that we also must make a further distinction in the theory of anaphora. He argues that not only must we distinguish the role of syntax and semantics, but also the role of predicate-argument structure. He develops his argument in the context of a puzzle in Toba Batak, pointing to a curiosity in the bound anaphor *dirina* in the language. The central contrasts are in (12)/(13) and (14)/(15), which are distinguished by voice, the former being in the *mang* voice, the latter the *di* voice:

(12)   Mangida dirina si   John
        see   self PM John

(13)   *Mangida si   John dirina
        see   PM   John self

(14)   Diida si   John dirina
        see   PM John self

(15)   *Diida dirina si   John
        see   self   PM John

The immediate problem is that if all that is relevant are c-command relations, then the differences between (12)/(13) and (14)/(15) are quite problematic, if both voices have the same structure.

While one could reject the latter assumption, Clark argues against this, proposing rather that observed asymmetries are a consequence of an anaphoric principle pertaining to argument structure. He gives this principle as follows:

(16)   The *n*-th argument of an *n*-place predicate may bind into
        the *m*-place predicate, where *m* is greater than or equal to
        n.

The application of (16) can be observed from the well-known active/ passive contrast in English:

(17) a.   John saw himself

  b   *John was seen by himself

Clark supposes that (17b) has the structure in (18):

(18) [$_S$ John$_i$ [$_{I'}$ was [$_{VP}$ [$_{VP}$ seen e_i] by himself]]]

This contravenes (16) because there is binding from an argument of a two-place predicate (*see*) to an argument of a one-place predicate (*see John*, relative to trace binding). In (17a), on the other hand, there is binding from an argument of a one-place predicate to an argument of a two-place predicate, and this is consistent with (16). For the Toba Batak cases, Clark proposes that they have the following structure, in which the two arguments mutually c-command (both are dominated by the same maximal projections) but differ in argument structure:

(19) a.   [$_{VP}$ [$_{V'}$ *mang*-V NP-theme] NP-experiencer]

  b.   [$_{VP}$ [$_{V'}$ *di*-V NP-experiencer] NP-theme]

The binding contrasts now follow on the assumption that the theme is always the internal argument, the experiencer, the external. Thus, both (12) and (14) satisfy (16), as the experiencer argument of a one-place predicate binds the theme argument of a two-place predicate, but neither (13) nor (15) do, as the theme, argument of a two-place predicate, binds the experiencer, argument of a one-place predicate. In both cases, however, c-command relations are exactly the same, but it is only when both Binding Theory requirements and predicate-argument requirements are met that the results are well-formed.

  It is well-known that relative to their syntactic position in logical form, quantifiers may interact in their scope. This sort of interaction extends beyond sequences of quantified phrases, to sequences of mixed quantifier phrases and *wh*-phrases. In May (1985), it is pointed out that there is a contrast in the scope possibilities of the sentences in (20):

(20) a.   What did everyone buy for Max

  b.   Who bought everything for Max

Whereas in (20a), *everyone* can be understood to have scope inside or outside the *wh*-phrase, this is not the case in (20b), where the universal must be understood as within the scope of *wh*. What May argued was that this distinction could be grouped together with two other phenomena — superiority and *that*-trace effects — as consequences of the Empty Category Principle (ECP). The idea presented there was that while the alternative scope orders are possible for (20a) in virtue of the structure in (21a),[4] (21b) is ill-formed, comparable to the ill-formedness of (22), the LF-representation of * *What did who buy for Max*:

(21) a. $[_{S'}$ What$_j$ $[_S$ everyone$_i$ $[_S$ e_i bought e_j for Max]]]

   b. *$[_{S'}$ Who$_i$ $[_S$ everything$_j$ $[_S$ e_i bought e_j for Max]]]

(22) $[_{S'}$ Who$_i$ what$_j$ $[_S$ e_i bought e_j for Max]]

These effects were taken by May as comparable to that found in (23):

(23)   *Who$_i$ did John say $[e_i$ that $[e_i$ left early]

Here it is the complementizer which is the cause of the proper government failure. Thus, all three cases are taken as being ruled out because there is improper antecedent government. What is not ruled out in this way is (24):

(24) $[_{S'}$ Who$_i$ $[_S$ e_i $[_{VP}$ everything$_j$ $[_{VP}$ bought e_j for Max]]]]

This represents the only present reading of (20b), where the universal has narrower scope, in virtue of being adjoined to VP.

   Osvaldo Jaeggli explores in his paper "Head Government in LF-Representations" these intervention effects for ECP, in the context of certain parametric contrasts between English and Spanish. It is well-known that Spanish differs from English in that its counterpart to (23) is well-formed:

(25)   Quién dijiste   que salió temprano
        who   you + say that left early

        'Who did you say left early'

This lack of *that*-trace effects is mirrored by the lack of superiority effects comparable to those in English, as Jaeggli (1982) observed in earlier work:

(26)   Què vio quièn
        what saw who

        'What did who see?'

The reason for this difference, deriving from ideas of Rizzi (1982), is that in Spanish the subject can be inverted to a post-verbal position, its trace being taken as an occurrence of an expletive, with subsequent extraction from the inverted position. This latter position will then be properly governed by the verb. Against this assumption, Jaeggli observes that Spanish shows the same properties as English regarding the scope interactions of quantifiers and *wh*-phrases. Thus, the scope relations in the sentences in (27) and (28) are just the same as in their English counterparts in (20):

(27)   A quièn examinó   cada   doctor
        whom   examined every doctor

        'Who did every doctor examine?'

(28)   Quièn examinò a cada   paciente
        who   examined   every patient

        Who examined every patient

To account for these differences, Jaeggli proposes that the ECP include a "head-government" clause, in addition to the requirement of ante-cedent government. He argues that on this basis an account is forth-coming, relative to certain parametrizations, of the differences between English and Spanish.

The head-government condition Jaeggli proposes centers around the idea that heads govern the specifiers of their complements. The implementation of this idea relative to the cases under consideration is based on two assumptions regarding the structure of COMP. First, Jaeggli follows Chomsky (1986) in assuming that COMP is an X-bar projection, containing a head C which projects the category CP (= traditional S′). Second, he assumes that there is agreement between the specifier of CP and its head. When the head of COMP is empty, this amounts to coindexing the specifier and the head. The account of superiority, that is, the ill-formedness of (22) is now as follows. At S-Structure, the specifier position of CP is occupied by *what*, so C will be coindexed with this phrase. At LF, with extraction of *who*, the resulting structure will be (29):

(29) $[_{CP}$ Who$_i$ what$_j$ $[_C$ $e_j]$ $[_{IP}$ e_i bought e_j for Max$]]$

The now present subject trace must be head-governed. But it cannot be, since it is not coindexed with C. Similarly, head-government fails in (21b). This is because the presence of the adjoined phrase blocks government of the specifier of the complement of C, that is, the subject.

To account for Spanish, Jaeggli proposes, again following Chomsky (1986), that the expletive *pro* resulting from inversion is subject, at LF, to replacement by a process of expletive substitution. Thus, we have for *Qué vio quién* 'What did who see', initially (30a), which becomes (30b):

(30) a. $[_{CP}$ quièn$_i$ què$_j$ $[_C$ $e_j]$[vio $[_{IP}$ *pro* $[_{VP}$ $[_{VP}$ $[_V$ $t]$ e_j $e_i]$]]]]

    b. $[_{CP}$ quièn$_i$ què$_j$ $[_C$ $e_j]$ [vio $[_{IP}$ e_i $[_{VP}$ $[_V$ $t]$ $e_j]$]]]]

The key to what is going on in Spanish, Jaeggli argues, is that in these structures the complex of the verb+INFL has been raised. In its raised position, it can head-govern the trace in the subject position, which has replaced the expletive. In contrast, even this sort of head-government will be blocked in (31), where there is a quantifier rather than a *wh*-phrase in-situ:

(31)   *$[_{CP}$ què$_i$ $[_C$ $e_i]$ [vio $[_{IP}$ cada estudiante$_j$ $[_{IP}$ e_i $[_{VP}$ $[_V$ $t]$ $e_j]$]]]]

As Jaeggli observes, the ill-formedness of (31) arises from essentially the same sort of failure of proper government as in its English counterpart. In contrast, if the quantifier phrase is attached to VP, then the result is well-formed:

(32) $[_{CP}$ què$_i$ $[_C$ $e_i]$[vio $[_{IP}$ e_i $[_{VP}$ cada estudiante$_j$ $[_{VP}$ $[_V$ $t]$ $e_j]$]]]]

Here there is head-government by the verbal-inflection complex, just as in (30b).

Verb fronting in Spanish as it interacts with constraints on S-Structure and LF also plays a central role in the chapter by Margarita Suñer "Two Properties of Clitics in Clitic-Doubled Constructions." Suñer observes an asymmetry in Spanish between certain constructions involving overt *wh*-movement of either the direct or indirect object, which requires the occurrence of "doubling" clitics, and comparable constructions containing quantified NPs (which by assumption involve QR in LF), in which the clitics are optional. In order to explain this asymmetry, Suñer first notes (after Torrego (1984)) that *wh*-movement in Spanish triggers verb fronting. She then assumes that when verb fronting takes place, neither the verb nor its trace can θ-govern an object. In constructions involving overt *wh*-movement, therefore, all direct and indirect object traces must be antecedent-governed, as required by the ECP. The clitic requirement in such constructions is then in place, Suñer argues, because clitics are able to serve as anchors (that is, antecedent governors) of the object traces. On the other hand, since the operation of QR onto LF does not trigger verb fronting at S-Structure, the verb in its base-generated position does θ-govern its direct and indirect objects. In case the direct or indirect objects are quantificational and undergo QR in LF, their traces are already θ-governed. Therefore, no clitics are required in non-interrogative quantificational sentences. Thus, although a different property is observed between overt *wh*-movement and QR, that difference is attributed to an independent difference regarding verb fronting, and not to a difference in the application of the ECP at S-Structure and at LF.

While as far as the ECP is concerned, clitics do not interact with LF movement in any essential way, Suñer shows that they do play an important role in LF in other respects. In particular, their existence in a sentence can serve to circumvent weak crossover violations. Thus, (33) contrasts with (34), with the indicated anaphoric connection possible only in the latter:

(33) *Su$_i$ madre   quiere   a todos$_i$.
       Their$_i$ mother likes   everybody$_i$.

(34) Su$_i$ madre   los$_i$ quiere   a todos$_i$.
      Their$_i$ mother them   likes   everybody$_i$.

The contrast between (33) and (34) is particularly interesting, in that the addition of a pronominal element (the clitic) that c-commands a quantified NP renders a bound variable interpretation possible for another pronoun. The structural relationship of the quantified phrase and the preceding pronoun *su* at S-Structure is identical in (33) and (34), and the addition of a clitic does not alter that relationship in any significant way at S-Structure. In neither case does the quantified NP c-command either pronoun. Assuming QR, however, Suñer shows that a crucial difference emerges between (33) and (34). The LF representations of (33) and (34) are as follows:

(35) [$_{IP}$ A todos$_i$ [$_{IP}$ su$_i$ madre   quiere t_i]]
          everybody   their mother likes

(36) [$_{IP}$ A todos$_i$ [$_{IP}$ su$_i$ madre   los$_i$ quiere t_i]]
          everybody   their mother them   likes

In (35), the quantified NP locally binds the possessive pronoun *su* and a variable, but in (36) the quantified phrase locally binds two pronouns (the possessive pronoun and the clitic), and the clitic in turn locally binds a variable. (36) is thus comparable, Suñer observes, to the sort of cases explored by Safir (1984). Safir observed that there is a parallelism constraint operant for weak crossover, so that all elements that are concurrently locally bound by an operator must be either all lexical or all empty categories. Thus Suñer's account of the anchoring effects of clitics, especially in their ability to overcome weak crossover effects, provides evidence for the existence of QR, and for the idea that the condition on the interpretation of a pronoun as a bound variable is not defined at S-Structure, but at LF.

The interaction of syntactic constraints with quantification was recognized as early as 1971, when Lakoff observed that scope interpretation of quantifiers is subject to locality conditions reminiscent of Ross' (1967) island constraints. In May (1977), the position was put forth that since QR is a syntactic rule, a transformation, it is subject to the same constraints as other transformations. Thus, since QR, *qua* rule, is òf the same form as *wh*-movement (movement to an Ā-position), the presumption was that the constraints on the latter would also be applicable to the former. A central constraint which May took as a case in point was the Subjacency Condition, based on the observation, among others, that complex noun phrase contexts are not only islands for overt movement, but also for scope, to wit, "covert" movement onto LF. This correlation , when taken in conjunction with other constraints, gives rise to what Longobardi (in his contribution) calls the "Correspondence Hypothesis," according to which constraints on overt movement, (and only those constraints), apply also to movement in LF. The correctness of this hypothesis would quite clearly provide evidence of the strongest kind for the postulation of LF-movement. In Huang (1982), however, it was observed that at least in this "strong" form, there are apparent problems with the Correspondence Hypothesis. This is because the interpretation of *wh*-in-situ is essentially free of island constraints, and although quantifier scope is generally clause bound, it is also free of such constraints where the relevant islands do not involve clauses.[5] Huang concluded that, although the ECP obtains both at S-Structure and at LF, the bounding conditions (Subjacency and the CED) only obtain with overt movement.[6]

Although this conclusion was satisfactory for the considerations in

Huang (1982), it raised two important problems. Theoretically, this conclusion amounts to adoption of a "weak" version of the Correspondence Hypothesis, according to which overt movement and LF-movement share certain crucial properties, but not all such properties. This scenario is not, by itself, necessarily implausible (since different levels need not have conditions defined over them in precisely the same ways), but it does raise the question of why "covert" and "overt" syntax should differ precisely in this way but not, say, the other way round, with bounding conditions applying at both levels and the ECP applying only at S-Structure. Empirically, certain other facts not previously considered would be left unaccounted for if neither Subjacency nor the CED were operative in LF. Such facts are the subjects of the contributions by Wahba; Barss, Hale, Perkins and Speas; Nishigauchi; and Longobardi.

"Movement in Iraqi Arabic" by Wafaa Abdel-Faheem Batran Wahba investigates the syntax of *wh*-questions in Iraqi Arabic, a language which allows a free choice between in-situ and movement strategies in the formation of *wh*-questions. Thus it offers a useful ground for the study of the syntax of LF in close comparison with the syntax of overt movement. Wahba first shows that, in addition to exhibiting standard weak crossover effects and scope properties whose generalizations are naturally captured at the linguistic level of LF, Iraqi Arabic in-situ questions exhibit COMP-to-COMP effects of a kind typifying overt *wh*-movement in familiar languages. This is so even though Iraqi Arabic allows *wh*-phrases to be "stranded" at S-Structure in an intermediate COMP, their derivation being completed at LF. Wahba further shows that the distribution and interpretation of in-situ *wh*-questions exhibit locality restrictions, as it is often impossible to interpret an in-situ *wh*-phrase located within an island as having scope larger than the island. In fact, LF extraction out of a tensed clause also appears to be excluded. Wahba shows that the island properties can be accounted for by the assumption that Subjacency applies both in the Syntax and in LF. In this way, she argues strongly for the existence of an abstract *wh*-movement in LF that has properties similar to those of overt *wh*-movement.

The contribution by Andrew Barss, Kenneth Hale, Ellavina Perkins and Margaret Speas, "Logical Form and Barriers in Navajo," investigates the syntax of "internally headed relative clauses" (IHRs) in

Navajo. The existence of this construction offers a particularly interesting way to look into the nature of LF.[7] IHRs are relative clauses
whose relativized arguments appear in their base-generated argument
position. Given the assumption that *wh*-in-situ undergoes movement in
LF, it is natural to assume that "relatives-in-situ" (as IHRs may well be
called), though they do not undergo overt relativization at S-Structure,
do undergo relativization in LF. Barss et al. observe that, in Navajo, it is
impossible to relativize an argument within a relative clause (both
IHRs). Following Platero (1978), they suggest that this is a Complex
Noun Phrase Constraint effect, and thus conclude that Subjacency
(subsumed, they assume, under the theory of Barriers (Chomsky
(1986)), is a condition that applies at LF. Barss et al. also argue that a
minimality condition on binding applies at this level. Thus, in addition
to disallowing double relativization, Navajo also prohibits double
questioning, double focusing, and the existence of both a focus and a
wh-phrase within a clause. The relevant generalization is that there can
be no more than one Question/Focus particle within a given sentence.
Barss et al. argue that in *wh*-questions and focus constructions, the
particle forms a functional chain with an empty head position of a
dominating CP. When two particles are present, there must be two
distinct CPs each containing an empty head forming a distinct functional chain with a particle. But then the lower functional binder
necessarily intervenes between the higher binder and the particle it
binds, resulting in a violation of some sort of "relativized minimality"
(Rizzi (1990)) at LF.

Taisuke Nishigauchi's paper "Construing *WH*" shows that the syntax
of the particles *mo* and *ka* in Japanese and their role in determining
the construal of "*wh*-phrases" provide important *prima facie* grounds
for the treatment of *wh*-in-situ as a case of unselective binding, in the
sense of Heim (1982). Central to Nishigauchi's observation is the fact
that so-called "*wh*-phrases" in Japanese cannot simply be treated as
interrogative pronouns in their own right, but that their interpretation
depends on the kind of particles that c-command them in certain, often
non-adjacent, positions in a sentence. In particular, when occurring in
the local c-command domain of *mo*, a *wh*-in-situ is interpreted as
having either the meaning of the universal quantifier *every*, or as the
negative polarity item *any*. But if in construction with the particle *ka*,
then a *wh*-in-situ has either the interpretation of a pure existential

quantifier or that of an interrogative pronoun. Thus in (37) below the *wh*-word *dare* "who" is construed as a universal quantifier, but in (38) the same element is treated as an existential:

(37)   dare-ga   ki-te   mo,   boku-wa   aw-a-nai.
        who-*nom* come   Q   I-Top   meet-not.

        'Whoever may come, I will not meet (him).'

(38)   dare-ka-kara   henna   tegami-ga   todoi-ta.
        who-Q-from   strange   letter-*nom* arrived

        'A strange letter came from somebody'

The interpretation of *dare* in (37), in particular, cannot be determined until the entire clause *dare-ga ki-te* is considered, to which the particle *mo* is attached. "*Wh*-phrases," then, do not have any quantificational force by themselves, Nishigauchi argues. Rather, they serve as free variables in the logical representation, and in this respect they behave like other indefinites, whose quantificational force varies depending on the kind of adverbs of quantification occurring elsewhere in the sentence (Heim (1982)). For example, the indefinite *a man* is appropriately interpreted as universal in (39) in the presence of *always*, and as existential in (40) in the presence of *sometimes*:

(39)   If a man owns a donkey, he always beats it.

(40)   Sometimes, if a cat falls from the fifth floor, it survives.

Nishigauchi assumes that *wh*-phrases are to be somehow represented as variables "unselectively" bound by the particles. Unlike Heim, however, who assumes that the binding relations are directly effected by coindexing the *wh*-phrases and the particles (the unselective binders), Nishigauchi assumes that *wh*-phrases move to the Spec position of the CP of which a given particle is the head, and from which it is governed by the particle. Thus in a representation of the form (41), the moved *wh*-phrase binds a standard variable (the trace that results from its movement in LF), but is in turn unselectively bound, licensed by a relation of government, by an appropriate particle that gives it the appropriate quantificational force:

(41) $[_{CP} [_{SPEC} wh_i] [_{C'} [_{IP} \ldots x_i \ldots] [_C mo/ka]]]$

As support for this movement analysis of the *wh*-phrases, Nishigauchi shows that the construal of *wh*-in-situ, whether as a universal, an existential, or an interrogative quantifier, is in principle unbounded, but otherwise exhibits effects of locality conditions (e.g. the *Wh*-Island Condition) typifying syntactic processes of movement. In certain cases, the construal of the *wh*-phrase appears to violate the Subjacency Condition, in particular the Complex NP Constraint:

(42) $[_{CP} [_{NP} [_{IP}$ dare-ga   kai-ta] hon]-o   yon-de mo],
      who-*nom* wrote book-*acc* read   Q

omosiro-katta.
interesting was

'For all *x*, *y*, *x* a person, *y* a book *x* wrote, *y* was interesting.'

(43) $[_{NP} [_{CP}$ dare-ga   kai-ta] hon]-ga   omosiroi-desu-ka?
      who-*nom* wrote book-*nom* interesting-be-Q

'Book that who wrote are interesting?'

In these sentences, the *wh*-word *dare* appears to be construed with the quantification particles *mo* and *ka* in violation of the CNPC, but Nishigauchi argues that what is directly construed with these particles is not the *wh*-word *dare*, but the entire complex NP that contains it. In LF, it is the complex NP that moves to the Spec of the CP, where it is governed by *mo* or *ka*. *Dare* also moves, but only to the specifier position of the complex NP. Neither movement violates Subjacency. A convention of feature percolation ensures that the specifier and the head of an NP share their features. Thus, in the LF representation of (42), the head of a complex NP acquires the force of universal quantification from the particle *mo* which governs it, as does its specifier *dare*, and both the complex NP and the *wh*-phrase indeed receive a universal interpretation. On the other hand, in (43), both *dare* and the complex NP containing it receive an interrogative interpretation. Evidence for this comes from the fact, pointed out in Nishigauchi (1986), that preferable answers to such questions often take the form that repeats the whole complex NP, rather than one that simply supplies the value for *dare*. Thus, *Bill-ga kai-ta hon desu* 'It is the book that Bill wrote' is a natural answer to (43), but *Bill desu* 'It's Bill' is not. Nishigauchi's paper thus turns around a set of important facts that might at first glance support a non-movement version of the theory of unselective binding, and shows that they actually support the hypothesis that *wh*-in-situ undergoes movement in LF.

In his article, "In Defense of the Correspondence Hypothesis: Island Effects and Parasitic Constructions in Logical Form," Giuseppe Longobardi explicitly argues for the strong form of the Correspondence Hypothesis on the basis of generalizations that hold of the trace of overt movement and of quantifiers. Relying on the distribution in Italian of negative quantifiers such as *nessuno* and phrases of the form *sole* + *XP* 'only XP', Longobardi shows that they both obey the range of island conditions, and display effects comparable to those shown by parasitic gaps. In looking at island effects at LF, Longobardi builds on Rizzi's (1982) observation that *nessuno* is sensitive to the ECP, showing that *sole*-phrases are also subject to this condition. Thus, in (44b) the scope of this phrase is limited to the embedded clause, while it can extend over the matrix in (44a):

(44) a   E' proprio necessario che ci venga a trovare solo Gianni
         'It is really necessary that come to visit us only Gianni' (i.e.
         'the others must not/need not come')

     b   E' proprio necessario che solo Gianni ci venga a trovare
         'It is really necessary that only Gianni come to visit us' ('the
         others must not/*need not come')

Not only are both types of expressions subject to ECP, but Longobardi also shows that they are subject to the full range of bounding effects, including the Complex NP Constraint, the Coordinate Structure Constraint, the Sentential Subject Constraint and Constraint on Extraction Domains (CED). (45) and (46) show this for the Complex NP Constraint:

(45) a. Non credo che sia possible che ci consenta di fare neinte
         'I do not believe that it is possible that he allows us to do
         anything'

     b. *Non credo alla possibilit̀ che ci consenta di fare niente
         'I do not believe the possibility that he allows us to do
         anything'

(46)   Cercavo una persona che si occupasse solo di lei
         'I looked for a person who would take care only of her'

Whereas (45b) is ungrammatical, as *niente* cannot escape the island to be properly associated with *non*, (46) is grammatical, but only with the scope of *sole*-phrase containing within the relative clause. This shows that Subjacency holds of LF; that is, at the level at which both *wh*-movement and QR have applied. Longobardi's second class of evidence for the Correspondence Hypothesis is based on showing that "parasitic" effects cut across traces of *wh* and quantifiers. Parasitic effects are seen when an occurrence of an element inside an island is licensed by some other element of the same type which occurs outside the island. The most broadly discussed case of this are parasitic gaps, where *e* inside the island is licensed by *t* outside:

(47)   What did John read *t* without filing *e*

With quantifiers, Longobardi, developing an observation made for English by Kayne (1983), observes sentences such as (48):

(48) a. Non fa niente paer aiutare nessuno
          'He doesn't do anything in order to help anyone'

  b. *Non fa questo davoro per aiutare nessuno
          'He doesn't do this work in order to help anyone'

As (48b) shows, *nessuno* cannot by itself occur within the island. It can, however, if it is licensed from outside, as in (48a) by *niente*. Thus, again these elements behave in a fashion comparable to the traces of overt *wh*-movement; their generalization is to be had relative to their structure at LF.

In summary, in this volume we have presented a collection of papers by scholars explicating the notion of Logical Form and its relation with syntactic structure on the one hand, and logical structure on the other. With extensive data drawn from a variety of languages, the papers provide cross-linguistic perspectives concerning such issues as phrase structure, scope interpretation, bound anaphora, the syntax and interpretation of *wh*-in-situ and the status of grammatical constraints. While the issues broached here remain open to further empirical inquiry, we hope the publication of these papers will stimulate further research in comparative semantics in this vein.

Many people have helped us in the preparation of this volume. We would like to thank Peter Cole, Mürvet Enç, Robert Freidin, Wayne Harbert, Howard Lasnik, Gita Martohardjono, Eduardo Raposo, Tim

Stowell, and Edwin Williams for their assistance in reviewing the papers collected here. We are also grateful to the anonymous reviewer who examined the entire volume again for us and made numerous pertinent suggestions which led to considerable improvement of the papers. Finally, in bringing this volume to fruition only after his untimely death, we would like to dedicate this volume to the memory of Osvaldo Jaeggli, our good friend, colleague, and fellow contributor, whose work has inspired not only those of us working on issues dealt with herein, but numerous others in the field of generative grammar.

REFERENCES

Bach, E.: 1968, 'Nouns and Noun Phrases', in E. Bach and R. T. Harms (eds.), *Universals in Linguistic Theory*, Holt, Reinhart, Winston, New York.

Chomsky, N.: 1976, 'Conditions on Rules of Grammar', *Linguistic Analysis* **2**, 303–351. Also appears in N. Chomsky, N.: 1977, *Essays on Form and Interpretation*, North-Holland, New York.

Chomsky, N.: 1986, *Barriers*, MIT Press, Cambridge, MA.

Cole, P.: 1987, 'The Structure of Internally Headed Relative Clauses, *Natural Language and Linguistic Theory* **5**, 277–302.

Evans, G.: 1980, 'Pronouns', *Linguistic Inquiry* **11**, 337–362.

Heim, I.: 1982, *The Semantics of Definite and Indefinite NounPhrases*, Doctoral dissertation, University of Massachusetts, Amherst, Massachusetts.

Higginbotham, J.: 1980, 'Pronouns and Bound Variables', *Linguistic Inquiry* **11**, 679–708.

Huang, C.-T. J.: 1982, *Logical Relations in Chinese and the Theory of Grammar*, Doctoral dissertation, MIT, Cambridge, MA.

Itô, J.: 1986, 'Head Movement in LF and PF: The Syntax of Head-Internal Relative Clauses in Japanese, in *University of Massachusetts Occasional Papers in Linguistics* **11**, 109–138.

Jaeggli, O.: 1982, *Topics in Romance Syntax*, Foris, Dordrecht.

Kayne, R.: 1983, 'Connectedness', *Linguistic Inquiry* **14**, 223–249.

Kiss, K.: 1987, *Configurationality in Hungarian*, Reidel, Dordrecht.

Koopman, H. and Sportiche, D.: 1982, 'Variables and the Bijection Principle', *The Linguistic Review* **2**, 139–161.

Kripke, S.: 1979, 'A Puzzle about Belief', in A. Margalit (ed.), *Meaning and Use*, Reidel, Dordrecht.

Lakoff, G.: 1971, 'On Generative Semantics', in D. Steinberg and L. Jakobovits (eds.), *Semantics*, Cambridge University Press, Cambridge.

Lasnik, H. and Saito, M.: 1984, 'On the Nature of Proper Government, *Linguistic Inquiry* **15**, 235–289.

May, R.: 1977, *The Grammar of Quantification*, Doctoral dissertation, MIT, Cambridge, MA.

May, R.: 1985, *Logical Form: Its Structure and Derivation*, MIT Press, Cambridge, MA.

May, R.: 1988, 'Bound Variable Anaphora', in R. Kempson (ed.), *Mental Representations: The Interface between Language and Reality*, Cambridge University Press, Cambridge, England.

May, R.: 1989, 'Interpreting Logical Form', *Linguistics and Philosophy* **12**, 387—435.

May, R.: 1991, 'Syntax, Semantics and Logical Form', in A. Kasher (ed.), *The Chomskyan Turn*, Basil Blackwell, Oxford.

McCawley, J.: 1970, 'Where do Noun Phrases Come from?', in R. A. Jacobs and P. Rosenbaum (eds.), *Readings in English Transformational Grammar*, Ginn & Co., Waltham, MA, pp. 166—183.

Nishigauchi, T.: 1986, *Quantification in Syntax*, Doctoral dissertation, University of Massachusetts, Amherst, MA.

Partee, B.: 1978, 'Bound Variables and Other Anaphors', in D. Waltz (ed.), *Proceedings of TINLAP 2*, University of Illinois Press, Urbana.

Partee, B. and Bach, E.: 1984 'Quantification, Pronouns and VP Anaphora', in J. Groenendijk, T. M. V. Janssen and M. Stokhof (eds.), *Truth, Interpretation and Information*, Foris Publications, Dordrecht.

Platero, P.: 1978, *Missing Noun Phrases in Navajo*, Doctoral dissertation, MIT, Cambridge, MA.

Reinhart, T.: 1983 *Anaphora and Semantic Interpretation*, Croon Helm, London.

Rizzi, L.: 1982, 'Negation, *Wh*-Movement and the Null Subject Parameter', in L. Rizzi (ed.), *Issues in Italian Syntax*, Foris Publications, Dordrecht.

Rizzi, L.: 1990, *Relativized Minimality*, MIT Press, Cambridge, MA.

Ross, J. R.: 1967, *Constraints on Variables in Syntax*, Doctoral dissertation, MIT, Cambridge, Massachusetts.

Safir, K.: 1984, 'Multiple Variable Binding', *Linguistic Inquiry* **15**, 603—638.

Saito, M. and Hoji, H.: 1983, 'Weak Crossover and Move-alpha in Japanese', *Natural Language and Linguistic Theory* **1**, 245—259.

Torrego, E.: 1984, 'On Inversion in Spanish and Some of Its Effects, *Linguistic Inquiry* **15**, 103—129.

Williamson, J.: 1984, 'An Indefiniteness Restriction for Relative Clauses in Lakhota', Paper presented at Groningen Conference on Indefiniteness.

NOTES

[1] For the extensional case. What I believe to be true in one language, however, I may not believe to be true in another. Thus, as Kripke (1979) points out, intentionally truth must be relativized to the language spoken.

[2] The former view of bound pronouns has been espoused by Partee (1978), for instance, the latter by Evans (1980). Note that to say that anaphoric occurrences of pronouns are variables is not exclude that they may co-refer with other expressions, only that this coreference is not grammatically determined.

[3] For a range of perspectives on crossover, cf. Chomsky (1976), Higginbotham (1980), Koopman and Sportiche (1982), May (1988), Partee and Bach (1984), Reinhart (1983) and Safir (1984).

[4] It is argued in May (1985, 1989) that such cases show the need for a symmetrical

theory of scope, where quantifiers which mutually c-command in their adjoined positions can be interpreted under any scope permutation. This contrasts with the asymmetrical theory of scope in May (1977), where the scope order mirrors the order of quantifiers at LF.

[5] Cf. May (1985), on inverse linking of quantifiers. There, May argues that scope outside of an NP is compatible to their island status if the quantified phrase is assumed to be adjoined to the NP itself. From this position, it can c-command outside of the NP, and hence can also have scope outside such domains.

[6] This is also the hypothesis assumed in Lasnik and Saito (1984), Chomsky (1986), and other work.

[7] See Platero (1978), Williamson (1987), Cole (1987) and Itô (1986) for further discussion of this type of construction.

JOSEPH AOUN AND NORBERT HORNSTEIN

BOUND AND REFERENTIAL PRONOUNS

0. INTRODUCTION

In this paper, we investigate the behavior of bound pronouns (i.e. pronouns linked to quantificational noun phrases) in English, Chinese and Japanese. It is commonly assumed that these elements obey two distinct requirements. The first requires these pronouns to be in the scope of the quantificational NP they are coindexed with. The second states that these pronouns obey the same anti-locality condition as the one applying to referential pronouns: they must be A-free in the same environment as referential pronouns. That is, they obey principle B of the Binding Theory (see Chomsky 1981). In this paper, we will argue for two conclusions. First, whether referential or bound, pronouns obey two distinct anti-locality requirements rather than one. They must be A-free as well as A'-free in some local environments. Second, across languages, the environment in which a pronoun has to be A'-free need not be identical to the environment in which it has to be A-free; thus, corroborating the conclusion of Manzini and Wexler (1987) according to which the definition of locality is subject to variation.

To illustrate, consider the following examples from Japanese (see Saito and Hoji 1983):

(1) a. John-ga   [Kare-ga atamaga ii to] omotteiru
        John-nom   he-nom   be-smart   COMP think

   'John thinks he is smart'

   b. daremo-ga [Kare-ga attamaga ii to] omotteiru
       everyone-nom

   'Everyone thinks he is smart.'

In (1a), the pronoun *Kare* can be coindexed with the name *John*. In (1b), however, this pronoun cannot be bound by the quantifier *daremo* ("everyone"). We show in section (1) how to account for the contrast between the two sentences by assuming that *kare* has to be locally A-free and A'-free throughout. In (1a), the pronoun is A-free in the

1

embedded clause. However, in the LF-representation (1b′) of (1b), the pronoun is A′-bound; this is why sentence (1b′) is not acceptable with a bound pronoun reading:

(1) b′. daremo-ga$_i$ [x_i [Kare-ga atamaga ii to] omotteiru]

In Mandarin Chinese, the behavior of pronouns will prove to be more complex. Pronouns must be A-free in the least Complete Functional Complex in which they occur and A′-free in the least Complete Functional Complex containing a subject (section 2). Consider the following pair of sentences from Chinese:

(1) c. Zhangsan xihuan [$_{NP}$ ta mama]
    'Zhangsan likes his mother'

    d. meiren xihuan [$_{NP}$ ta mama]
    'nobody likes his mother'

In (1c), the pronoun can be coindexed with the name *Zhangsan*. In (1d), however, the pronoun cannot be bound by the quantificational element *meiren*. The LF-representation of sentence (1d) is given in (1d′):

(1) d′. [meiren$_i$ [X_i xihuan [ta$_i$ mama]]]

In (1c), the pronoun is A-free in NP. In the LF representation (1d′) of (1d), the pronoun is A-free in NP but is A′-bound in the minimal Complete Functional Complex containing the subject -the whole clause-. This is why sentence (1d′) is unacceptable with a bound pronoun reading.

In English, the environment in which pronouns have to be A-free and A′-free happen to be the same. This has obscured the fact that pronouns must meet two distinct disjointness requirements. However, we will see in section (3) that there are speakers of English who adopt the same disjointness requirements as the ones holding in Chinese. The distribution of bound and referential pronouns for these speakers will prove to be similar overall to the distribution of bound and referential pronouns for Chinese speakers.

1. THE LF-STRUCTURE OF PRONOMINAL VARIABLES

Pronouns linked to quantificational noun-phrases (henceforth bound pronouns) are usually taken to obey two distinct requirements. The first states that the bound pronoun interpretation may arise just in case the pronoun is in the scope of a quantificational NP (QP), i.e., c-commanded by this QP (see Chomsky 1977; Higginbotham 1980). In the following sentence (from Higginbotham 1980, p. 684), the pronoun cannot be bound by the quantificational NP. The reason is that the LF rule of Quantifier-Raising is essentially clause-bound (see May 1977, Aoun and Hornstein 1985). Consequently, the scope of the QP *everybody* in (2) is restricted to the relative clause in which it is contained:

(2)   Somebody who liked everybody lent him money.

This scope requirement holds in the LF component. It is only at this level that the QP will c-command the pronoun in a sentence like (3a). (3b) is the LF representation of (3a):

(3) a.   Everybody's mother said he dislikes beer.

    b. $[_s$ everybody$_i$ $[_s[_{NP}$ X_i's mother$]$ said he dislikes beer$]]$

Assuming LF-representations such as (3b), Weinberg and Hornstein (1986) argue that the relationship between the bound pronoun and the QP does not need to be mediated by the variable (X in 3b). That is, the c-command requirement must hold between the QP and the pronoun and not necessarily between the variable and the pronoun. This observation, which will play a crucial role in the subsequent discussion, suggests that weak cross-over effects should not be accounted for in terms of the Bijection Principle of Koopman and Sportiche (1982).

The second requirement concerning bound pronouns is an anti-locality requirement: "A pronoun can be bound to a quantificational NP only if it could overlap in reference with a referential NP occupying the same position as the quantifier" (Higginbotham 1980). In the following sentence, for instance, the referential and bound pronouns must be disjoint from the name and the QP respectively. The reason is that principle B is taken to constrain both types of pronouns:

(4) a.   *John$_i$ expected PRO$_i$ to see him$_i$

    b.   *No one$_i$ expected PRO$_i$ to see him$_i$

The second requirement concerning bound pronouns subsumes three logically distinct sub-requirements. The first, a disjointness requirements, states that the bound pronoun has to be free in some

local environment E. The second, a parallelism requirement, states that
the local environment E in which the bound pronoun has to be free is
the same as the one in which the referential pronoun has to be free. The
final one states that both bound and referential pronouns have to be
free in E with respect to the same type of element. That is, in terms of
the binding principles (see Chomsky 1981, 1986), both bound and
referential pronouns have to be A-free in E.

While the first subrequirement seems to hold across languages, the
last two have to be qualified as shown by the behavior of pronouns in
Japanese. In this language, as argued in Saito and Hoji (1983), an overt
pronoun can never be used as a bound pronoun:

(5) a. John-ga   [Kare-ga atamaga ii to] omotteiru
        John-nom   he-nom   be-smart   COMP think

        'John thinks he is smart'

    b. daremo-ga [Kare-ga atamaga ii to] omotteiru
        everyone-nom

        'Everyone thinks he is smart.'

Unlike (5a), (5b) is unacceptable in case the overt pronoun *Kare* is
bound by the quantifier *daremo* ("everyone"). Sentence (6), however, is
perfectly acceptable with the non-overt element *e* interpreted as a
bound variable:

(6)   daremo-ga [[e] atamaga ii to] omotte iru

        'Everyone thinks (he) is smart'

For the sake of completeness, notice that the "reflexive" form *zibun*
("self") can be linked to a quantificational NP in Japanese (see 7 from
Saito and Hoji 1983):

(7)   daremo-ga   [zibun-ga Mary-ni   kirawareteiru] to
        everyone-nom self-nom   Mary-by   be-dislike   COMP
        omoikondeiru (koto)
        be convinced

        'Everyone is convinced that he is disliked by Mary.'

Principle (8) describes the anti-locality requirement that Japanese
overt pronouns are subject to:

(8)   *Kare* cannot be bound by a quantificational NP.

Requirement (8), however, cannot be taken as a primitive principle in the grammar. Disjointness requirements are generally stated with respect to a position P; not with respect to the types of element that occurs in P. Thus the binding principle B (Chomsky 1981) states that the pronoun has to be A-free, i.e. free with respect to an element in an A-position (argument-position), in some local environment. It does not require the pronoun to be free in E with respect to a name, another pronoun or an anaphor. In (9a—c), for example the pronoun in the embedded object position has to be disjoint from the embedded subject position:

(9) a.   Mary thinks John likes him.

  b.   Mary thinks he likes him.

  c.   They expect each other to dislike them.

Similarly, principle C states that a name has to be A-free (in all environments). In (10a—c), the name *John* has to be disjoint from any c-commanding NP:

(10) a.   He likes John.

  b.   Peter expects himself to dislike John.

  c.   The bastard thinks John dislikes good food.

The problem raised by formulation (8) can be solved when the LF representation of sentences such as (5, 6) in Japanese are considered. At LF, after the process of Quantifier-Raising, the quantificational NP will be in an A′-position (non-argument-position). Assuming, that the disjointness requirement for *Kare* involves A′-positions, (11) can replace (8):

(11)   *Kare* must be A′-free.

Requirement (11) solves the problem of disjointness raised earlier. The unacceptability of (5b) is due to the position of the binder rather than to its intrinsic quantificational content. The following facts support formulation (11) over formulation (8).

In Japanese, the so-called reflexive form *zibun* can have a long distance binder. There also exist limitations on the interaction of *zibun* and the pronominal form *Kare*. As pointed out in Lasnik (1986), *zibun* cannot bind *kare*. This prohibition is illustrated in the following contrast (we wish to thank H. Hoji, F. Katada and N. Yoshimura for their help with the Japaneses examples):

(12) a. John-ga   [[Kare-ga Kare-no hahaoya-o   koroshita] to]
      John-nom   he-nom   his   mother-acc killed   that
      omotte ita (koto)
      thought

      '(The fact that) John thought he killed his mother'

b. John-ga [[zibun-ga Kare-no hahaoya-o   Koroshita] to]
          self   he-nom   mother-acc killed   that
      omotte ita
      thought

      'John thought that (self) killed his mother'

In sentence (12a) *John* and the two occurrences of *Kare* can be understood as coreferential. In (12b), however, this option is not available: *zibun* and *Kare* cannot both be bound by *John*. Chomsky (1986) and Lebeaux (1983) suggest that anaphors raise at LF and are adjoined to a position governed by their antecedent. Assuming that their analysis extends to *zibun*, the fact that this element cannot bind *kare* may be accounted for by constraint (11) as follows. As a result of the raising process, *zibun*, at LF, will be in a configuration where it A'-binds *Kare* in (12b); thus, violating requirement (11). (12b') is the LF representation of sentence (12b) (non-relevant details omitted):

(12) b'. $[_{I'}$ John-ga$_i$ $[_{I'}$ zibun-ga$_i$ $[[x_i$ Kare-no$_i$ hahaoya-o koroshita] to] omotte ita]]

Let us return, now, to the proper formulation of the disjointness requirement for *kare*. We indicated that by assuming that *zibun* raises at LF, the contrast between (12a) and (12b) can be accounted for by constraint (11) which prohibits *kare* from being A'-bound. But this contrast cannot be accounted for if formulation (8) is adopted because *zibun* is not a quantificational NP. We thus conclude that the disjointness of *Kare* is with respect to an A'-position (formulation 11) rather than a QP (formulation 8).[1]

We wish to clarify one point before closing the discussion of bound elements in Japanese. For many speakers, there is a marked contrast between *zibun* and *zibun-zisin* in contexts such as (12b). In (13), *zibun* is replaced by *zibun-zisin*. Binding of *zibun-zisin* and *kare* by *John* is more readily available:

(13)   John-ga zibun-zisin-ga kare-no hahaoya-o koroshita to omotte ita

'John thought that (self) killed his mother'

Zibun is traditionally considered to be a long distance dependent element; it can have a long distance antecedent. This is not the case with *zibun-zisin* which needs a more local antecedent. The contrast between (12b) and (13) suggests that only long distance dependent elements (i.e., the so-called long distance anaphors) raise at LF. Our aim in this section was to establish the correct disjointness requirement applying to pronominals in Japanese and not to provide an extensive analysis of long distance anaphors. For a thorough analysis of the contrast between *zibun* and *zibun-zisin*, the reader is referred to Katada (1987).

So far, we have established the existence of constraint (11) in Japanese which prohibits the pronominal form *Kare* from being A'-bound. Recall that the following three generalizations concerning bound pronouns are usually assumed: (a) a bound pronoun must be free in some local environment E; (b) the local environment E in which the bound pronoun has to be free is the same as the one in which the referential pronoun has to be free; (c) both bound and referential pronouns have to be A-free in E. The existence of constraint (11) indicates that two types of disjointness requirements apply to the pronominal *Kare* in Japanese. This pronominal element has to be *A'-free* as well as A-free (generalization c).[2] Furthermore, the local environment in which this pronominal has to be A'-free is different from the one in which it has to be A-free (generalization b). *Kare* has to be A'-free throughout (in all the clauses in which it is contained) and A-free essentially in the minimal clause in which it occurs; see the contrast between (5a) and (5b). In other words, *kare*'s properties bear on both claims we made at the outset. Both A and A' restrictions need to be separately stated and their domain of application are rather different.

Notice furthermore, that the existence of two separate disjointness requirements (A-disjointness and A'-disjointness) suggests that at least

for the pronominal element *Kare* in Japanese, the binding theory ought
to be generalized to make reference to A'-relations as well as A-rela-
tions, i.e., it has to be generalized to a theory of A'-binding and
A-binding along the lines of Aoun (1985, 1986a), Aoun and Hornstein
(1966), Finer (1985), Hornstein (1984). In the forthcoming section, we
will show that such a binding approach is necessary to account for the
behavior of pronominal elements in Chinese and English as well.

2. BOUND PRONOUNS IN CHINESE

In contrast to Japanese, pronouns in Mandarin Chinese can function as
bound variables. Of course, these pronouns may also be used deictically
or have a non-quantificational antecedent:

(14) a. Zhangsan$_i$ shuo Lisi taoyen ta$_i$
         'Zhangsan said Lisi hates him'

  b. Meiren$_i$ shuo Lisi taoyen ta$_i$
      'No one said Lisi hates him'

However, despite considerable overlap, there appear to be important
differences between the distribution of bound and referential pronouns
in Chinese. This is shown by the contrast between (15c) and (15d):

(15) a. * Zhangsan$_i$ xihuan ta$_i$.
         'Zhangsan likes him.'

  b. * Meiren$_i$ xihuan ta$_i$.
      'No one likes him.'

  c. Zhangsan$_i$ shuo ta$_i$ yao lai.
      'Zhangsan said he would come.'

  d. * Meiren$_i$ shuo ta$_i$ yao lai.
      'No one said he would come.'

The behavior of bound pronouns in Chinese may be accounted for
once we observe that this language does not have an AGR marker as
indicated in Huang (1982): indeed, in Chinese, there is no overt
evidence that subjects agree with predicates. Moreover, the distribution
of anaphors also suggest that there is no AGR marker:

(16)   Zhangsan$_i$ shuo [taziji$_i$ hui lai]
         'Zhangsan said self would come.'

Sentence (16), contrary to its English counterpart (17), is grammatical:

(17)   *John$_i$ said (that) himself$_i$ would come.

As argued in Huang (1982), these contrasts follow if we assume that Chinese, in contrast to English, has no AGR marker. As such, the environment for the anaphor in the subject position of the embedded clause in (16) and (17) would be the matrix clause in Chinese and the embedded one in English. The anaphor is bound in its local environment in Chinese but not in English, hence the grammaticality of (16) and the ungrammaticality of (17).

The assumption that Chinese has no AGR marker will also allow us to account for the behavior of bound pronouns in this language. The relevant example is (15d). In this example, *ta* is a bound pronoun. The LF structure of (15d) is given in (18):

(18) $[_{I_2}$ meiren$_i$ $[_{I_1}$ X$_i$ shuo $[_{I_0}$ ta$_i$ yao lai]]]

Let us assume that pronouns in Chinese have to be A'-free in the same local environment in which anaphors have to be bound. In (18), the local environment for *ta* will be the matrix clause since AGR is missing in Chinese.[3] In this clause, the pronoun is A'-bound; thus violating the binding theory. As for the grammaticality of sentence (15c), it may be accounted for once it is assumed that pronouns in Chinese essentially have to be A-free in the minimal clause or NP in which they occur (see Aoun 1986a, chapter 1, section 1.4). In (15c), the pronoun *ta* is free in the embedded clause. In brief, the local environments in which pronouns have to be A-free and A'-free are distinct in Chinese:

(19) B. A pronoun has to be A-free in the least Complete Functional Complex containing this pronoun and its governor.

B'. A pronoun has to be A'-free in the least Complete Functional Complex containing this pronoun, its governor and a c-commanding SUBJECT.

SUBJECT will be characterized as in Chomsky (1981): A is a SUBJECT for B iff A c-commands B and A is a subject or AGR. Since in Chinese, AGR is missing (Huang 1982), SUBJECTS are equivalent to subjects. Furthermore, along the lines of Chomsky (1986), we characterize a governing category as a Complete Functional Complex (CFC) in the sense that all grammatical functions compatible with its head are realized in it (see Chomsky 1986). In contexts of predication, subjects are required; thus, a CFC has to include a subject in these contexts. In contexts where predication is not operating, as in noun phrases, a CFC does not have to include a subject; this last assumption is slightly different from the characterization of CFC given in Chomsky (1986).[4]

The analysis of bound pronouns in Chinese makes the following prediction. If it is true that the lack of AGR in Chinese prevents the pronoun from meeting the binding principle (19B') in constructions such as (15d), then we expect that a bound pronoun should be possible in case it is more deeply embedded. This appears to be correct:[5]

(20) a. meiren$_i$ shuo Lisi xiangxin ta$_i$ hen congming
'No one said Lisi believes he is intelligent.'

Sentence (20a) is acceptable with the bound pronoun interpretation as our theory leads us to expect. The LF representation of sentence (20a) is (20b):

(20) b. [meiren$_i$ [$_{I_2}$X$_i$ shuo [$_{I_1}$ Lisi xiangxin [$_{I_0}$ ta hen congming]]]]

In (20b), the local environment for the pronoun *ta* is the intermediate clause I_1''. Observe that in this clause *ta* is A'-free. The binding principle (19B') is satified. Thus, (20a) is fully acceptable.

To further illustrate the application of principles (19B—B'), consider the distribution of pronouns that occur within noun phrases as in (20c—d):

(20) c. Zhangsan$_i$ xihuan [$_{NP}$ta$_i$ mama]

     d. *meiren$_i$ xihuan [$_{NP}$ta$_i$ mama]

The contrast illustrated in (20c—d) is again accounted for by (19B—B'). In (20c), the pronoun is A-free in the NP which is the least CFC containing the pronoun and a governor. In (20d), the pronoun is A'-bound in the matrix clause which is the least CFC containing a subject; thus, this sentence is ungrammatical. The contrast between (20c) and (20d) provides more evidence for the relevance of the notion SUBJECT in the formulation of principle (19B') and indicates that the head of the noun phrase *mama* in (20d) does not count as a SUBJECT (see Raposo 1985).

Notice that in the LF representation of all the Chinese examples discussed so far, the pronoun is at the same time A'-bound by the operator and A-bound by the trace of this operator. In other words, if only the sentences discussed so far were considered, it would be possible to claim that bound pronouns, in contrast to referential pronouns, obey a special binding requirement: they have to be A-free in the least CFC containing them and a subject. In that case no reference to A'-positions or to principle (B') would be required. In order to establish the relevance of principle (19B'), it is necessary to study constructions where the bound pronouns are A'-bound by the operator without being A-bound by the trace of the operator. Sentences (21a—c) have the required form.[6]

(21) a. *meiren de   xin   shuo ta bei-jiegu le.
       nobody DE letter say he by-laid off

   'Nobody's letter said that he was laid off.'

   b. *meiren de   xin   jinule   tade pengyou
        nobody DE letter angered his   friend

   'Nobody's letter angered his friend.'

   c. meiren de   xin   shuo Mali hui qu jie ta
      nobody DE letter say Mary will go pick-up him

   'Nobody's letter said that Mary would go to pick him up.'

These examples support the claim that pronouns have to be A'-free. The LF representation of sentences (21a), (21b) and (21c) are given in (21d), (21e) and (21f) respectively:

(21) d. $[_{I'}$ meiren$_i$ $[_{I'}$ $[_{NP}$ X$_i$ de xin] shuo $[_{I'}$ ta bei-jiegu le]]]

   e. $[_{I'}$ meiren$_i$ $[_{I'}$ $[_{NP}$ X$_i$ de xin] jinule tade pengyou]]

   f. $[_{I'}$ meiren$_i$ $[_{I'}$ $[_{NP}$ X$_i$ de xin] shuo $[_{I'}$ Mali hui qu jie ta]]]

Observe that in (21d—f), the pronoun is A'-bound without being A-bound. In (21d—e), it is A'-bound in its local environment — the matrix clause — and therefore violates the binding principle (19B'). In (21f), the pronoun has the embedded clause as its local environment since *Mali* ("Mary") is a subject. The pronoun, thus, is A'-free in its local environment and the structure is well formed.

The necessity of two separate binding requirements (19B and 19B') in Chinese adds further support to the view that there is a grammatical level LF, distinct from S-structure. The reason is that only at LF is it possible to state principle (19B′) and to make the requisite distinction between A′-bound and A′-free pronouns as illustrated in the paradigm (21).

3. BOUND PRONOUNS IN ENGLISH

To this point, we have suggested that postulating the existence of the binding principle (19B′) allows us to account for the interesting behavior of bound pronouns in Chinese. We have also indicated that in this language, the contrast between bound and referential pronouns (e.g., 15c and 15d) may be accounted for once we acknowledge that the local environment in which a pronoun has to be A′-free (19B′) is different from the local environment in which this pronoun has to be A-free (19B).

Let us turn now to the behavior of bound and referential pronouns in English. In English, these two types of pronouns have very similar distribution as illustrated in the following paradigm:

(22) a. *John$_i$ likes him$_i$

   b. *No one$_i$ likes him$_i$

   c. *John$_i$ believes him$_i$ to be intelligent.

   d. *No one$_i$ believes him$_i$ to be intelligent.

   e. John$_i$ believes that he$_i$ is a fool.

   f. No one$_i$ believes that he$_i$ is a fool.

In (22a), the pronoun *him* is bound in its local environment, the matrix clause, by the coindexed antecedent. In (22e), on the other hand, the pronoun *he* is free in its local environment, the embedded clause. Consider, now, the cases where the pronoun is functioning as a bound variable in English. The LF representations of the English sentences (22b, d and f) are given in (22b′, d′ and f′) respectively:

(22) b′. No one$_i$ [$_I$ [X$_i$ [$_{VP}$ likes him]]

   d′. No one$_i$ [$_I$[X$_i$ [$_{VP}$ believes [$_I$him to be intelligent]]]

   f′. No one$_i$ [$_I$ X$_i$ believes [$_C$ that he$_i$ is intelligent]]

In (22b′—d′), the local environment in which the bound pronominal has to be free is the matrix clause and in (22f′), it is the embedded clause.

The main difference between (22d′) and (22f′) is that the embedded clause in the former structure is infinitival. As such, the local environment for the bound pronominal must be the matrix clause; just as in the simplex sentence (22b′). In brief, it seems that the local environments in which a pronoun has to be A-free and A′-free are essentially the same in English; see Chomsky (1986), section (3.5.2.3):

(23) B. A pronoun has to be A-free in the least CFC containing this pronoun and its governor

B′. A pronoun has to be A′-free in the least CFC containing this pronoun and its governor

Further evidence for (23B—B′) may be provided by considering the behavior of bound pronouns which occur within noun phrases:

(24) a. I showed John's mother pictures of him

b. I showed everyone's mother pictures of him

In (24a), the pronoun *him* can be coindexed with *John*. Similarly in (24b), the pronoun *him* can be bound by *everyone*. Sentence (24b) is specially relevant. At LF, the quantifier can be adjoined to the VP or to IP; in case, it is adjoined to NP, it will not c-command the pronoun. For concreteness, we assume that *everyone* adjoins to VP.

(25)   I [$_{VP}$everyone$_i$ [$_{VP}$showed [$_{NP}$X$_i$'s mother] [some pictures of him]]]

The well-formedness of (25) in English indicates that the local environment in which the pronoun has to be A′-free does not take into account the notion subject. Indeed, in case the pronoun *him* were to be A′-free in the local environment of a subject, representation (25) would be ungrammatical: the pronoun would be A′-bound in the local environment of [NP, S]. In brief, the acceptability of sentence (24b) indicates that the binding domain for the pronoun is the minimal NP is which it is contained; in this domain, it has to be A′-free.

Interestingly, however, we found speakers of English who distinguish between (24a) and (24b). These speakers accept (24a) but reject (24b). It is tempting to say that for them, the local environment in which the pronoun has to be A′-free takes into account the notion SUBJECT. That is to say that for these speakers, the pronoun has to be A′-free in the local environment of a SUBJECT. Essentially, they adopt a binding requirement similar to the Chinese requirement (19B'). For these speakers, the LF representation (25) of sentence (24b) is not well-formed because the pronoun is not A'-free in the environment defined by the subject of the clause. A confirmation of this analysis is provided by the fact that sentence (24b) becomes acceptable for these speakers when a subject intervenes between the pronoun and the quantificational NP as illustrated in sentence (26a). In the LF representation (26b) of sentence (26a), the pronoun is A'-free in the NP *John's pictures of him* which is the minimal NP containing a subject (the [NP, NP] *John*):

(26) a. I showed everyone's mother John's pictures of him.

  b. I [$_{VP}$ everyone [$_{VP}$ showed [X$_i$'s mother] [John's pictures of him]

Interestingly, the speakers rejecting the bound variable interpretation for the pronoun in (26b) appear to disallow sloppy identity interpretation of the pronoun in cases such as (27a) though they accept the coreferrential reading of the pronoun indicated in (27b):

(27) a. John destroyed pictures of him and Bill did too

  b. John destroyed pictures of him

  c. John [λx [x destroyed pictures of him]] and Bill [λx [x destroyed pictures of him]]

We expect these different acceptability judgments if the pronoun in sloppy identity cases is in reality a pronoun bound by a lambda operator, as has been suggested in Williams (1977), Reinhart (1983) and Weinberg and Hornstein (1986). In the logical representation (27c) of sentence (27a), the pronoun would be A'-bound by the lambda operator in the domain of the subject. In contrast, the pronoun in (27b) is not a pronoun bound by a lambda operator but is simply a coreferential pronoun.

Consider, now, the following paradigm involving predicative phrases which was pointed out to us by R. Clark:

(28) a. *No one$_i$ became [$_{NP}$ a comfort to him$_i$]

  b. *John$_i$ became [$_{NP}$ a comfort to him$_i$]

  c. *No one$_i$ became [$_{AP}$ proud of him$_i$]

  d. *John$_i$ became [$_{AP}$ proud of him$_i$]

According to the analysis given so far, the pronoun in (28b) is free in the least CFC -the NP- in which it is contained. Thus, it should be possible to A-bind it from the subject position; which is not the case. The same remark can be made with respect to (28d) if CFCs include APs. Notice that the noun phrase in (28b) and the adjectival phrase in (28d) are predicational. As we said earlier (see the discussion of 19B—B'), in contexts of predication, subjects are required: a CFC has to include a subject in these contexts. We can now assume that the ungrammaticality of (28b) and (28d) arises because the pronoun is bound in the CFC that include the subject. There are many ways to instantiate this proposal: it is possible to consider that the CFC is the whole clause in (28b) and (28d) because this clause is the least CFC containing a subject. In this CFC, the pronoun would be bound; thus these sentences are ungrammatical. Another possibility is to adopt a proposal made to us by R. Clark who suggests a small clause analysis for sentences (28). In this case, the D-structure of (28b), for example, would be as in (29a):

(29) a. $[[e] [_{VP} \text{ became } [_{NP} \text{ John}_i [_{NP} \text{ a comfort to him}_i]]]]$

The associated S-structure would be as in (29b):

(29) b. $[\text{John}_i [_{VP} \text{ became } [_{NP} t_i [_{NP} \text{ a comfort to him}_i]]]]$

In (29b), the pronoun is bound in the least CFC containing a subject -the maximal NP-; hence, this sentence is ungrammatical.

From the previous discussion, it appears that there are speakers of English who essentially adopt the same A'-disjointness requirement as the one holding in Chinese (19B'). Let us turn now to the formulation of the Binding principle B for the speakers of English who adopt (19B'). For some of the speakers adopting (19B'), there is a contrast between sentence (30a) and sentence (30b). They allow the pronoun *him* to be indexed with *John* in (30a), but do not allow this pronoun to be bound by *everyone* in (30b):

(30) a.   I showed John some pictures of him

     b.   I showed everyone some pictures of him

It seems that for these speakers, the environment in which the pronoun has to be A-free is the least CFC containing this pronoun and its governor. This is the binding principle given in (31B):

(31) B. A pronoun has to be A-free in the least CFC containing this pronoun and its governor

We also found speakers who do not allow the pronoun to be indexed with *John* in (30a) or with the quantifier in (30b). These speakers also disallow the bound variable reading in examples such as (24b) and do not allow the pronoun to be coindexed with the subject in (27b). That is, these speakers adopt an A-disjointness requirement where the notion SUBJECT seems to be relevant:

(32) B. A pronoun has to be A-free in the least CFC containing this pronoun, its governor and a c-commanding SUBJECT

In brief, some of the English speakers who adopt the A'-disjointness requirement (19B') repeated for convenience adopt (31B) and some adopt (32B):

(19) B'. A pronoun has to be A'-free in the least CFC containing this pronoun, its governor and a c-commanding SUBJECT

3.1. *Some Structure Differences between Chinese and English*

In the previous section we saw that there are speakers who essentially adopt the same A'-disjointeness requirement (19B') as the one holding in Chinese. Thus, we expect the distribution of bound pronouns for these speakers to be parallel to the distribution of bound pronouns for Chinese speakers. In this section, we will discuss instances where this expectation does not hold and will claim that the various differences concerning the behavior of bound pronouns can be traced back to independent structural differences between English and Chinese.

The analysis presented so far explains why English and Chinese pattern together in cases such as the following:

(33) a. no one$_i$ [X$_i$ said [Lisi hates him$_i$]]

b. meiren$_i$ [X$_i$ shuo [Lisi taoyen ta$_i$]]

The local environment for both *him* and *ta* is the embedded clause. In this local environment both elements are A'-free. Consequently both sentences are acceptable with a bound pronoun reading.

Consider, now, the cases where Chinese and English differ. Sentence (22f), in contrast to the similar Chinese sentence (15d), is acceptable for the English speakers adopting the A'-disjointness requirement (19B'). The LF representations (22f') of (22f) and (18) of (15d) are repeated below:

(22) f'. No one$_i$ [$_I$-X$_i$ believes [$_C$- that he$_i$ AGR is intelligent]]

(18)   [$_{I_2}$ meiren$_i$ [$_{I_1}$X$_i$ shuo [$_{I_0}$ ta$_i$ yao lai]]]

Recall that in representation (18), the local environment in which the bound pronoun should be A'-free is the matrix clause since AGR does not exist in Chinese. This is why the pronoun *ta* cannot be A'-bound by the QP *meiren* ("no one"). On the other hand, for the English speakers adopting (19B'), the local environment in which the pronoun *he* has to be A'-free in (22f') is the embedded clause since AGR functions as SUBJECT (see Chomsky, 1981). In the embedded clause, the pronoun is A'-free. Nothing prevents it from being A'-bound by the QP *no one* which occurs outside the local environment of the pronoun.

In the previous paragraph, we saw that for the speakers of English who adopt the binding requirement (19B'), the grammaticality of representation (22f') can be traced back to the presence of AGR. On the other hand, the fact that these speakers accept sentences such as (34a) despite the fact that the corresponding sentences in Chinese are unacceptable raises a problem for the analysis presented so far.[7]

(34) a. No one$_i$'s friend killed him$_i$

   b. * meiren$_i$ de pengyou sha-diao ta$_i$
      'no one's   friend   killed   him'

In (34a), the indicated relationship between the quantified antecedent and the pronoun is quite acceptable, in contrast to the Chinese case in (34b). The assumption according to which sentences (34a) and (34b) have similar LF-representations (35a–35b) leads us to expect these sentences to be ungrammatical for the speakers of English adopting (19B'): in representations (35a) and (35b), the pronoun is A'-bound in its local environment:

(35) a. [$_I$- no one$_i$ [$_I$- [X$_i$'s friend]   killed him]]

   b. [$_I$- meiren$_i$ [$_I$- [X$_i$ de pengyou] sha-diao ta]]

We can remedy this problem by adopting a suggestion made by Kitagawa (1986), Koopman and Sportiche (1985), Kuroda (1985),

Zagona (1982) among others. For several syntactic reasons, these linguists suggested that the basic structure for an English sentence is as follows:

(36) $[_{I'} NP_2 [_{I'} I [_{VP} NP_1 VP]]]$

That is, all subjects in English are generated in the Specifier of VP (NP_1) and are then moved to the Specifier of IN (NP_2) in order to be case-marked. Their proposal, in essence, is that all clauses in English are like raising constructions with NP movement applying to yield the attested surface form. In case their proposal is adopted, the LF representation of sentence (34a) will be (37) instead of (35a):

(37) $[_I$ no one$_i$ $[_{I'} [_{NPK} X_i$ friend$]$ $[_{I'} I [_{VP} t_K [_{VP}$ killed him$_i]]]]]$

In (37), the trace of the raised NP (t_K) is in the subject position (the specifier position) of VP. Observe that for the purpose of the binding theory, this VP contains a subject and constitutes a CFC; it is a local environment for the pronoun. The pronoun is A'-free in this local environment (19B'); hence, the grammaticality of sentence (34a).[8]

We saw in the previous paragraph that it is possible to account for the grammaticality of sentence (34a) in case a base structure like the one given in (36) is adopted. On the other hand, the ungrammaticality of the Chinese sentence (34b) suggests that in Chinese, subjects are not derived via NP-movement from a small clause. This is the proposal made in Aoun and Li (1989) who argue that in Chinese, such raising process does not occur. The syntactic representation of standard sentences in Chinese is given in (38):[9]

(38) $[_{I'} NP [_{I'} I VP]]$

Returning to the contrast between sentence (34a) and sentence (34b), the LF representation of the Chinese sentence (34b) will not contain any subject trace in the specifier position of VP. Thus, VP in Chinese, contrary to the VP in English, will not constitute a domain for binding purposes. Representation (35b) is repeated in (39):

(39) $[_{I'}$ meiren$_i$ $[_{I'} [X_i$ de pengyou$]$ sha-diao ta$]]$

In (39), the pronoun is A'-bound in its local environment; thus violating principle (19B') of the binding theory.

Recapitulating, we saw that for English, there are speakers who assume a binding principle similar to the one postulated for Chinese (19B'). Since these speakers adopt a binding requirement similar to the one holding in Chinese, it is natural to expect that they allow bound pronouns to occur in the same contexts allowed in Chinese. This basically seems to be correct: sentences (24b), like their Chinese counterpart (30b), are unacceptable for the relevant speakers:

(40)   *Chinese   English*
       *   *   I showed everyone$_i$'s mother pictures of him$_i$
       *   *   I showed everyone$_i$ some pictures of him$_i$

As for the difference concerning the acceptability of certain sentences, we claimed that they can be traced back to independent (structural) differences between English and Chinese. For instance, the contrast between (22f) and (15d) can be traced back to the existence of AGR in English but not in Chinese (see representations 22f' and 18):

(41)   *Chinese   English*
       *   OK No one$_i$ believes that he$_i$ is intelligent

Similarly the contrast between (34a) and (34b) can be traced back to the existence in English (but not in Chinese) of a process which raises the subject generated in the specifier of VP to the specifier of INFL:

(42)   *Chinese   English*
       *   OK No one$_i$'s friend killed him$_i$

4. CONCLUSION

In this paper we have tried to provide evidence for two different propositions. First, we have tried to show that there exist two types of anti-locality requirements for pronominal elements in natural languages: these elements have to be A-free as well as A'-free in some local environments. We have argued that in Japanese, Chinese and English, there are several restrictions on pronominal binding that cannot be adequately accounted for unless A'-antilocality conditions are made explicit.

Second, we argued that across languages, the environment in which a pronoun has to be A'-free is not always identical to the environment in which it has to be A-free; thus, corroborating Manzini and Wexler's (1987) claim that locality effects are subject to variation.

We have also indicated that the reference to A′-antilocality requirements must be made at the level of Logical Form (LF): as indicated in the paper (see the discussion of sentences 21), it is only after the LF rule of Quantifier-Raising level that the A′-disjointeness of pronouns with respect to quantifiers can be stated. This favors the hypothesis that LF constitutes an autonomous level of linguistic representation (see Chomsky 1981; Higginbotham 1989; May 1977; Weinberg and Hornstein 1986 among others).

The existence of an A′-disjointness requirements applying to pronouns raises the question of its extension to other contexts where pronouns enter into A′-relations. Assuming a Generalized Binding approach, Borer (1984) devise an analysis incorporating the notion of A′-disjointness to account for the behavior of resumptive pronouns (see also Sells 1984 for a different account of resumptive pronouns based on Generalized Binding). Similarly, in Finer (1985) which contains the first detailed discussion of the notion of A′-disjointness, it is argued that the phenomenon of switch reference can be accounted for if it is assumed that the elements subject to switch reference effects have to be A′-free in certain environments. In brief, the notion of A′-disjointness allows us to account for a variety of phenomena such as switch reference effects, the distribution of bound pronouns and of resumptive pronouns. It is clear that the notion of A′-disjointness is a fruitful notion that has a wide empirical coverage and as such needs to be incorporated in the grammatical theory.

ACKNOWLEDGEMENTS

We wish to thank R. Clark, C.-T. J. Huang, A. Li and W. Hudson.

NOTES

[1] Our aim is to establish the existence of constraint (11) in Japanese. Space limitation prevents us from going into the exact working out of the raising rule (see Katada 1987 for an analysis of the raising rule in Japanese).

[2] For completeness, sentence (i) is provided. It illustrates the fact that *Kare* has to be A-free:

(i)   *John$_i$-ga kare$_i$-ga sukida
             John-nom he-acc like

             'John$_i$ likes him$_i$.'

[3] In Aoun (1986a), Chapter 1, it is argued that the domain of the matrix subject in a construction such as (18) includes the node created by adjunction (I$_2''$).

[4] Notice that as formulated, (19B') embodies a redundancy: both the notion of SUBJECT and that of CFC refer to subject. This redundancy, as customary, may be taken to indicate a deficiency in the formulation of the Binding requirements for pronouns. We will not undertake the elimination of the redundancy in the present work. The relevance of the notion governor for principle B in Chinese is motivated in Aoun (1986a, chapter 1 section 1.4.). We include the notion of governor in the formulation of principle B' for the sake of symmetry; we do not have any evidence for or against including it. The inclusion of the notion SUBJECT makes the notion of governor non-crucial; see the discussion of "Binding Category" in Chomsky (1981, chapter 3).

There are substantial dialectal variations affecting bound pronouns in Chinese; they are analyzed in Aoun (1986b).

[5] Montalbetti (1984) discusses the behavior of bound pronouns in Spanish and establishes an Overt Pronoun Constraint which essentially prohibits an overt pronoun from being used as a bound variable when a non-overt pronominal is available for such a use. His analysis cannot be extended to Chinese, since there are contexts such as (i) where both an overt and a non-overt pronominal can be construed as bound variable. The reader is referred to Aoun (1986b) for a discussion of such cases:

(i) a.   meiren   hui xihuan ta mei de jiang zheijian shi
            nobody   will like   he not get prize matter   this

            'nobody will like the fact he hasn't got the prize'

    b.   meiren   hui xihuan [pro] mei de jiang zheijian shi
            nobody   will like   pro   not get prize matter   this

            'nobody will like the fact he hasn't got the prize'

[6] The following examples illustrate the contrast between the behavior of bound pronouns and referential pronouns in contexts where the antecedents of the pronouns do not c-command them:

(i) a.   Zhangsan de pengyou sha diao ta le
                         friend   killed him asp

            'Zhangsan's friend killed him.'

    b.   *meiren de pengyou sha-diao ta
            'No one's friend killed him.'

In (ia), the pronoun can be related to the name *Zhangsan*. In (ib), this pronoun cannot be construed as bound by the OP meiren ("no one").

Our purpose in this work is to establish the existence of the two kinds of disjointness requirements. In Aoun and Li (1988), it is shown that the A'-disjointness requirement is subject to a minimality effect.

[7] There are speakers of English who require the quantifier to c-command the pronoun at s-structure. For these speakers, (34a) and (i) are ungrammatical:

(i)   No one$_i$'s mother said Mary dislikes him.

[8] The proposal according to which subjects in English are generated in the Specifier position of VP still allows us to rule out the bound pronoun interpretation in (24b). Indeed, it is argued in Aoun and Hornstein (1985) that Quantifier-Raising is sensitive to principle A of the binding theory. That is, the empty category left by the raised quantifier must be A'-bound in the domain of the subject. This will prevent the quantifier *everyone* in (24b) from being directly adjoined to the clause. Rather, this quantifier must first adjoin to the VP (as in the LF-representation 25) and then may adjoin to the clause. As such, the LF representation of (24b) will always contain an A'-binder for the variable x in the domain of the subject, i.e. in the VP:

$$i\text{-}I_j \, [_{VP}\text{everyone}_i \, [_{VP} \, t_j \, [\text{showed} \, [_{NP}X_i \, 'mother] \, [\text{pictures of him}]]]]$$

In the LF representation (i), the pronoun is A'-bound in the domain of the subject which is the VP dominating *everyone* (see note (3)).

[9] Alternatively, it is possible to assume that for Chinese, the subject is generated in the Specifier of VP; see Aoun and Li (1989) for a discussion of this possibility.

REFERENCES

Aoun, J.: 1985, 'A Grammar of Anaphora', *Linguistic Inquiry* monograph 11, MIT Press, Cambridge, MA.
Aoun, J.: 1986a, *Generalized Binding*, Foris, Dordrecht.
Aoun, J.: 1986b, Bound Pronouns in Chinese', *NELS* 16.
Aoun, J. and Hornstein, N.: 1985, 'Quantifier Types', *Linguistic Inquiry* 16, 623—637.
Aoun, J. and Li, Y.: 1988, 'Two Case of Logical Relations', ms. USC.
Aoun, J. and Li, Y.: 1989, 'Constituency and Scope', *Linguistic Inquiry* 20, 141—172.
Aoun, J. and Li, Y.: 1990, 'Syntax of Scope', MIT Press (to appear).
Borer, H.: 1984, 'Restrictive Relatives in Modern Hebrew', *Natural Language and Linguistic Theory* 2, 219—260.
Chomsky, N.: 1977, *Essays on Form and Interpretation*, North-Holland, Amsterdam.
Chomsky, N.: 1981, *Lectures on Government and Binding*, Foris, Dordrecht.
Chomsky, N.: 1986, *Knowledge of Language*, Praeger, New York, p. 169.
Chomsky, N. and Lasnik, H.: 1977, 'Filters and Control', *Linguistic Inquiry* 8, 1—46.
Finer, D.: 1985, 'The Syntax of Switch-Reference', *Linguistic Inquiry* 16, 35—55.
Higginbotham, J.: 1980, 'Pronouns and Bound Variables', *Linguistic Inquiry* 11, 679—708.
Hornstein, N.: 1984, *Logic as Grammar*, MIT/Bradford Press, Cambridge, MA.
Huang, C.-T.: 1982, 'Logical Relations in Chinese and the Theory of Grammar', Doctoral dissertation, MIT, Cambridge, MA.
Katada, F.: 1988, 'What can Long-distance Anaphors Say about Operator Systems of Syntax', *NELS* 195 (to appear).

Kitagawa, Y.: 1986, 'Subjects in Japanese and English', Doctoral dissertation, University of Massachusetts, Amherst.

Koopman, H. and Sportiche, D.: 1982, 'Variables and the Bijection Principle', *The Linguistic Review* **2**, 139—160.

Koopman, H. and Sportiche, D.: 1987, 'Subjects', ms., University of California, Los Angeles.

Kuroda, S.Y.: 1985, 'Whether We Agree or Not', ms., University of California, San Diego, *Linguisticae Investigationes* (to appear).

Lebeaux, D.: 1983, 'A Distributional Difference between Reciprocals and Reflexives', Linguistic Inquiry **14**, 723—730.

Manzini, MR. and Wexler, K.: 1987, 'Parameters, Binding Theory and Learnability' *Linguistic Inquiry* **18**, 423—444.

May, R.: 1977, 'The Grammar of Quantification', Doctoral dissertation, MIT, Cambridge, MA.

May, R.: 1985, *Logical Form: Its Structure and Derivation*, MIT Press, Cambridge, MA.

Montalbetti, M.: 1984, 'After Binding', Doctoral dissertation, MIT, Cambridge, MA.

Reinhart, T.: 1983, *Anaphora and Semantic Interpretation*, Croom-Helm, London.

Raposo, E.: 1985, 'Some Asymmetries in the Binding Theory in Romance', ms. University of California, Santa Barbara.

Saito, M. and Hoji, H.: 1983, 'Weak Crossover and Move-alpha in Japanese', *Natural Language and Linguistic Theory* **1**, 245—259.

Tang, C-C.: 1989, 'Chinese Reflexives', *Natural Language and Linguistic Theory* **6**, 93—122.

Weinberg, A. and Hornstein, N.: 1986, 'On the necessity of LF', *Linguistic Inquiry* (to appear).

Williams, E.: 1977, 'Discourse and Logical Form', *Linguistic Inquiry* **8**, 101—139.

Zagona, K.T.: 1982, 'Government and Proper Government of Verbal projections', Doctoral dissertation, University of Washington, Seattle.

ANDREW BARSS, KEN HALE, ELLAVINA TSOSIE PERKINS
AND MARGARET SPEAS[1]

LOGICAL FORM AND BARRIERS IN NAVAJO

0. INTRODUCTION

In a recent discussion of the syntax of Logical Form (LF) in Navajo (Barss, Hale, Perkins and Speas 1986, hereafter BHPS) data was given which indicated that the general transformational rule Move-Alpha (Chomsky 1981, 1986), applying at that level of linguistic representation (with some exceptions, cf. Schauber 1979), was subject to certain constraints. Specifically, it appears, the rule cannot apply in such a way that the associated movement "crosses" certain barriers, the most prominent of which is the configuration arising from a prior application of the same rule. In short, some principle blocks extraction of two constituents from the same "domain."

The purpose of the study just mentioned was primarily reportative and, consequently, concerned itself merely with presenting what its authors perceived to be certain elementary facts. In the present paper, we explore these constructions further, clarifying what they have in common as well as how they differ. We begin with a brief review of the data and then we proceed to suggest a tentative explanation for them.

1. LF MOVEMENT IN NAVAJO

In the favored form of the Navajo relative clause, the nominal expression corresponding semantically to the head (i.e., the "relative NP") appears overtly in its argument position internal to the relative clause — i.e., it is not in an external (left- or right-) head position, as it would be in Japanese or English. The clause itself is "nominalized" by means of the definite determiner — -yígíí (-ígíí) 'nonpast', -yę́ę (-ę́ę, -ą́ą) 'past'. In other words, Navajo employs what is sometimes called the "internally headed" relative clause, as illustrated in (1) below, where the understood head is represented overtly by a nominal expression (ashkii 'boy') which is flanked by material (an adverb and a verb) belonging to the subordinate clause.

25

(1)　　[Tł'éédą́ą́' ashkii ałhą́ą́'-ą́ą]
　　　　[last night boy　　snore-REL]
　　　　yádoołtih. (Platero 1974, 204)
　　　　will:speak

　　　　'The boy who was snoring last night will speak.'

We follow a number of our colleagues in the field in assuming that the logical form of an internally headed relative clause is derived by movement resulting in the extraction of the relative NP to a peripheral position — yet to be characterized. We will assume initially that the extracted NP is adjoined to the clause and that a trace is left in the source argument position (cf. Williamson 1984; Cole, 1987, among others, for recent relevant discussion of relative clauses of this type). Thus, the LF of the complex nominal subject of (1) is approximately as follows, in our initial representation of the matter:

(1')　　[[ł'éédą́ą́' t_1 ałhą́ą́'-ą́ą] ashkii$_1$]

For some speakers, (1') is in fact an acceptable surface structure (cf. Platero 1974, 1978), though the right-headed relative clauses are rather rare in the language generally, and they are not universally accepted. For those speakers who do accept them, we can assume that Move-Alpha applies in syntax as well as at LF. Our interest here is primarily with movement in LF, however.

A second Navajo construction which evidently involves movement in LF is the content question, illustrated in (2) and (3) below. These frequently take a form in which the question word appears in situ, accompanied by a particle (*-lá*, or alternatively *-sh*) appearing either on the question word itself or else "moved" to Wackernagel's (i.e., second) position in the clause over which the question word has scope in LF:

(2) a.　　Jáan háí-lá　　yiyiiłtsą́? (Schauber 1979, 1971)
　　　　　John who-PRT saw

　　　　　'Who did John see?'

　　b.　　Jáan lá háí yiyiiłtsą́?

(3) a.　　Jáan ha'át'íí-lá　nayiisnii'? (Schauber 1979, 186)
　　　　　John what-PRT bought

　　　　　'What did John buy?'

(3) b.   Jáan lá ha'át'íí nayiisnii'?

We will assume, with Huang (1982) and others, that a question word appearing in situ at s-structure is in fact moved in LF to the position defining its scope, i.e., to the relevant clause margin. We will assume initially (as we did in BHPS) that the moved element is simply adjoined, as in the case of relativization, thus attributing the following LF representation to (2), in which the right- or left- linear ordering of the adjunct is chosen arbitrarily, being irrelevant to the questions at issue here:

(2′)   [[Jáan t_1 yiyiiłtsą́] háí$_1$]

Overt movement of the question word is also possible here, as pointed out by Schauber (1979). In this case, the direction of movement is leftward, not rightward as depicted in (2′) and as observed overtly in indirect questions (Schauber 1974, 1979) and relativization (Platero 1978).

Finally, the Navajo focus constructions (as in (4—7) below) also involve movement in LF, we contend (cf. BHPS). These constructions contain a focus particle (i.e., the positive *ga'*, the negative *hanii*, illustrated below, the interrogative *-ísh* (cf. Schauber 1979), or the element *ndi* 'even', not illustrated here) which occurs immediately after the focused constituent.

(4)   Ashkii ga'   łį́į́'   nabííłgo'. (Schauber 1979, 177)
         boy   FOC   horse   threw

         'It's the BOY that the horse threw.'
         'The horse threw the BOY.'

(5)   Ashkii łį́į́'   ga'   nabííłgo'. (Schauber 1979, 178)
         boy   horse   FOC   threw

         'It's the HORSE that threw the boy.'
         'The HORSE threw the boy.'

(6)   Jáan hanii   chidí yiyííłchǫ'.
         John NEGFOC   car   wrecked
         (Chii ga'.) (cf. Perkins 1978, 25)
         (Chee FOC)

         'It's not JOHN that wrecked the car.' ('It's CHEE.')
         'JOHN didn't wreck the car.' ('CHEE did.')

(7)   Jáan chidí hanii   yiyííłchǫ'. (Tsinaabąąs ga'.)
        John car   NEGFOC wrecked   (wagon FOC)

'It's not the CAR that John wrecked.' ('It's the WAGON.')
'John didn't wreck the CAR.' ('But rather the WAGON.')

Given our prelminary assumptions, the LF representation of (4), for example, is approximately as in (4'), the direction of the adjunction being immaterial:

(4')   [[t_1 łį́į́' nabííłgo'] ashkii$_1$ ga']

In summary, assuming that LF movement is involved in the three constructions just considered, the effect of the rule is to extract a constitutent from its source clause and to place it at some clause-periphery. Our preliminary assumption has been that the extracted constituent is simply adjoined to the clause, as depicted in (8) below:

(8)   [[. . . t . . .] NP] direction immaterial)

This represents the position taken in BHPS, and our purpose here will be to reexamine this elementary proposal. As a part of this effort, we consider now a particular kind of constraint which must be placed on the extraction process.

2. DOUBLE EXTRACTIONS

Schauber (1979) showed that long distance construal of WH in-situ is possible in Navajo, at least among some speakers. For example, there are speakers who admit both interpretations of (9):[2]

(9)   Jáan ha'át'íí-sh   nahideeshnih ní
        John what-PRT   will:buy   say

    a. 'What did John say he'll buy?'
    b. 'John asked what he should buy' (Schauber 1979, 151–
        153)

We would analyze (9)a as a case of long-distance LF movement of *ha'át'íísh*.

Although long-distance LF-movements do seem to be permitted in Navajo, each of the three constructions are resistant to certain *multiple* extractions. We now turn our attention to these cases.

Platero (1974) has observed that sentence (10) below cannot receive an interpretation according to which both *hastiin* 'the man' and *łééchąą'í* 'the dog' are relativized:

(10)   *Hastiin łééchąą'í bishxash-éę bee'eldǫǫh néidiitá(n)-éę
        man   dog   bit-REL   gun   picked:up-REL
        nahał'in.
        bark

        NOT = '*The dog that the man who was bitten by picked up the gun is barking.' (Platero 1974, 220)

As mentioned in BHPS, the Navajo string (10) can, with some difficulty, receive a "stacked reading" (e.g., approximately: 'the man that the dog bit (and) that picked up the gun . . .' or 'the dog that bit the man (and) that picked up the gun . . .' — this is, however, irrelevant to our point here, which is that the string does not have an interpretation according to which hastiin 'man' is relativized at the innermost clause and in which leechaa'i 'dog' is relativized at the next clause up. The relevant — ill-formed — derived LF structure has approximately the following form, with t_1 the trace of *man*, t_2 the trace of dog:

(11)   [[[[t_1 t_2 bit-REL] man] gun picked:up-REL] dog] bark

However, the well-formedness of (12) below shows that the relation between t_1 and *man* in (10) is permissible, and the fact that the same string (12) also represents a relative clause with the meaning 'the dog that bit the man' indicates that there is nothing in principle blocking LF extraction of dog.:[3]

(12)   hastiin łééchąą'í bishxash-éę
        man   dog   bit-REL

        'the man whom the dog bit',
        'the dog that bit the man'[4]

Platero (1974) has suggested that the excluded interpretation of (10) has the character of an island violation, in the sense of Ross (1967). If so, then some configuration in (10) constitutes a "barrier" (Chomsky

1986) in relation to the long extraction (i.e., of 'dog'), assuming, of course, that LF movement is involved here.

In any event, it is evidently not possible to relativize two arguments from one and the same clause. And it is reasonable to expect the same effect to be observed in the case of the other putative LF movement constructions. Thus, double questions, in which the particle -lá appears on both question words, are ill-formed, as shown in the following (from Saito 1984, 94):

(13)   *Háí-lá   ha'át'íí-lá   nayiisnii'?
        who-PRT   what-PRT   bought
        'Who bought what?'

The focus constructions also show this resistance to double extraction, as illustrated in (14):[5]

(14)   *Ashkii hanii   łį́į́   ga'   nabíiłgo'.
        boy   NEGFOC   horse   FOC   threw

And, as expected, a content question containing a focused element is likewise ill-formed, as illustrated by the following (from Schauber 1979, 178):

(15)   *Háí-lá   łį́į́   ga'   nabíiłgo'.
        who-PRT   horse   FOC   threw

It is evident from this that the configuration associated with LF extraction in Navajo is correlated with the presence of a barrier (or barriers) for subsequent extractions. The ill-formedness of a sentence like (14), for example, is roughly comparable to that of such English "double clefts" as *It wasn't the boy that it was the horse that threw; and (15) is roughly comparable to the ill-formed *Who was it the horse that threw?. Thus, assuming LF extraction and adjunction are involved in the constructions we have examined, the principle embodied in (16) below (from BHPS) is observationally correct, accounting for the relevant ill-formed cases so far considered — i.e., (10, 13—15), in which, by hypothesis, movement out of an adjunction configuration has taken place:

(16)   The adjunction configuration[6]
        $[_{XP} YP [_{XP} z]]$ is a barrier for extraction of z. (where XP and
        YP are maximal X-bar projections).

While this is observationally correct, we doubt that it is linguistically correct, and it is the purpose of this paper to suggest a more plausible explanation for the limitations on LF extraction which we have identified in the Navajo data.

Before suggesting an alternative to (16), however, let us consider briefly a construction which might appear to be a counterexample to the observation which (16) embodies, namely, constructions of the type represented by (17) below:

(17) Łį́į́ʼ hanii   nabííłgo'-ę́ę ashkii shik'ihodíí'á.
      horse NEGFOC threw-REL boy   blamed:me

      'It's not the boy that the HORSE threw who blamed me.'
      (Schauber 1979, 271)

This sentence contains a (right-headed) relative clause which, in turn, contains a (negatively) focussed constituent (cf. Perkins (1978), for detailed discussion of negative focus in Navajo). Assuming that focus involves LF movement, then (17) would be a counterexample to (16). But that would be true only if the putative LF movement actually *extracted* the focus constituent out of the relative, adjoining it to the matrix clause. However, the interpretation which (17) receives indicates clearly that the negative focus is on the complex noun phrase as a whole, not on łį́į́ʼ 'horse' — the latter only receives "contrastive" focus, not negative focus. This suggests that, in the case of (17), the LF movement which we have assumed to be associated with focus in Navajo extracts the entire complex NP — i.e., this entire constituent is "pied-piped" (cf. Choe (1987); Nishigauchi (1985), for detailed discussion of LF pied-piping in relation to apparent LF violations of subjacency). If this is so, then the LF representation of (17) is roughly as follows:

(18) $[_{XP} [_{XP} \cdots t_1 \cdots] [_{YP} \cdots t_2 \cdots \text{-REL}] \text{NP}]]$

In this configuration, t_1 is the trace of the moved category YP (i.e., the entire relative clause, extracted and adjoined to XP), and t_2 is the trace of NP (the head of the relative clause construction). This is not, after all, a counterexample to (16), since the moved constituent does not cross an adjunction configuration.

It should be pointed out that (16) is nothing more than a descriptive comment. We must seek to explain why the adjunction configuration is a barrier to LF extraction, if it is in fact. In the most carefully elaborated theory of barriers (Chomsky 1986), an adjoined category is, technically, neither *excluded* nor *dominated by* the category to which it is adjoined. Thus, each node in an adjunction configuration is merely a segment of the relevant projection, and consequently, does not count as an autonomous boundary. Under this interpretation of the adjunction configuration, it cannot, in and of itself, count as a barrier.

In pursuing the questions raised by these observations, it will be useful, in fact vital, to determine whether double extractions are ill-formed for the same reasons as are certain single extractions which, in some sense yet to be determined, cross a barrier. For example, as pointed out in BHPS, the ill-formedness of (19) and the necessity of pied-piping in (20—21) indicate that extraction from an adjunct clause is not possible:

(19)   *Ashkii yah'ííyáa-go   hadeeshghaazh-ę́ę
        boy   entered-COMP   I:shouted:out-REL
        sitsilí át'é.
        my:younger:bro is

        '*The boy that I shouted when t came in is my younger brother.'

(20)   Q: ni-zhé'é   háágóó-lá   ííyáa-go   nicha.
        your-father   whither-prt   he-went-COMP   you-cry

        'Your are crying because your father went where?'

        A: Kinłání-góó ííyáa-go   yishcha.
        Flagstaff-to he-went-COMP   I-cry

        'I am crying because he went to Flagstaff.'
        (Schauber 1979)

(21)   Jáan hanii   chidí yiyíiłchǫ'-go   t'ááni' naashá.
        John NEGFOC car   wrecked-COMP   on:foot I:walk

        a. 'It's not because John wrecked the car that I'm on foot.'
        b. 'It's not because JOHN wrecked the car that I'm on foot.'
        (Perkins 1978)

The tags appropriate to the negative focus construction illustrated by (21) are consistent with the interpretation according to which the entire subordinate clause assumes the adjoined position in relation to the matrix in LF (and this is the position defended in greater detail in Perkins (1978) see also BHPS for brief discussion):

(22)   Tag for (a): . . . Łahgo áhóót'įįd-go ga' t'ááni' naashá.

'I'm on foot because something else happened.'

Tag for (b): . . . Mary ga' chidí yiyíiłchǫ'-go t'ááni' naashá.

'I'm on foot because MARY wrecked the car.'

The first tag is appropriate for the use of (21) according to which the negative focus is applied to the reason clause as a whole, with no ancillary contrastive focus, while the second is appropriate to the case in which, in addition to denying the reason, the construction serves to identify, by contrastive focus, a particular constituent of the reason clause which is at issue in the disagreement implicated in the sentence. Under neither interpretation, we suggest, does LF movement involve extraction over an adjunction configuration. If movement is involved in these cases, and our assumption is that movement is involved, then we suggest it is movement of the focussed reason clause to the periphery of the matrix. Though we have not attempted to give an account of the "contrastive" component of negative focus, we suspect that this does not involve extraction, at least, it does not involve extraction of the sort we are considering here.

There appears to be some empirical support for the recognition of certain barriers to LF extraction in Navajo, and in particular, to recognition of the notion that an LF extraction itself creates a barrier. Since adjunction *per se* should not create a barrier, we are faced with the problem of explaining why the Navajo data are as they appear to be.

3. TOWARD AN EXPLANATION OF THE CONSTRAINTS ON MULTIPLE LF EXTRACTION IN NAVAJO

Navajo multiple questions shed light on the problem of accounting for the observations we have reported in the foregoing discussion. The ill-formedness of (13) above, repeated here as (23), stems not from the

double extraction itself, it appears, but rather from the fact that both
question words are accompanied by the particle lá:

(23)   *Háí-lá   ha'át'íí-lá   nayiisnii'?
       who-PRT   what-PRT   bought
       'Who bought what?'

Paul Platero (personal communication), and a number of Navajo-
speaking students consulted by Speas, have reported that the sentence
improves considerably — to the point of being perfect, for some
speakers — when one of the occurrences of this particle is omitted:

(24)   Háí-lá   ha'át'íí   nayiisnii'?
       who-PRT   what-PRT   bought
       'Who bought what?'

While not all speakers accept multiple questions in Navajo, many do,
and we will assume that the judgments of these speakers must be
accommodated in a general theory of Navajo grammar. In this regard, it
is perhaps relevant to point out that other languages using LF movement in the derivation of content questions — i.e., in which content
question words are *in situ* at S-structure — also permit multiple
questions. Winnebago, another language of the New World, is an
example:

(25)   Peezhe-ga jaagu ruwin?
       who-DET what bought
       'Who bought what?'

And it might be relevant, further, that Winnebago does not employ
interrogative particles in association with its content question words.
There is an interrogative "marker," realized as a particular dip-and-rise
in intonation on the final foot, which is clearly distinct from declarative
intonation. But this is in complementary distribution with the overt
declarative marker and, like the latter, forms a part of the rich
Winnebago complementizer system. Thus, it follows that there can be
only one interrogative marker in a given clause, as seems to be the case
in Navajo.

If the observed difference between (23) and (24) is significant, then
it would appear that the ill-formedness of the first of these is related not

so much to the extractions themselves, but rather to the presence of the two markers. It is reasonable, therefore, to turn our attention to these elements.

In the formation of a well-formed Navajo content question, two elements are involved — to wit, the "question word" itself, and an interrogative particle. Similarly, in a well-formed focus construction, two elements are involved — the focussed constituent and the focus particle. We believe that this is significant and that it reflects the presence of a structural configuration not immediately evident in the surface structures of the Navajo sentences.

It is instructive to compare the content question and focus constructions with the relative clause. The latter also involves two elements — the relativized argument, located within the dependent clause, and the relativizing complementizer (glossed REL in our examples). In our elementary theory of relativization (above and in BHPS) this complementizer was essentially ignored as irrelevant to the fundamental LF process. We portrayed the derived LF structure as a simple adjunction in (1'), leaving tacit any commitment either to the precise character of the sentential structure hosting the adjunct or to the structural position of the complementizer.

Let us now take the complementizer into account in our analysis of Navajo relative clauses. And let us assume that the Navajo complementizer, like its counterpart in other languages, belongs to the functional category C and that its maximal projection immediately dominates the specifier position characteristic of all categories, including functional categories (cf. Fassi Fehri 1982; Abney 1987; Chomsky 1986; Fukui and Speas 1986), as depicted in (26) below, in which the order of constituents is immaterial):

(26)

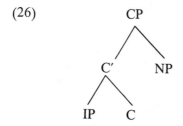

The specifier position, when filled, is occupied by a phrasal category — i.e., **XP**, represented by NP in (26). We can assume that (26) is essentially the configuration which results from the application of Move-Alpha (whether in "overt" syntax or in LF) in the formation of Navajo relative clauses. If this is correct, then the moved NP can be regarded as an operator which binds a variable — its trace — in the IP, i.e., in the clause governed by the complementizer C. We will further suppose, following Chomsky (1986), that the XP in specifier position is coindexed with the head C, through the general relation of spechead agreement.

On the assumption that Navajo relative clauses have the derived structure (26), it is not surprising that they should resist further extractions. The configuration which defines this construction is not the adjunction structure, as assumed earlier, but rather the complementation structure headed by the functional category C. This complementizer "type marks" the construction and identifies its function — in this case, its function as an argument and as a referentially definite expression.

Since C is not a lexical category, but a functional one, it does not "select" its complement — i.e., IP — in the same sense as does a verb, say. To put it in terms of current "barrier" theory (Chomsky 1986), C does not L-mark IP. The latter is, therefore, a "blocking category" for any constituent which it contains — e.g., in this circumstance, IP is a blocking category for any trace within it. It is this that creates the potential for a barrier to extraction, given the provisions of barrier theory as formulated in Chomsky (1986, 14):

(27) a. g is a Blocking Category (BC) for b iff
          g is not L-marked and g dominates b.

   b. g is a barrier for b iff (i) or (ii):
        (i) g immediately dominates d, d is a BC for b;
        (ii) g is a BC for b, g is not IP.

Given that IP is a blocking category and CP immediately dominates IP, it is clear that by the above definition, CP of (26) is a barrier for any b contained within IP. It follows, then, that anything extracted out of CP from a position with IP will cross a barrier.

Let us assume for the present that a single barrier is enough to block LF extraction of the type putatively involved in the formation of Navajo relative clauses.[7] Under this assumption, barrier theory, as represented by (27) above, predicts the ill-formedness of (10), whose structure is approximately that set out in (11), repeated here as (28), in which *t-m* and *t-d* are traces resulting from LF extraction of the relative arguments:

(28)   [[[[*t-m t-d* bit-REL] man] gun picked:up-REL] dog]bark
                                        CP

In conformity with (27b), the innermost CP in this structure is a barrier for *t-d*, the trace bound by the argument extracted from the CP — i.e., the subject of the innermost clause, *łééchą́ą́'í* 'dog'. The relevant CP is repeated more accurately as (29) below, embodying our assumption that the element we have heretofore glossed REL is in fact C, head of CP, and our assumption that the LF head is in specifier position in CP:

(29)   [[[*t-m t-d* bit]-REL] man]
              IP   C'   CP

Given that the first and third brackets here correspond, respectively, to the categories CP and IP, the trace symbolized *t-d* is separated from its antecedent by at least one barrier, namely, CP.[8]

Persisting with our elementary assumption that one barrier is enough to block extractions of the type we are considering, we would like to explore the possibility that the other cases of ill-formed multiple extraction in Navajo are to be explained in terms of the barrier theory, in the manner suggested here for the relative clause.

We will look first at the type represented by (15) above, repeated here as (30), in which one argument (the subject) is questioned while another (the object) is focussed:

(30)   *Háí-lá   łį́į́'   ga'   nabííłgo'. (Schauber 1979, 178)
         who-PRT   horse   FOC   threw

Fundamental to a barrier explanation of the ill-formedness observed here, we believe, is the idea that the particles which occur in association with content questions and focussed constituents reflect the presence of a complementizer projection. The particles can be viewed as "type markers" which identify the specific content of the functional category C — let us, therefore, refer to them as "C-type" particles. Syntactically, we propose, such a particle forms a "functional" chain with C, and its surface location serves to identify the clause-internal constituent which, in LF, occupies the specifier position within the complementizer projection. The particle is, so to speak, a "local" representative of the C itself, inasmuch as it is the surface syntactic realization of that element. If this is correct, then any clause containing such a particle is a CP-over-IP construction and, therefore, extraction from it, across the CP, will necessarily involve extraction across a barrier:

(31)

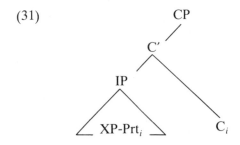

In this structure, CP is a barrier for any category within IP. The presence of a complementizer, and therefore of CP, is signaled by the particle. This forms a functional chain with the complementizer, a relation which is symbolized by means of coindexing; the particular particle identifies the "type" of the complementizer (e.g., content question, focus, negative focus, etc.), and its surface location identifies the syntactic position which enters into the operator-variable relation in LF. And, by hypothesis, the latter relation is defined through the application of Move-Alpha, which extracts the relevant maximal projection, a noun phrase, for example, to the "Spec of CP" position, leaving a trace. This trace functions as a variable; it is bound by the operator identified with the moved constituent — i.e., it is bound, in the usual manner, by the "head" of the chain formed by movement. We will not go into the question here of precisely how the different operator-variable relationships are interpreted semantically (as content question, positive focus, negative focus, etc.), assuming simply that the necessary syntactic relationships are properly defined by the mechanisms we have just discussed and that the semantic analysis will be straightforward given the structures defined by the syntax.

The structure depicted in (31) corresponds to the structures of the following well formed sentences:

(32) a. Háí-lá   łį́į́'   nabííłgo'.
         who-PRT   horse   threw

         'Who did the horse throw?'

   b. Ashkii łį́į́'   ga'   nabííłgo'. (Schauber 1979, 178)
       boy   horse   FOC   threw

       'It's the horse that threw the boy.'

In each of these cases, a C-type particle accompanies the XP which undergoes LF movement. According to our hypothesis, this particle reflects the presence of a complementizer C, with which it is coindexed to form a functional chain. Movement of the relevant XP is, of course, within the CP projected by C. No barrier is crossed, and the structure is, therefore, syntactically well-formed.

By contrast, in (30) — a composite of (32a) and (32b) — the presence of two C-type particles reflects the presence of two complementizers. The ill-formedness of (30) is surely related to this fact. If both of these complementizers occupy the head position of a single CP, the structure will be ruled out by general principles which forbid a single COMP to bear two indices. Alternatively, if each particle reflects the presence of a distinct CP projection, (30) is ill-formed because one of the extractions necessarily moves the focussed phrase "too far" (in a sense to be elaborated below) from its trace, as shown in (33).[9]

(33)

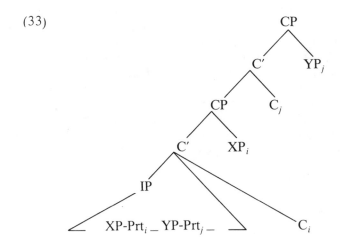

We will assume here that the possibility depicted in (33) is the correct one, that is, that each particle bears its own index and is associated with the head of a distinct CP projection. Accordingly, (30) is ill-formed for the same reason that (10) (cf. (28)) is ill-formed — one of the phrases must occupy the spec of the higher CP, which puts it "too far" from its trace. Presumably, therefore, for the types of LF-extractions we are considering here, any two (or more) from the same clause would lead to ungrammaticality. Thus, the ill-formedness of (13) (= (23)) is also predicted, since this involves two extractions of a questioned constituent, and one of these extractions will always cross an "extra" CP node.

Now we must address the question of in what sense the projection of an additional CP node places the focussed phrase "too far" from its trace at LF. Notice it is not sufficient simply to say that the CP node is a barrier for movement, since although we are supposing, following Choe (1987) and Nishigauchi (1985) that Subjacency may hold of movement at LF, in the representation shown in (33), CP is the only barrier which is crossed, and so we would predict that the Navajo sentences which contain two focus particles have a level of ungrammaticality equivalent to a subjacency violation. In fact, these sentences are much worse than a mere subjacency violation.

We suggest that this level of ungrammaticality is due to the constraints on the relation we have posited between the head of CP and the particle with which it must be indexed at S-Structure. In particular, we suggest that the head of CP must be *locally indexed* with the focus particle in its surface position. Although an exploration of the exact nature of this "local indexing" relation is beyond the scope of the present article, it seems clear that under our analysis the COMP in a focus construction serves as a sort of antecedent to the focus particle itself.[10] Suppose that this antecedence relation is identical to other relations of antecedence in that it is constrained by a *minimality condition* (as in Rizzi 1987), whereby a word or phrase may be the antecedent of another word or phrase only if no other potential antecedent intervenes between the two.

(34)   Relativized Minimality (Rizzi 1987:6)
        $X \alpha$ — governs Y only if there is no Z such that
        (i) Z is a potential α — governor for Y and
        (ii) Z c-commands Y and does not c-command X.

The severe ungrammaticality of sentences with multiple particles is now predicted, since, in addition to the fact that LF movement of the focussed phrase will cross a barrier in such constructions, such constructions will also violate the minimality condition on the local indexing between the COMP and the surface position of the focus particle. This is due to the fact that the presence of two particles corresponds to the presence of two separate projections of C. Hence, the lower C will always constitute an intervening potential antecedent, blocking local indexing of the higher C with the relevant position within IP.

It may be suggested that once we posit the local indexing relation between C and the surface position of the focus particle, it is not necessary to invoke the minimality condition, since there is a barrier, CP, between the higher C and the surface position of the focus particle. However, evidence from embedded focus indicates that it is not correct to say that the local indexing relation between C and the focussed constituent is necessarily blocked by one CP node. Recall that the interpretation of constructions in which a question or focus particle is embedded in an adjunct clause in one which necessarily involves pied piping. As discussed above, this indicates that long-distance extraction out of an adjunct clause is not possible. However, notice that the appropriate answer for such a sentence clearly indicates that the entire adjunct phrase, *including the complementizer*, is questioned/focussed.

(35) Q: ni-zhé'é   háágóó-lá   ííyáa-go   nicha.
         your-father whither-prt he-went-COMP you-cry

      'Your are crying because your father went where?'

      A: Kinłání-góó ííyáa-go   yishcha.
         Flagstaff-to he-went-COMP I-cry

      'I am crying because he went to Flagstaff.' (Schauber 1979 273—274)

In other words, the focus particle has scope *outside of* the surface complementizer. Thus, it seems that the local indexing relation between a focus COMP and the surface position of the focus particle may cross (at least) one CP node, as long as the head of that CP is not one which would count as a closer potential antecedent, in violation of the minimality condition.

This analysis suggests an explanation for why it is possible to have multiple content questions in Navajo, as long as there is only one question particle. Recall that (24) possible, for some speakers. We repeat that sentence as (36) below:

(36)   Háí-lá   ha'át'íí   nayiisnii'?
        who-PRT   what-PRT   bought

        'Who bought what?'

The well-formedness of this question, we suggest, stems directly from the fact that only one particle appears, indicating that only one complementizer — and therefore, just one CP — is present in the structure. If this is so, no barrier can have been crossed in extracting the questioned elements to specifier of CP. This means, of course, that both questioned constituents are, somehow or other, moved to the Spec, CP position. This is consistent with the standard assumption that two operators may occupy the same Spec, CP position at LF, as long as they are eligible to undergo "absorption", in the sense of Higginbotham and May (1981). According to their theory, certain extracted content question operators which are adjacent in LF may be "absorbed" into a single coordinate operator (see Higginbotham and May 1981, 49 ff, for detailed discussion). Presumably, the absorption operation results in a COMP which bears a unique index, namely that of the coordinate operator.

(37)

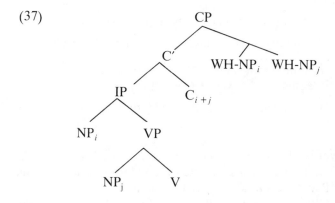

Under these assumptions, no barrier is crossed in deriving the LF representation of (36). The same is true, of course, for the corresponding Winnebago double question (25), in which the single overt question complementizer (the fall-rise intonation) is associated with the canonical complementizer position, i.e., sentence-final position.

In the Navajo data, we see that when two separate complementizers are present, (each triggered by a separate focus or interrogative particle) absorption cannot "save" the construction. We suggest that this is because each particle must be associated with a unique COMP, and each COMP must be coindexed at LF with its specifier, and hence must bear a unique index. If there are two particles, there are two CP projections, and either one XP movement would cross a barrier, as discussed above, or the higher COMP would remain unindexed, as schematized in (38).

(38)

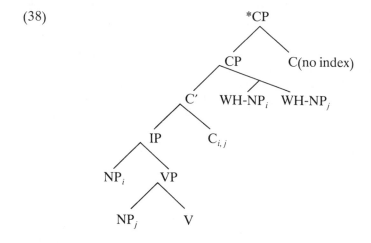

Thus, our proposal that each particle is associated with a separate projection of C predicts the ill-formedness of such sentences.

4. CONCLUDING REMARKS

We have suggested a barrier theory of the ill-formedness of certain Navajo sentences which, by hypothesis, involve extraction at the LF level of representation. The extractions at issue here, we suggest, are LF extractions to the specifier position of CP. That is to say, these movements are not to an adjoined position. By definition, an extraction which crosses both IP and CP (without utilizing the intermediate specifier position) necessarily crosses a barrier. This, we assume, is relevant to the ill-formedness we have observed in certain cases of double LF extraction from a single clause. Further, we have suggested that the particles which may be present in Navajo questions and focus constructions are each associated with a C position, with which they must be locally indexed. This local indexing obeys a minimality condition. Under these assumptions, we can predict that multiple questions are well-formed as long as they do not contain multiple *particles*, and that sentences with multiple particles are ill-formed to a degree which exceeds that of a simple subjacency violation.

We have assumed in this paper that the direct object nominals in Navajo are properly governed by the verb, but we suggested in note 7 that this assumption is controversial for Navajo. In fact, Jelinek (1984) has suggested that all overt nominals in Navajo are actually adjuncts, with the rich agreement morphology serving as the actual arguments. Our primary reason for following Speas (1986, forthcoming) in assuming, contra Jelinek, that Navajo direct objects are governed by the verb is that if all nominals are adjuncts, then all multiple questions ought to involve multiple adjunct traces, and should therefore be impossible. As we have seen, multiple questions in Navajo *are* possible, as long as no more than one question particle is present. Therefore we assume that at least one of the traces must be a lexically governed argument trace. However, we believe that further research is needed to settle this question.

As a final remark, we briefly return to the constructions which were mentioned earlier as apparent counterexamples to our proposal. Sentences of the type represented by (19) above can presumably be explained in terms of the barrier theory. Extraction from the adjunct clause is impossible, without crossing a barrier, since the adjunct clause is marked by means of the complementizer -go, indicating the presence of a CP. Extraction from an adjunct CP is presumably impossible, since the CP would constitute a barrier. The ill-formedness of (19), then, is to be expected.

But why, then, is the question in (20) — repeated here (with its answer) as (39) — well-formed?

(39)   Q: ni-zhé'é   háágóo-lá   ííyáa-go   nicha.
           your-father whither-prt he-went-COMP you-cry

        'Your are crying because your father went where?'

(39)   A: Kinłání-goo ííyáa-go   yishcha.
            Flagstaff-to he-went-COMP I-cry

            'I am crying because he went to Flagstaff.' (Schauber
            1979, 273—274)

The question portion of (39), as its answer indicates, is well-formed because there is no extraction of the question word itself across CP (although we have suggested above that there may be a local indexing relation between the focus COMP and the surface position of the particle which does cross CP). The questioned constituent itself is not extracted out of the adjunct clause — instead, the latter is moved as a whole to serve as a complex operator binding a unitary variable corresponding to the reason whose identification the question seeks to ascertain — the question asks not where? but rather why?, limiting the range of relevant answers to places the addressee's father might have gone. Analogous remarks apply to sentence (21), a type which is fully discussed in Perkins (1978).

We do not plan at this point to suggest precisely how these "pied piped" interpretations are derived, or what their precise LF representation is. But we are nonetheless relatively certain that whatever their LF representations prove to be, they will not involve the illicit crossing of barriers.

NOTES

[1] The authors are listed in alphabetical order.

[2] The sentence given here is an example of a direct discourse complement. The agreement morphology on the embedded verb indicates a 3rd person object and 1st person subject, and there is no overt complementizer. The two translations might more accurately be given as: '(about) what did John say "I'll buy (it)"' and 'John asked "What should I buy?"'. Navajo does have indirect discourse complements, but investigation of extraction from such complements is complicated by the fact that these appear, according to Schauber 1979, always to have the abstract structure of a complex NP:

   (i)   Kii naakaii tł'óól yizhbizhigii   yiyiinii'
            Kii Mexican rope   3.3.P.braid-COMP 3.3.P.hear (Schauber 1979, 31)

            'Kii heard (the fact) that the Mexican braided the rope'

We believe that the fact that some speakers accept sentences like (9) indicates that long-distance LF movement is not ruled out altogether in Navajo. Future investigations will certainly have to explore whether long-distance LF movement is possible in sentences like (i). For the movement, we set these cases aside.

[3] The verb in this clause bears a morpheme (*bi*) which indicates that the order of arguments is inverted. The basic word order in Navajo is SOV, but if the morpheme *bi* occurs on the verb, the order is OSV. See Perkins (1978) for details.

[4] Jelinek (1987), following judgments from Willie (1987), indicates that Navajo relative clauses are not ambiguous. In our example (12), their judgments would admit only the first reading. We do not know if this represents a geographic dialect variation, or simply variation among individuals. In the absence of a study of this issue, we will continue to follow the our judgments and those of Platero (1974).

[5] A reviewer has suggested that there are pragmatic reasons to disallow multiple focus, as such a construction would represent conflicting discourse goals. We do not consider such a possibility here for several reasons. First, as will become apparent, the problem in sentences like (14), as in the multiple questions like (13), has more to do with the presence of multiple particles than with the attempt to focus two elements. Second, we cannot see a priori why it should not be pragmatically acceptable to want to indicate multiple elements of a sentence as focussed. For example, in English it is possible to focus the coordinate phrase 'John and Mary' in a sentence like 'It is JOHN AND MARY who love each other', yet it is impossible to focus both 'John' and 'Mary' in a sentence like *'It is JOHN who it is MARY who loves'. This contrast indicates to us that the problem is syntactic rather than pragmatic.

[6] Our intention in BHPS was to suggest that Navajo extractions obey some version of the 'Freezing Principle' of Wexler and Culicover (1980).

[7] This assumption is not without problems, since Chomsky (1986) proposes that one barrier is sufficient to block proper government, but that crossing one barrier does not yield a subjacency violation. We are assuming that the trace of "dog" in our example is not properly governed by the verb, since it is the subject of the sentence (although it is adjacent to the verb — see note 2. We suspect however that similar examples in which the direct object is long-extracted will also be ungrammatical. If this turns out to be the case, we might adopt the position of Jelinek (1984), that all overt nominals in Navajo are adjuncts, so that representations like (28) with object long-extraction do involve ECP violations. This, and other issues raised by our analysis, will be discussed in the closing remarks.

[8] As it stands, our theory would seem to allow successive cyclic movement of the head of the relative clause, since the CP node would be L-marked by the verb, and therefore would not be a barrier for extraction directly out of spec, CP. We have no substantive suggestion to prohibit such movement, but perhaps it is related to structural restrictions on the predication relation which holds between a relative clause and its head NP.

[9] One might suppose that the language simply does not permit a CP to be immediately contained within another, but this is unlikely, in view of the fact that "stacked complementizers" are commonplace in Navajo surface structures.

[10] It is possible that the focus particle is actually in COMP at S-Structure, and that the locality restriction observed here is a constraint on the operation of lowering from COMP to the position adjoined to the focussed NP.

REFERENCES

Barss, A., Hale, K., Perkins, E., and Speas, M.: 1989, 'Aspects of Logical Form in Navajo', in: Cook and Rice (eds.), *Studies in Athabaskan Syntax*, J. Benjamins.

Choe, J.W.: 1987, 'LF WH-Movement and Pied Piping', *Linguistic Inquiry* **18.2**, 348–353.

Chomsky, N.: 1973, 'Conditions on Transformations', in: Anderson and Kiparsky (eds.), *A Festschrift for Morris Halle*, New York: Holt, Rinehart and Winston.

Chomsky, N.: 1981, *Lectures on Government and Binding*, Dordrecht: Foris.

Chomsky, N.: 1986, *Barriers*, MIT Press, Cambridge, MA.

Cole, P.: 1987, 'The Structure of Internally Headed Relative Clauses', *Natural Language and Linguistics Theory* **5.2**, 277–302.

Higginbotham, J. and May, R.: 1981, 'Questions, Quantifiers, and Crossing', *The Linguistic Review* **1**, 41–79.

Huang, C.-T.J.: 1982, 'Move WH in a Language without WH Movement', *The Linguistic Review* **1**, 369–416.

Jelinek, E.: 1987, '"Headless" Relatives and Pronominal Arguments: A Typological Perspective', in: Kroeber and Moore (eds.), *Native American Languages and Grammatical Typology*, Indiana University Linguistics Club, 136–148.

Jelinek, E.: 1984, 'Empty categories, case, and configurationality', *Natural Language and Linguistic Theory* **2**, 39–76.

Kaufman, E.: 1974, 'Navajo Spatial Enclitics: A Case for Unbounded rightward Movement', *Linguistic Inquiry* **5**, 507–33.

Nishigauchi, T.: 1985, 'Japanese LF: Subjacency vs. ECP', in: Lee (ed.), *Seoul Papers in Formal Grammar Theory*, Hanshin Publishers, Seoul.

Perkins, E.: 1978, 'The Role of Word Order and Scope in the Interpretation of Navajo Sentences', Ph.D. dissertation, University of Arizona, Tucson.

Platero, P.: 1974, 'The Navajo Relative Clause', *IJAL* **40**, 202–46.

Platero, P.: 1978, 'Missing Noun Phrases in Navajo', Ph.D. dissertation, MIT, Cambridge, MA.

Rizzi, L.: 1987, 'Relativized Minimality', ms. Universite de Geneve.

Ross, J.R.: 1967, 'Constraints on Variables in Syntax', Ph.D. dissertation, MIT, Cambridge, MA.

Saito, M.: 1985, 'Some Asymmetries in Japanese and their Theoretical Implications', Ph.D. dissertation, MIT, Cambridge, MA.

Schauber, E.: 1979, *The Syntax and Semantics of Questions in Navajo*, New York: Garland. Speas, M.: 1986, 'Adjunctions and Projections in Syntax', Ph.D. dissertation, MIT, Cambridge, MA.

Williamson, J.: 1984, 'An Indefiniteness Restriction for Relative Clauses in Lakhota', Paper Presented at the Groningen Conference on Indefiniteness.

Wexler, K. and Culicover, P.: 1980, *Formal Principles of Language Acquisition*, MIT Press, Cambridge, MA.

Willie, M.: 1987, 'Why There is Nothing Missing in Navajo Relative Clauses', in Cook and Rice (eds.), *Athabaskan Linguistics*, Mouton.

ROBIN CLARK

TOWARDS A MODULAR THEORY OF COREFERENCE

0. INTRODUCTION

In this paper, I will defend the notion that the theory of coreference involves at least three distinct modules. One component, codified in the binding theory, takes into account configurational relations between elements in the syntactic representation. A second module filters potential pairs of bound elements and their antecedents according to the interpretive properties of the elements themselves. Finally, I will argue that a third component filters pairs of elements according to their thematic relations to predicates.

In section 1, I will argue that the theory of coreference is modular in at least two ways; the theory must be sensitive both to syntactic relations and to semantic properties of NPs. In section 2, I will apply the results of the binding theory to explicating possible constituent structures and attempt to determine the constituent structure of Toba Batak, a language spoken in northern Sumatra, and I will show that the results are inconsistent with other aspects of the language. In section 3, I will resolve the dilemma by appeal to a theory of predicate argument structure, a theory which is closely related to thematic theory, as that term is understood in government binding theory. Finally, in section 4, I will outline the implications which this approach has for the analysis of psych verbs and to the "absorption" operation proposed in Higginbotham and May (1981).

1. OVERVIEW OF A MODULAR THEORY OF COREFERENCE

The key insight of the Binding Theory is that syntactic structure (the hierarchical grouping of linguistic elements into phrases) plays a crucial role determining possible coreference relations between NPs in a sentence. Pretheoretically, this result seems surprising since the relations *X is/is not coreferent with Y* rely on the notion of reference which is a core relation of semantic theory. After all, for two elements to be coreferential means that they refer to the same entities or covary over

49

the same sets. It appears, then, that reference and covariance are a matter of establishing the denotation set for NPs and interpreting NPs with respect to this set. One might hold the following line:

(1)   Coreference follows from reference which, in turn, follows from interpreting syntactic structures with respect to, e.g., a model.

The complete theory of reference and coreference, of which the binding theory is a part, will have to provide an account of the denotation of NPs, perhaps with an eye toward distinguishing possible coreference relationships.

By way of illustrating the above point, consider a sentence like that in (2):

(2)   [every student]$_i$ thinks he$_i$ is smart

As shown by the indexation, the pronoun *he* may be interpreted as a variable bound by the quantified NP, *every man*. We can conclude from example (2) that an element in the matrix subject position of a clause may bind a pronoun in an embedded S. Consider, next, the following set of examples:

(3) a.   Some students think they're smart.

   b.   Some students think he's smart.

   c.   Every student thinks he's smart.

   d.   Every student thinks they're smart.

Example (3a) is ambiguous. The pronoun *they* may be taken as bound by the NP *some student*; that is, each member of some set of students has a belief about himself, namely, "I am smart." On another reading, each member of some set of students has a belief about this set, namely, "We are smart." Let us refer to the former reading as the *bound* interpretation and to the latter reading as the *group* interpretation.

Given the observation that an element in the subject position of a clause may enter into either the *bound* or *group* interpretation with a pronoun in an embedded clause, how are we to account for the facts in (3b) and (3d)? The pronoun, *he*, in (3b) may not be interpreted as bound by *some students*, even though this NP is in a structural position to bind the pronoun. Example (3d) poses an analogous problem; *every student* is in a structural position to bind the pronoun *they*, but may not do so.[1] Furthermore, the pronoun cannot be taken as coreferent with the set which *every student* ranges over (the group reading).

We will want a theory of possible coreference to account for these judgements. We might allow the purely structural module of the theory of coreference to overgenerate under the following hypothesis:

> The structural theory of coreference specifies, for any pair of structural positions X and Y whether X may bind Y in principle. Whether or not a particular NP in position X actually binds a pronoun in position Y will depend, in part, on the sets in which the NP and the pronoun may take their denotation.

In other words, structural binding is subject to filtering by the interpretive component.[2] The method of overgeneration and filtering has been quite fruitful for linguistic theory (cf., the discussion in Hale, Jeanne and Platero 1977), and has played an important role in the development of general subtheories of syntax, as discussed in Chomsky (1986a).

The interpretive component is primarily concerned with the possible denotations of NPs. Returning to the examples in (3), the NP, *every student*, ranges over the set of students, taking individual members as its value, but does not refer to the set of students. The NP, *some students*, both ranges over the set of students and refers to a subset of the set of students; thus, *some students* may license either the bound interpretation or the group interpretation. The interpretive component filters pairs of possibly coreferent NPs from the group interpretation if the putative antecedent fails to refer either to an individual or to a set of individuals.

The classical form of the binding theory, as developed in Chomsky (1981), takes *binding* as its core relation:

(4) X *binds* Y just in case X c-commands Y and X is coindexed with Y.

For present purposes, we will say that X c-commands Y just in case the maximal projection dominating X also dominates Y.[3] The set of NPs is partitioned into three classes (anaphors, pronominals and R-expressions) which exhibit different behavior with respect to their abilities to enter into coreference relations. Putting aside the case of R-expressions, for the moment, the relevant conditions are as follows:

(5)   *Condition A*: Anaphors must be bound in their minimal
        syntactic domain.

(6)   *Condition B*: Pronouns must be free in their minimal
        syntactic domain.

(7)   *Condition C*: An R-expression may not be bound by an
        expression which lacks inherent reference.

(8)   *A* is the minimal syntactic domain for *B* (with respect to the
        binding theory) just in case *A* is the minimal projection
        containing *B* and a SUBJECT accessible to *B*.

The core cases which conditions A and B of the binding theory account
for are illustrated by the examples in (9) and (10), respectively:

(9) a.   John$_i$ saw himself$_i$

    b.   *John$_i$ believes that [$_S$ Mary saw himself$_i$]^4

    c.   John$_i$ saw [$_{NP}$ a picture of himself$_i$]

    d.   *John$_i$ saw [$_{NP}$ Mary's picture of himself$_i$]

(10) a.   *John$_i$ saw him$_i$

     b.   John$_i$ said Mary saw him$_i$

     c.   [$_{NP}$ John$_i$'s father]$_j$ saw him$_i$

     d.   *[$_{NP}$ John$_i$'s father]$_j$ saw him$_j$

In examples (9a) and (9c), the anaphor is bound by an element
contained in its local syntactic domain. In examples (9b) and (9d), the
putative antecedent of the anaphor is syntactically too far away since it
is not contained in the same local syntactic domain that contains the
anaphor. The relevant structural property that defines the local syntactic domain is the presence or absence of a SUBJECT accessible[5] to the
anaphor. Thus, the NP in (9d) contains a SUBJECT for the anaphor
and may, then, act as the local syntactic domain for that anaphor. The
examples in (10) illustrate that the distribution of bound pronouns is
nearly complementary to that of anaphors. The binding theory accounts
for this by requiring that pronouns be free within the local syntactic
domain where anaphors must be bound.

The effects of the version of condition C given above are illustrated
in (11):

(11) a.   *he$_i$ admires Oscar$_i$

   b.   *he$_i$ thinks that Mary$_j$ admires Oscar$_i$

   c.   *?Oscar$_i$ admires Oscar$_i$

   d.   If everyone admires Oscar then Oscar$_i$ admires Oscar$_i$.

   e.   *If everyone admires Oscar$_i$ then he$_i$ admires Oscar$_i$.

Example (11a) and (11b) show that a (potentially) referentially dependent element like a pronoun may not bind an R-expression. Example
(11c) reflects my judgement that, in the unmarked case, elements with
inherent reference may not stand in a binding relation. Consider,
however, examples (11d) and (11e) (from Evans 1980); in the consequent clause of (11d), one token of an element with inherent reference
stands in the binding relation to another token and the result seems
fully natural. In the consequent clause of (11e), on the other hand, a
referentially dependent element (a pronoun) stands in the binding
relation to the name with ungrammatical results. The distinction
between (11d) and (11e) implies that a name may be bound given an
appropriate context just so long as its binder is not a referentially
dependent element.

   The above account of condition C makes crucial appeal to the
modular character of the theory of coreference: Semantic binding need
not consider all and only the pairs of NPs provided by syntactic
binding. In particular, it can ignore pairs consisting of two tokens of the
same R-expression. While the full range of data is quite complex, we
will take the statement of Condition C given in (7) as definitive for
purposes of the discussion below.

2. CONSTITUENT STRUCTURE AND THE DISTRIBUTION OF ANAPHORS IN BATAK

In the previous section, I argued for a modular theory of coreference
relations. The theory involves a syntactic component, which makes
reference to tree geometry and indices on syntactic constituents, and an
interpretive component, which makes reference to the denotation sets
of NPs.[6] We might suppose that the syntactic theory of binding determines a list of ordered pairs:

(12)   ⟨binder, bound element⟩

of possible binding relationships in a given syntactic structure; these pairs are then filtered by the interpretive component which takes into account the referential properties of the binder and the bound element.

We can use information about coreference to induce a plausible constitutent structure for a given sentence. Suppose, for example, that a particular element, Z, is an anaphor and that W is the antecedent for Z in a structure:

(13)   ...W...Z...

Then, according to the structural theory of binding, W must both c-command and be coindexed with Z in (13). But if W must c-command Z, then we have ruled out a number of a priori possible constituent structures. In particular, a plausible representation for (13) must be such that W c-commands Z, since it is only then that we can prove that W binds Z in our theory.[7]

Let us turn to a concrete example of this implication. Toba Batak is an Austronesian language spoken in northern Sumatra. The canonical word order for a simple sentence involving a monotransitive verb is:

(14)   Verb NP NP

(15)   Mang-ida si   John si   Bill[8]
        Voice-see PM John PM Bill

        'Bill saw John.'

Toba Batak has two voices: the *mang* voice and the *di* voice. Consider the assignment of the AGENT and PATIENT θ-roles. The *mang* voice associates AGENT with the right-most NP and PATIENT with the left-most NP. The *di* voice associates the AGENT θ-role with the left-most NP and the PATIENT θ-role with the right-most NP. There is, therefore, an apparent 'inversion' of the NPs in pairs of sentences that differ only with respect to voice:

(16) a. Mangallang [sassing i]   [dengke i]
         eat   worm DET fish   DET

     b. Diallang [dengke i]   [sassing i]
         eat   fish   DET worm DET

         'The fish ate the worm.'

Information about potential antecedent/anaphor relations can be used to limit the range of hypotheses about constituent structure in Toba Batak. We can minimally assume the following from the information above:

(17)   [$_\text{clause}$ V NP$_1$ NP$_2$]

We are now in a position to examine the distribution of anaphors in Toba Batak and to consider the implications that their distribution has for fixing the constituent structure of the language.

Consider the examples in (18):[9]

(18) a. Mangida dirina$_i$ si   John$_i$.
         see   self   PM John

         'John saw himself.'

    b. *Mangida dirina$_j$ si   John$_i$.
         see   self   PM John

The above examples show that the element, *dirina*, is obligatorily taken as coreferent with another NP in the sentence; example (18b) is ungrammatical because *dirina* is taken as disjoint from *John*, leaving *dirina* free. The examples in (19) should reinforce the hypothesis that the relationship between *dirina* and its antecedent is syntactic.

(19) a. Manghatahon dirina$_i$ tu si   Bill$_j$ si John$_i$.
         talk   self   to PM Bill   PM John

         'John$_i$ talked about himself$_i$ to Bill.'

    b. *Manghatahon dirina$_j$ tu si   Bill$_j$ si John$_i$.
         talk   self   to PM Bill   PM John

         'John talked to Bill$_j$ about himself$_j$.

In example (19a), *John* may serve as the antecedent for *dirina*; note that *John* must be in a position to c-command *dirina* since *John* is a bare NP argument. *Bill*, on the other hand, is embedded in a PP and, so, may not c-command an element external to the PP. Example (19b) confirms the assumption that c-command is relevant in determining the antecedent for *dirina* since *Bill*, a non-c-commanding NP, may not act as antecedent.

Finally, the examples in (20) show that syntactic locality is important in fixing the antecedent for *dirina*:

(20) a. *Mangidok [$_{S'}$ na [$_S$ patandahon si   Bill tu si   Ria
        say   that   introduce PM Bill to PM Ria
        dirina$_i$]] si John$_i$.
        self   PM John

        *'John said that himself introduced Bill to Ria'

     b. Mangidok [$_{S'}$ na [$_S$ patandahon si   Bill tu si   Ria
        say   that   introduce PM Bill to PM Ria
        imana$_{i/j}$]] si John$_i$.
        he   PM John

        'John$_i$ said that he$_{i/j}$ introduced Bill to Ria.'

John may not act as antecedent for *dirina* since *John* is contained in a clause that is superordinate to the clause containing *dirina*. Note that (20b) shows that a pronoun may optionally be bound by *John*. The examples in (20) establish that the governing category of *dirina* is relevant in determining its possible syntactic antecedents.

The data above indicate that *dirina* is an anaphor in the classical sense: It must be taken as coreferent with a c-commanding antecedent contained in a local syntactic domain. The data in (18—20) are not completely decisive since one might adopt the hypothesis that *dirina* is a subject-oriented anaphor and, as a result, is subject to restrictions not associated with anaphors in English. The example in (21) shows that *dirina* is not subject-oriented but may be bound by a non-subject:

(21)   Manghatahon si   Bob$_i$ tu dirina$_{\{i/j\}}$ si   John$_j$
       talk   PM Bob to self   PM John

       'John talked about Bob to himself.'

Both NPs in the above example c-command the anaphor and are potential antecedents. If *dirina* were truly subject-oriented, we would expect the example in (21) to be unambiguous. Since either interpretation is well-formed, we conclude that *dirina* is not a subject-oriented anaphor.

Having established the basic nature of the anaphor, *dirina*, we can investigate the relationship between binding and constituent structure:

(22) a. Mangida dirina si John.
   see self PM John

  'John saw himself.'

 b. *Mangida si John dirina
   see PM John self

  'John saw himself.'

It would appear from the examples in (22) that the right-most NP asymmetrically c-commands the left-most NP. The above facts are compatible with the following constituent structure:

(23) $[_S [_V max$ V NP-1] NP-2]

(24) a. $[_S [_V max$ mangida dirina] si John]

 b. *$[_S [_V max$ mangida si John] dirina]

NP-2 may bind NP-1 in (23), but not vice versa. The anaphor in (24a) is locally bound as required by condition A of the binding theory. The structure in (24b) would violate both condition A (*dirina* is free) and condition C (since a referentially dependent element, *dirina*, binds a name, *John*).

The data in (25) is rather problematic:

(25) a. Diida si John dirina.
   see PM John self

  'John saw himself.'

 b. *Diida dirina si John
   see self PM John

  'John saw himself.'

The example in (25a) shows that the left-most NP may bind the right-most NP; the left-most NP must c-command the right-most NP. Example (25b) indicates that the right-most NP may not bind the left-most NP. The obvious conclusion is that the left-most NP asymmetrically c-commands the right-most NP. The facts in (25) indicate that Toba Batak has a constituent structure similar to (26):

(26) $[_V max$ V NP-1 $[_X max$ NP-2]]

(27) a. [$_V$*max* diida si John$_i$ [$_X$*max* dirina$_i$]]

   b. *[$_V$*max* diida dirina$_i$ [$_X$*max* si John$_i$]]

In (27a), the R-expression, *John*, asymmetrically c-commands the anaphor, *dirina*; conditions A and C of the binding theory are satisfied since *dirina* is locally a-bound by *John* while *John* remains A-free. In (27b), on the other hand, the anaphor, *dirina*, asymmetrically c-commands the R-expression, *John*; conditions A and C of the binding theory are violated since *dirina* locally A-free (violating condition A) and *John* is A-bound by a referentially dependent element (violating condition C).

We are faced with an apparent disunity in surface constituent structure depending upon the voice of the verb. The situation can be represented as follows:

(28) a. *Mang* voice: [[mangida dirina]   si John]
                             | |
                          THEME   EXPERIENCER

   b. *Di* voice: [diida$_V$ si John [t_V dirina]]
                             | |
                     EXPERIENCER   THEME

The contrast in surface constituent structure is mediated by a morphological process (voice) and, furthermore, there is surface evidence for the contrast: Namely, the distribution of overt anaphors differs according to the voice on the verb. Given the structural theory of binding, the language learner would be forced to posit particular constituent structures in order to guarantee c-command.

The issue at hand is directly related to the Uniformity of Theta Assignment Hypothesis advanced in Baker (1985):

(29)   *The Uniformity of Theta Assignment Hypothesis*

   Indentical thematic relationships between items are represented by identical structural relationship between those items at D-structure.

If the hypothesis is correct, then (22a) and (25a) must share a nearly identical D-structure representation (up to the morpheme for the voice contrast). Assume that the structure is as shown in (30) (details omitted):

(30)

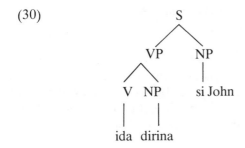

The *mang-* and *di-* morphemes occur as independent elements at D-structure, perhaps adjoined to the left of S. The *di-* morpheme triggers verb raising in the syntax and the complex *di*+V assigns Case to the structural subject under adjacency (see Stowell 1981). In the *mang-* voice, the verb remains in situ and assigns Case to the structural object. The adjacency requirement on Case assignment would trigger the gross word order difference observed between the two voices.

The above hypothesis, however rough, provides an account of the possible surface loci of adverbs in Batak (data from Schachter 1984):

(31) a. *Nantoari* mangida si Bill si John.
     yesterday see   PM Bill PM John

   b. *Mangida *nantoari* si Bill si John
      see   yesterday PM Bill PM John

   c. Mangida si Bill *nantoari* si John.
      see   PM Bill yesterday PM John

   d. Mangida si Bill si John *nantoari*.
      see   PM Bill PM John yesterday

   'John saw Bill yesterday.'

(32) a. *Nantoari* diida si John si Bill.
     yesterday see PM John PM Bill

   b. *Diida *nantoari* si John si Bill
      see   yesterday PM John PM Bill

   c. Diida si John *nantoari* si Bill.
      see   PM John yesterday PM Bill

(32) d. Diida si   John si   Bill *nantoari*.
        see   PM John PM Bill yesterday

'John saw Bill yesterday.'

Since Case is assigned under government and adjacency, we can account for the ungrammaticality of (31b) and (32b) by saying that Case assignment to the left-most NP has been blocked by the intervening adverb, *nantoari*. But then the following must hold:

(33) a.   *mang-V* NP-1 NP-2

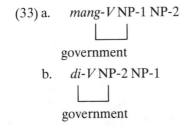

government

     b.   *di-V* NP-2 NP-1

government

That is, the verb must govern the NP which is right-adjacent to it.

The above hypothesis presents some difficulties for the account of extraction in Toba Batak. As pointed out in Clark (1985), the NP which is governed by the verb may never be extracted. This effect holds no matter what the voice of the governing verb is. Furthermore, the right-most NP may always be extracted. Again, this holds no matter what the voice of the verb is. The following data illustrate this point:

(34) a. Mangida si   John ise?
        see   PM John who

     b. Ise$_i$ mangida si   John t_i?
        who saw   PM John

     c. Diida ise   si   John?
        see   who PM John

     d. *Ise$_i$ diida t_i si   John?
         who saw   PM John

        'Who saw John?'

(35) a. Mangida aha   si   John?
        see   what PM John

     b. *Aha$_i$ mangida t_i si   John?
         what see   PM John

(35) c. Diida si   John aha?
       see   PM   John what

   d. Aha$_i$ diida si   John t_i?
      what   see   PM   John

      'What did John see?'

The above asymmetry persists across overt syntactic movement and the assignment of scope to quantifiers:

(36) a. Manopot tolu   soridadu ganup presiden.
        visit   three   soldier   every president

   b. *Disopot ganup presiden tolu   soridadu
      visit   every   president three soldier

   c. Manopot tolu   soridadu angka presiden.
      visit   three   soldier   every president

   d. Disopot angka presiden tolu   soridadu.
      visit   every   president three soldier

      'Every president visited three soldiers.'

The quantifiers *angka* and *ganup* both have the force of universal quantification; they differ in that *ganup* takes wide scope obligatorily. Thus, example (36a) is unambiguous with the interpretation that every president is such that he visited a group of three soldiers (not necessarily the same group of soldiers). Examples (36c) and (36d) are ambiguous. We can account for this if we assume that *ganup* induces movement to Comp at LF, not unlike the treatment accorded to wh-in situ. Example (36b) would then be ruled out by the same principle that rules out examples (34d) and (35b); presumably, some form of the Empty Category Principle (Chomsky 1981; Chosmky 1986b).

If we adopt the structures in (37) as a working hypothesis:

(37) a. [$_s$ *mang*- [$_v$max V NP] NP]

   b. [$_s$ *di*- V NP [$_v$max t_v NP]]

our theory will have to derive the following properties:

(38)   *mang*- voice
         (a) The subject NP may be antecedent governed (which allows leftward extraction).
         (b) The object NP is not properly governed.

(39)   *di-* voice
(a) The subject NP cannot be antecedent governed (which blocks leftward extraction).
(b) The object NP is properly governed.

Property (38a) is unproblematic given that the subject may be antecedent governed from Comp; property (39a) entails first that the fronted verb does not lexically govern the subject NP but does block antecedent government from Comp.[10] Properties (38b) and (39b) are more problematic; we must ensure that the lexical verb is not a proper governor while the trace of the verb allows for proper government of the object.[11] Either the trace of a verb may act as a proper governor for the object or the raising of the verb makes VP transparent to antecedent government from Comp. If the latter case is correct, then we must account for how the fronted verb blocks antecedent government of the subject but not the object.

While a fully developed version of the analysis of Batak presented above would involve subtleties not mentioned here, it does seem that the constituent structure presented in (37) is consistent with the distribution of anaphors but problematic for the distribution of wh-traces. An apparently simpler solution would be to assign distinct D-structure representations to the two voices; such an analysis would violate the Uniformity of Theta Assignment Hypothesis.

Let us assume that the difference between the *mang* and *di* voices is precisely that the morphology affects thematic role assignment (cf., Marantz 1984). The *mang* voice applied to the verb *ida* allows the THEME role to be assigned to the NP governed and Case-marked by the verb. The *di* voice applied to the verb *ida* allows the EXPERIENCER role to be assigned to the NP governed and Case-marked by the verb. In the *mang* voice, the EXPERIENCER may be extracted but the THEME may not. The *di* voice invokes the opposite: The THEME may be extracted and the EXPERIENCER may not be. The generalization regarding extraction would make reference to government relations alone. But the government relations would be mediated by the morphological form of the verb. This analysis is consistent with the following bracketings:

(40) a.   [[mang-V NP-1] NP-2]

   b.   [[di-V NP-2] NP-1]

ccommands NP-1 in the *mang* voice and that NP-1 c-commands NP-2 in the *di* voice. A labelling consistent with the apparent c-command relations is:

(41) a. $[_V max [_{V'} \text{mang-V NP-1}] \text{NP-2}]$

  b. $[_V max [_{V'} \text{di-V NP-2}] \text{NP-1}]$

Such a language should lack true anaphors in subject position or object position since such an anaphor/antecedent pair enter into a mutual c-command relation and the anaphor would bind its antecedent. Hence, an anaphor would always bind its antecedent. The only pair syntactically compatible with this configuration would be a pair of anaphors; but their interpretation would be a case circular referential dependence (cf., Higginbotham 1983).

3. BINDING AND PREDICATES

The puzzle may be summarized as follows: The structural theory of binding along with the assumption that *dirina* is a true anaphor supports separate surface constituent structures for the two basic voices in Toba Batak. These two constituent structures, however, present problems for a unified theory of proper government.

I would like to propose a solution to this dilemma that both allows us to retain the classical notion of binding along with a unified treatment of surface constituent structure for Toba Batak. The idea is simply this: The complete theory of coreference makes reference not only to syntactic relations and denotation sets, but is also sensitive to the predicate structure (in a sense to be made precise).

Consider sentences of the following type (cf., Postal 1971):

(42) a. John$_i$ saw himself$_i$

  b. *John$_i$ was seen by himself$_i$

In (42b), the prepositional phrase, *by himself*, is taken to be an agent *by* phrase. Following the analysis of passives given in Jaeggli (1986), let us suppose that the agent *by* phrase is adjoined to VP. The structure of (42b) is, therefore:

(43) $*[_S \text{John}_i [_{Infl'} \text{was} [_{VP} [_{VP} \text{seen } t_i] \text{ by himself}_i]]]$

By virtue of its position as structural subject, the NP *John* c-comands the anaphor contained in the *by* phrase. Despite this fact, *John* may not be taken as the antecedent for *himself*, in the above structure. Notice that *John* bears the THEME θ-role by virtue of being in a chain with the object trace; the anaphor, *himself*, will bear the EXPERIENCER θ-role.

The facts regarding anaphora in English passive constructions are quite reminiscent of the facts regarding anaphora in the Toba Batak voice system:

(44) a. *Mangida si   John$_i$ dirina$_i$
         see   PM John   self

     b. *Diida dirina$_i$ si   John$_i$
         see   self   PM John

     *'himself saw John'

In both (44a) and (44b), *dirina* bears the EXPERIENCER θ-role and *John* bears the THEME θ-role. In neither case may *John* act as the antecedent for *dirina*. The English example suggests that this fact holds irrespective of the c-command relations between the antecedent and the anaphor.

It is tempting to conclude from the above that binding is directly sensitive to thematic roles. One might, for example, attempt to arrange thematic roles into a hierarchy with the constraint that an argument assigned a particular thematic role can only bind another argument if the second argument is assigned a thematic role lower on the hierarchy (see, for example, the treatment of coreference in Jackendoff 1972).[12] Presumably, EXPERIENCER is higher on such a hierarchy than THEME so that an argument assigned EXPERIENCER could bind an argument assigned THEME, but not vice versa. This approach to binding does not provide a clear account of examples like the following:

(45)   John persuaded [every student]$_i$ [that he$_i$ should take a comprehensive exam]

Since *every student* in (45) is a PATIENT and the pronoun, *he*, is an AGENT, we would not expect that *every student* could bind *he*. This would leave accidental coreference as the remaining possible coreference relation between the two arguments. For reasons discussed in section 1, an NP quantified with *every* never enters into accidental coreference relations with another NP. We would therefore expect that *every student* and *he* should be interpreted as obligatorily disjoint, which is counter to fact.

Suppose, however, we were to approach the problem in the following way. Thematic roles, in addition to giving a certain amount of cognitive information about the roles various arguments play in the event or state described by a sentence, also relate argument positions to n-place predicates; this is essentially the account of θ-roles given in Higginbotham (1985). To take a simple example, consider the following:

(46) a. John saw Bill.

    b. see, $[-N, +V]$, $\langle$EXPERIENCER, $\langle$THEME$\rangle\rangle$

In example (46a), the two-place predicate, *see*; this is indicated by the inclusion of the thematic roles in angled brackets. The distinction between the internal thematic role assigned by the two-place predicate and the external thematic role assigned by the one-place predicated is indicated by an extra pair of angled brackets around the internal thematic role. Thus, *see* takes as its internal argument an NP which it marks as THEME. Assignment of this θ-role under government allows *see* to project to a phrase (in the sense of X'-theory) and to project to the one-place predicate *see Bill*. This one-place predicate may assign the EXPERIENCER thematic role to its argument, in this case *John*. Assignment of the θ-role allows the complex *John saw Bill* to project to a zero-place predicate (i.e., a proposition). We are able to construe θ-role assignment both as a form of functional application which maps argument positions to places in a relation and as assignment of cognitive roles to arguments.

Suppose this theory of predicate formation places the following constraint on binding pairs:[13]

(47)   The nth argument of an n-place predicate may only bind into the m-place predicate where m is greater than or equal to n.

Notice that principle (47), unlike thematic hierarchies, makes no reference to the content of thematic roles. We will assume, instead, that thematic roles are related to positions in a predicate in some principled manner (see Marantz 1984 for one such proposal). Principle (47) makes reference to predicate argument structure and not the conceptual content of thematic roles.

Consider, for example, (42b) (*John was seen by himself). Here, the verb assigns the THEME θ-role to *John*, projecting from a two-place predicate to a one-place predicate (*see John*). This one-place predicate combines with the passive morpheme to form a zero-place predicate. The passive morpheme may optionally transmit the EXPERIENCER θ-role to the object of *by* yielding the following D-Sructure:

(48)   [$_S$ [e] [$_{Infl'}$ was [$_{VP}$ [$_{VP}$ seen John] by himself]]]

The expletive empty category in subject position is, of course, forced by the Extended Projection Principle. The inability of the passive participle to assign Case forces movement of *John* from the D-Structure object position to S-Structure subject position leaving behind a trace:

(49)   [$_S$ John$_i$ [$_{Infl'}$ was [$_{VP}$ [$_{VP}$ seen t_i] by himself]]]

This movement allows *John* to c-command the anaphor at S-Structure and at LF. Following various researchers (Aoun 1986; Weinberg, Aoun, Hornstein and Lightfoot 1987; Weinberg and Hornstein 1986), let us assume that binding applies at LF. The only possible binding pair admitted by the structural theory of binding is ⟨John, himself⟩. This pair is rejected by the theory of predicate formation (θ-theory construed as above) since *John* is an argument of a two-place predicate (*see*) and so may not bind *himself* which is an argument of the one-place (*was seen John*).

Note that c-command and coindexation are still necessary prerequisites for binding. Hence, we will still rule out (50) as impossible since the antecedent does not c-command the anaphor:

(50)   *himself$_i$ was seen by John$_i$

Furthermore, the approach is not sensitive to the cognitive content of particular thematic roles; it is specifically sensitive to the relation between thematic role assignment and n-place predicate formation.

Returning to an earlier example:

(51)   John persuaded [every student]$_i$ [that he$_i$ should take a comprehensive exam]

The verb, *persuade*, is a three-place predicate; it takes a proposition and a PATIENT to map to a one-place predicate (*persuade every student that he should take a comprehensive exam*). Since *every student* is the second argument, it may bind into the proposition. Hence, the binding relation between *every student* and *he* in (51) is unsurprising.

Huang has pointed out (personal communication) that the internal arguments of the head need not be treated as unstructured. Consider the well-known contrast between *promise* and *persuade*:

(52) a.   John$_i$ promised Bill$_j$ [PRO$_{\{i/*j\}}$ to see Mary]

   b.   John$_i$ persuaded Bill$_j$ [PRO$_{\{j/*i\}}$ to see Mary]

The verb *persuade* allows its internal argument to control the PRO in the embedded clause while *promise* requires its external argument to act as the controller.

We might distinguish *promise* from *persuade* by means of its argument structure; *promise* is a three-place predicate which combines with a DATIVE argument to form a two-place predicate. The two-place predicate combines with a proposition to form a one-place predicate:

(53)   promise, $[-N, +V]$, $\langle\text{AGENT}, \langle\langle\text{DAT}\rangle, \text{PROP}\rangle\rangle$

(54)

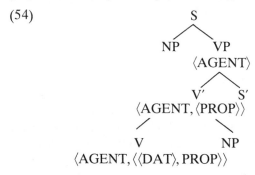

If the structural theory of binding allows the pairs $\langle$John, PRO$\rangle$ and $\langle$Bill, PRO$\rangle$, the thematic component of binding will filter the latter pair since *Bill* is an argument in the third place and, so, cannot bind into the second place of the predicate.

A similar account holds for the contrast in (55):

(55) a.   John$_i$ talked to Bill$_j$ about himself$_{\{i, j\}}$

   b.   John$_i$ talked about Bill$_j$ to himself$_{\{i/*?j\}}$

The verb *talk* is a three-place predicate which takes a THEME (marked with the preposition, *about*) and maps to a two-place predicate. This predicate takes a DATIVE (marked by *to*) and forms a one-place predicate. Even given free reanalysis of either preposition with the verb, the THEME argument will be unable to bind the DATIVE argument. Since both the THEME and the DATIVE are governed by prepositions, Case theory places no restriction that either argument of the verb must be adjacent to it.

Let us return to Toba Batak; the examples in (56) are ill-formed:

(56) a. *Mangida si   John$_i$ dirina$_i$
         see   PM John self

     b. *Diida dirina$_i$ si   John$_i$
         see   self   PM John

        (*'himself saw John')

The difference between the two examples in (56) is essentially morphological. The verb, *ida*, is a two-place predicate which takes a THEME and maps onto a one-place predicate. This one-place predicate takes an EXPERIENCER and maps onto a proposition. Both (56a) and (56b) will have essentially the same LF representations since their truth conditions do not vary and their predicate argument structure is, intuitively, equivalent; this is a desirable result given that the two voices have the same truth conditions.

Given this account, we would not expect *John* to bind *dirina* since *John* is an argument of a two-place predicate and *dirina* is an argument of a one-place predicate. The structural relation of binding admits two possible pairs for each of the examples in (56), ⟨John, dirina⟩ and ⟨dirina, John⟩. The theory of predicate formation simple rejects ⟨John, dirina⟩ as an impossible antecedent/anaphor pair since *John* is an internal argument and *dirina* is an argument of the one-place predicate. The remaining pair, ⟨dirina, John⟩, for both examples in (56) violates our formulation of condition C; *dirina* may bind *John* given that it c-commands *John* and it is binding into a two-place predicate. But then *John* is bound by a referentially dependent element.

We can contrast the examples in (56) with some well-formed examples of antecedent/anaphor pairs:

(57) a. Mangida dirina$_i$ si   John$_i$
         see   self   PM John

(57) b. Diida si   John$_i$ dirina$_i$
         see   PM John   self

'John saw himself'

Again, the structural relation of binding returns two possible pairs for each example, ⟨John, dirina⟩ and ⟨dirina, John⟩. In both of the above cases, *dirina* is an argument of a two-place relation (*ida*) while *John* is an argument of the one-place predicate (*ida dirina*). Hence, *John* may bind *dirina*, but not vice versa; the other pair, ⟨dirina, John⟩, is simply ruled out as a possible binding pair. The examples in (57), then, obey both conditions A and C of the binding theory.

Our approach allows us to adopt a unified constituent structure for Toba Batak, as desired:

(58) $[_{V}max [_{V'} V NP-1] NP-2]$

This is so since c-command and coindexation are not sufficient to establish a binding relationship. Properties of thematic structure (in particular, predicate formation) must be taken into account.

4. TWO APPLICATIONS

I have, so far, defended the view that the linguistic theory of coreference consists of three modules:

(59) (i) A binding theory based on syntactic relations.

      (ii) An interpretive theory of the denotations of arguments.

      (iii) A theory of predicate argument structure.

The three modules are simple, but may interact in subtle ways. The binding theory makes reference to relations defined on constituent structure to derive a set of possible binding pairs. The interpretive theory checks the pairs to guarantee that each member of the pair has an appropriate type of denotation. Finally, the theory of predicate argument structure ensures that no element binds an argument outside of its predicate; that is, if an NP combines with a verb to form a one-place predicate, then that NP cannot bind the semantic subject of that predicate, even if it is in a structural position to do so.

The approach advocated here serves to constrain the possible analyses that can be accorded to a variety of phenomena; in this section, I will sketch the treatment of two such phenomena: psych verbs and absorption.

Pysch verbs (Belletti and Rizzi, forthcoming) present an apparent counterexample both to the binding theory and to "Burzio's Generalization" (Burzio 1986). Descriptively, it appears that the surface object can bind into the surface subject:

(60) a. [stories about himself$_i$] bother John$_i$

  b. [these pictures of herself$_i$] annoy Mary$_i$

  c. [insulting each other$_i$] amuses the boys$_i$

Examples like those in (60) have led to the hypothesis that the surface subject originates as a complement of the verb at D-structure (adapted from Belletti and Rizzi, forthcoming):

(61)

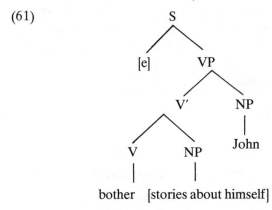

Since the verb cannot assign Case to both objects, NP movement is forced by the Case Filter:

(62)   [[stories about himself]$_i$ [bother t_i John]]

The surface binding facts are unproblematic if we adopt the analysis of Belletti and Rizzi (forthcoming) that condition A applies opportunistically at any level of representation. Since *John* c-commands the anaphor at D-structure, condition A is satisfied at that level and need not reapply at S-structure (or LF).

Belletti and Rizzi note, however, that the above analysis appears to violate the following generalization (from Burzio 1986):

(63)   All and only the verbs that can assign a θ-role to the subject
         can assign (accusative) Case to an object.

Psych verbs cannot assign an external θ-role since movement to subject
position would be impossible. If this is correct, then a psych verb
cannot assign Case to any NP and we would expect the examples ·in
(60) to violate the Case Filter. Belletti and Rizzi argue that the surface
object in psych verb constructions bears inherent (thematically related)
Case and, so, this construction does not provide a true counterexample
to (63).

In the framework proposed here, the D-structure analysis in (61) is
the only possibility; if the surface subject were a D-structure argument
of the one-place predicate (VP), then binding by the object would
minimally be ruled out by the theory of predicate argument structure.
The surface subject and object must be at least coequal at some level of
representation for there to be binding.

The S-structure in (62) remains problematic. In particular, the
apparent surface object must be adjacent to the verb:

(64) a.   These photos annoyed John *yesterday*.

    b.   *these photos annoyed *yesterday* John

    c.   *Yesterday* these photos annoyed John.

The contrast in (64) indicates that the verb is in a Case-marking
relation with the surface object; adjacency between the verb and the
apparent object is forced because the object must receive Case from the
verb. If the post-verbal NP bore inherent Case, perhaps as a function of
the thematic relations in the sentence, the word order facts in (64)
would be somewhat surprising; thematic role assignment is not sensitive
to adjacency. If this reasoning is correct, then psych verbs are problematic for the generalization in (63).

We might adapt the analysis of verb movement from Koopman
(1984). Briefly, Koopman argues that the main verb may raise to Infl to
license Case assignment to some position. Like NP movement, then,
local movement of the verb is forced by Case theory. We might
suppose that the same process underlies Case assignment in psych verb
constructions; the verb alone is not sufficient to assign Case to the
postverbal NP, but the combination of V+Infl is sufficient. The verb
must, then, obligatorily raise the Infl to assign Case:

(65)

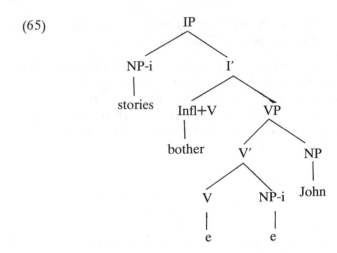

The VP in (65) is transparent to government from V+Infl since the two are coindexed; *John*, then, may be Case-governed. We may assume that either *John* fronts to the left-periphery of VP or that the traces, being Caseless, are invisible for purposes of adjacency. No phonologically realized material may interven between the post-verbal NP and the V+Infl, however.

Note that the *John* could not have raised to subject in (65), leaving the structural object in situ. In this case, either the verb could fail to raise. Since the V+Infl complex is crucial for Case-marking, the object would then violate the Case Filter. If the verb were to raise, then direct government by the V+Infl complex would be blocked due to the presence of a closer governor, the verbal trace. This latter condition is related to the Minimality Condition of Chomsky (1986b).

We turn, finally, to cases of crossing coreference (Higginbotham and May 1981; May 1985; Clark and Keenan 1985; May forthcoming). Crossing coreference bears some superficial resemblance to the binding possible in psych verb constructions; the surface object may bind a position contained in the surface subject:

(66)   [every pilot who shot at it$_i$]$_j$ hit [some MIG that chased him$_j$]$_i$

The binding in (66) is problematic both for the treatment of bound pronouns (Higginbotham 1983; Haik 1984; Koopman and Sportiche 1982).

In order to derive both the correct interpretation for crossing sentences and to account for the binding found there, Higginbotham and May (1981) define the operation of absorption which maps a sequence of simple operators onto a single complex operator; roughly:

(67) $[_{NP1}\ Qx: N'x]\ [_{NP2}\ Qy: N'y] \rightarrow [Qx:Qy: N'x\ \text{and}\ N'y]$

where NP1 and NP2 are in a government configuration. Higginbotham and May then give a semantic interpretation for absorbed operators which correctly accounts for the interpretation of crossing sentences. It is observed in Clark and Keenan (1985) that the absorption operation fails to preserve truth conditions in simple cases of non-crossing coreference, as in (68):

(68)   Every student read a book.

The theoretical problem is to force absorption in the crossing case while preventing (or filtering) its application in the simple, non-crossing case. Intuitively, we might suppose that absorption is simply a means for circumventing the filtering effects of the theory of predicate argument structure; the operators combine to form a single complex predicate; in particular, both operators become coequal in terms of predicate argument structure at LF. Thus, if absorption fails to apply, the theory of predicate argument structure will filter the LF representation of a crossing sentence for the familiar reason outined above.

We are left with the question of what filters absorption in the case of simple, non-crossing structures like (68). Following a suggestion in Clark and Keenan (1985), we might suppose that absorption is blocked unless both operators bind a variable in both NPs the absorption operation might best be stated as in (69):

(69) $[_{NP1}\ Qx:N'x, y]\ [_{NP2}\ Qy:N'x, y] \rightarrow [Qx:Qy:N'x, y\ \text{and}\ N'x, y]$

where NP1 and NP2 are in a government configuration. The restatement of absorption in (69) allows crossing constructions to circumvent constraints on binding that follow from predicate argument structure; absorption is, however, blocked in the simple cases.

6. CONCLUSION

I have argued in this paper that a modular approach to coreference which takes into account thematic relations (predicate argument structure), denotations of NPs (interpretation) and structural relations (binding) can yield a simple account of a variety of problems including accidental coreference, antecedent/anaphor relations in English passives and in Toba Batak. The theory, furthermore, constrains the analysis of psych verb constructions and crossing coreference.

Given the modular character of the theory, we can distinguish it from the classical binding theory (Chomsky 1981) and from more recent proposals like θ-binding (Williams 1986). In justifying a module, it is necessary to show that it reflects general linguistic properties that are evidenced by a wide variety of prima facie unrelated structures. While I have not attempted to do so here, it seems that the notion of predicate argument structure is independently required in constraining the relation between lexical representation and D-structure representation, for example. The theory may also play a role in relating adjuncts to heads as "secondary" predicates and in constraining certain morphological representations (cf., Levin and Rappaport 1986):

(70) a.   The workers loaded the wagon with hay.

   b. *the workers unloaded the wagon with hay

Furthermore, the question of the relationship between predicate formation and bound pronouns remains to be setlled. For example, I have not explicated the binding in so-called "donkey" sentences (Heim 1982; Haik 1984; Hornstein 1984; May 1985):

(71)   Every man who owns *a donkey* beats *it*.

Finally, as pointed out by J. Whitman, bound pronouns in the agent phrase of full passives appear problematic:

(72)   *every boy* is loved by *his* mother.

In particular, the subject in (72) should not be able to directly bind into the agent phrase. I will leave these questions for future research, although (72) may be a marked structure.

The theory of predicate argument structure is primarily a theory that relates syntax with the interpretive component. It is only natural to expect that predicate argument structure acts to constrain coreference relations. The theory of predicate argument structure cannot fully determine potential coreference any more than the interpretive theory or the binding theory can. It seems that, once again, we must appeal to the modular character of grammar for an explanation of the observed facts.

ACKNOWLEDGEMENTS

I gratefully acknowledge Wilson Manik for his clear judgements on Toba Batak. Many of the ideas in this paper were developed over the course of a number of consversations with Joseph Aoun. Finally, I wish to thank Jim Huang, John Whitman and anonymous reviewers for their many comments on an earlier draft of this paper. I, of course, bear all responsibility for errors and misrepresentations.

NOTES

[1] Innovative dialects which have circumvented certain agreement constraints on binding to avoid sexism may treat *they* as bound by *every student* in (3d).

[2] We will also want to include constraints on the morphological shape of elements. For example, taking ϕ features to be those features which express gender and number we will no doubt want to require that a bound element must agree in ϕ features with its binder; but cf., note 1.

[3] This is the definition of *m-command* given in Chomsky (1986b). It should be noted that a stricter version of command may be necessary for the binding theory. In particular, the binding involved in *ne* cliticization (Chomsky 1981; Belletti and Rizzi 1981; Burzio 1986) may require a very strict locality condition given the contrast in (i):

(i) a. $*[_{VP}$ *ne*$_i$ telefonano$]$ [molti e_i]]

        'Many of them telephoned.'

   b. $[_{VP}$ *ne*$_i$ arrivano [molti e_i]]

         'Mary of them arrived.'

The clitic in (ia) may be unable to command out of the minimal VP and therefore cannot license the clitic trace in the NP adjoined to VP. For present purposes, I will simply assme that the clitic must adjoin to a verb, or verbal complex, which theta-governs the clitic trace. This will distinguish between the intransitive case in (ia) and the ergative case in (ib).

[4] Note that the existence of this syntactic locality requirement on the antecedent of an anaphor adds further weight to the argument that a syntactic theory of binding must be added to supplement the semantic theory of coreference. Ed Keenan (personal communication) has pointed out that there is no obvious semantic reason why an anaphor could not have as its antecedent an NP that is arbitrarily far away from the anaphor in a syntactic structure; see, also, Keenan (to appear) where parts of the binding theory are recast in terms of "semantic case theory." It is quite plausible that the locality conditions on binding are syntactic for reasons having more to do with acquisition than logic.

[5] A subject is accessible to anaphor is an element *A* which is structurally a subject and which may in principle be coindexed with the anaphor. That is, coindexing *A* with the anaphor does not violate any principle of grammar (cf., Aoun 1985). We note without discussion that a tensed Infl may count as a subject for the purposes of binding (cf., Chomsky (1981) and the references cited there).

[6] We will no doubt wish to extend this to categories other than NP; there is nothing anomalous in taking projections of A, N, P, V, etc. as having denotations (it is, in fact, virtually necessary given compositionality). The binding theory may itself extend to these categories. For the sake of discussion, however, let us limit our attention to NP.

[7] Presumably, information of this sort may be accessible to the Language Acquisition Device and serve to rule out some a priori plausible mental representations.

[8] I use 'PM' to denote a person marker which occurs before names.

[9] The data in (18—21) are from Sugamoto (1984) and Schachter (1984).

[10] The Minimality Condition of Chomsky (1986) may block antecedent government from Comp given that the verb is the minimal governor for the subject NP in the *di* voice.

[11] It is important to bear in mind the observation of Torrego (1984) that verb fronting often inverts subject/object asymmetries. Apparently, the trace of a verb is not sufficient to properly govern the object, which can only be antecedent governed from Comp. Note further that the fronted verb in Spanish acts like a proper governor for the subject, which licenses "long extraction" of subjects. Thus, the rough analysis of Batak in the text brings us to a near contradiction when compared with the facts in Spanish. A full analysis of extraction in Batak, and a comparison with the relevant structures in Spanish, is far beyond the scope of this paper, although the general nature of the problem is clear.

[12] Indeed, Schachter (1984) and Sugamoto (1984) have both suggested that antecedent/anaphor relations in Toba Batak is sensitive to a "thematic hierarchy":

(i)   Actor > Patient > Dative

I reject this proposal for reasons cited in the body of the text.

[13] The theory of Pica (1984) makes crucial reference to the position of the anaphor; in particular, true anaphors must occur in theta-bar positions. This constraint may form a part of the thematic component of binding (referred to as predicate argument structure here). I will not, however, investigate the relationship between Pica's work and the theory outlined here.

REFERENCES

Aoun, J.: 1985, *A Grammar of Anaphora*, The MIT Press, Cambridge, MA.
Aoun, J.: 1986, *Generalized Binding*, Foris Publications, Dordrecht, the Netherlands.
Baker, M.: 1985, *Incorporation: A Theory of Grammatical Function Changing*, Unpublished Ph.D. Dissertation, MIT.
Belletti, A. and Rizzi, L.: 1981, 'The Syntax of *ne*: Some Theoretical Implications', *The Linguistic Review* 1, 117—54.

Belletti, A. and Rizzi, L.: 1990, forthcoming, 'Psych Verbs and Theta- Theory', *Natural Language and Linguistic Theory* (forthcoming).

Burzio, L.: 1986, *Italian Syntax*, Reidel, Dordrecht, The Netherlands.

Chomsky, N.: 1981, *Lectures on Government and Binding*, Foris Publications, Dordrecht, the Netherlands.

Chomsky, N.: 1986a, *Knowledge of Language*, Praeger, New York.

Chomsky, N.: 1986b, *Barriers*, The MIT Press, Cambridge, MA.

Clark, R.: 1985, 'The Syntactic Nature of Logical Form: Evidence from Toba Batak', *Linguistic Inquiry* **16**, 663—69.

Clark, R. and Keenan, E.: 1985, 'The Absorption Operator and Universal Grammar', *The Linguistic Review* **5**, 113—35.

Evans, G.: 1980, 'Pronouns', *Linguistic Inquiry* **11**, 337—62.

Haïk, I.: 1984, 'Indirect Binding', *Linguistic Inquiry* **15**, 185—223.

Hale, K., Jeanne, L. M., and Platero, P.: 1977, 'Three Case of Overgeneration', in P. Culicover, T. Wasow and A. Akmajian (eds), *Formal Syntax*. The Academic Press, New York, 379—416.

Heim, I.: 1982, *The Semantics of Definite and Indefinite Noun Phrases*, Doctoral Dissertation, University of Massachusetts, Amherst.

Higginbotham, J.: 1983, 'Logical Form, Binding, and Nominals', *Linguistic Inquiry* **14**, 395—420.

Higginbotham, J.: 1985, 'On Semantics', *Linguistic Inquiry* **16**, 547—93.

Higginbotham, J. and May, R.: 1981, 'Questions, Quantifiers and Crossing', *The Linguistic Review* **1**, 41—79.

Hornstein, N.: 1984, *Logic as Grammar*, The MIT Press, Cambridge, MA.

Jackendoff, R.: 1972, *Semantic Interpretation in Generative Grammar*, The MIT Press, Cambridge, MA.

Keenan, E.: 'On Semantics and the Binding Theory', to appear in: J. Hawkins (ed.), *Explaining Language Universals*. Basil Blackwell, Oxford.

Keenan, E. and Faltz, L.: 1985, *Boolean Semantics for Natural Language*, Reidel, Dordrecht, the Netherlands.

Koopman, H.: 1984, *The Syntax of Verbs*. Foris Publications, Dordrecht, the Netherlands.

Koopman, H. and Sportiche, D.: 1982, 'Variables and the Projection Principle', *The Linguistic Review* **2**, 139—61.

Levin, B. and Rappaport, M.: 1986, 'The Formation of Adjectival Passives', *Linguistic Inquiry* **17**, 623—61.

May, R.: 1985, *Logical Form*. The MIT Press, Cambridge, MA.

May, R.: 1989, 'Interpreting Logical Form', *Linguistics and Philosophy* **12**, 387—435.

Marantz, A.: 1984, *On the Nature of Grammatical Relations*, The MIT Press, Cambridge.

Pica, P.: 1984, 'Subjects, Tense and Truth: Towards a Modular Approach to Binding', in: Gueron, J., H.-G. Obenauer and J.-Y. Pollock (eds.), *Grammatical Representation* 259—91.

Postal, P.: 1971, *Cross-Over Phenomena*, Holt, Rinehart and Winston, New York.

Schachter, P.: 1984, 'Semantic-Role-Based Syntax in Toba Batak', in: P. Schachter (ed.), *Studies in the Structure of Toba Batak*, UCLA Occasional Papers in Linguistics, Number 5.

Stowell, T.: 1981, *Origins of Phrase Structure*, Ph.D. Dissertation, MIT.

Sugamoto, N.: 1984, 'Reflexives in Toba Batak', in: P. Schachter (ed.), *Studies in the Structure of Toba Batak*, UCLA Occasional Papers in Linguistics, Number 5.

Torrego, E.: 1984, 'On Inversion in Spanish and Some of Its Effects', *Linguistic Inquiry* **15**, 103—29.

Weinberg, A. and Hornstein, N.: 1986, 'On the Necessity of LF', ms. University of Maryland.

Weinberg, A., Aoun, J., Hornstein, N., and Lightfoot, D.: 1987, 'Two Notions of Locality', *Linguistic Inquiry* **18**, 537—77.

Williams, E.: 197, 'Implict Arguments, the Binding Theory and Control', *Natural Language and Linguistic Theory* **5**, 151—80.

OSVALDO A. JAEGGLI

HEAD GOVERNMENT IN LF-REPRESENTATIONS

0. INTRODUCTION

May (1985) argues that the interpretive contrast found in the sentences in (1) should be attributed to the Empty Category Principle (cf. Chomsky 1981, 1982, 1986 and references cited there).

(1) a.   What did everyone buy for Max?

    b.   Who bought everything for Max?

In (1a) *everyone* can have scope over the wh-element. Thus, it is possible to answer such a question by saying: "Bill bought him a tie, Mary bought him a pipe, Peter bought him records, . . .". But this is not possible in (1b). May points out that if the quantifier *everything* were to undergo QR and adjoin to S in (1b), yielding an LF representation as in (2):

(2) $[[\text{Who}_1] [\text{everything}_2] [t_1 \text{ bought } t_2 \text{ for Max}]]$

an ECP violation would obtain, as the trace in subject position will not be properly governed. The only possibility available is for *everything* to adjoin to VP, an option which May claims should be allowed on general grounds. In its VP-adjoined position, however, *everything* does not have wide scope over the wh-phrase. The situation is different in (1a), as the trace of *what* meets the ECP by being properly governed by *buy*. It need not be antecedent-governed from COMP. Hence, the quantifier in subject position may, and in fact must (for independent reasons), adjoin to IP. This allows it to have scope over the wh-phrase in COMP, as in (3):

(3) $[[\text{What}_2] [\text{everyone}_1] [t_1 \text{ bought } t_2 \text{ for Max}]]]$

The Empty Category Principle, which has been the focus of much research in recent years, accounts for a large range of facts including *that* trace effects as in (4), adjunct extraction effects as in (5), Superiority effects as in (6),[1] and many other facts which at first sight appear unrelated to each other.

(4) a.   Who did you say left early?

   b.   *Who did you say that left early?

(5) a.   Why did you say Bill left?

   b.   *Why do you wonder when Bill left?

(6) a.   Who saw what?

   b.   *What did who see?

It is well known that the counterpart to (4b) is grammatical in Spanish. Cf.:

(7)   ¿Quién dijiste   que salió temprano?²
       Who   you+say that left   early

       'Who did you say left early?'

This contrast between Spanish and English is usually accounted for by assuming that in Spanish the trace left by long-distance extraction of a subject is properly governed even in the presence of a lexical complementizer, while this is not the case in English. In English, the trace of a subject is properly governed only in the absence of a lexical complementizer. This difference has been attributed to the fact that Spanish can freely invert the subject, while this possibility does not exist in English, cf. Jaeggli (1982), Rizzi (1982).

Spanish also contrasts with English concerning certain Superiority violations. The Spanish counterpart to (6b) is fully grammatical. Cf.:

(8)   ¿Qué vio quién?
       what saw who

       'What did who see?'

This is predicted by an ECP analysis of Superiority. Under the assumption made above that the trace of a subject in Spanish is properly governed even in the presence of lexical material in COMP, the LF representation of (8) after wh-Raising of the subject *quién* would not involve an ECP violation.

On the other hand, Spanish and English pattern alike with respect to adjunct extraction. The trace of an adjunct, in both Spanish and English, can be properly governed only if its antecedent (or its trace) is in the local COMP. Hence, Spanish also shows the following contrast:

(9) a. ¿Porqué dijiste   que Juan salió temprano?
        why   you+said that J   left   early

   'Why did you say that Juan left early?'

   b. *¿Porqué no   sabes   cuándo salió Juan?
       why   not you+know when   left   J

   'Why don't you know when Juan left?'

Thus, Spanish differs from English with regard to ECP effects involving extraction of a subject over a lexically filled COMP, but it patterns with English with regard to adjunct extraction out of a wh-island.

In this paper we will consider how Spanish patterns with English with respect to the facts in (1). If the interpretive constrast found in English is to be analyzed under the ECP, the logic of previous analyses leads us to predict that Spanish should differ from English. The Spanish counterpart to (1b) should allow an interpretation in which the quantifier has scope over the wh-phrase. Traces of subject extraction are assumed to be properly governed in their inverted position in Spanish, irrespective of what relation holds between the trace and the nearest COMP. Adjunction of a quantifer to S should not affect the status of the subject trace with respect to the ECP.

Unfortunately, this expectation is not realized. Cf.:

(10) a. ¿A quién examinó   cada   doctor?
         whom   examined every doctor

   'Who did every doctor examine?'

   b. ¿Quién examinó a cada   paciente?
       who   examined every patient

   'Who examined every patient?'

In Spanish, as in English, (10b) does not allow wide scope for the universal quantifier. Sentence (10a) does. If this fact is to be attributed to the ECP, as argued by May, previous accounts of subject extraction in Spanish must be modified. More importantly, previous accounts of the Empty Category Principle must also be modified.

In this paper, we undertake these tasks. In section 1, we consider data as in (10) in some depth. We show that similar facts hold with a wide variety of verb types: transitives, unergative intransitives, and ergative intransitives.[3] In section 2, we show how the standard account of the Empty Category Principle is incapable of providing a satisfactory analysis of these facts. In section 3, we re-consider the structure of Comp, as well as the central notions invovled in the Empty Category Principle. Adopting a conception of 'government' which incorporates the notion of a 'barrier' as in Chomsky (1986), we provide an analysis in terms of this modified theory of the ECP, which accounts for these facts as well as certain facts related to the Superiority Condition. The central claim is that the ECP should be considered a conjunction of two conditions: a *head government* condition holding between an $X°$ category and a trace, and an *antecedent government* condition. We argue here that the head government relation holds at LF. In Jaeggli (1987) we showed that the head government requirement at S-structure accounts for *that*-t effects and other ECP effects that can be captured at that level of representation. Stowell (1987) argues further that this requirement also holds at D-structure. Thus, this part of the ECP can be considered to constitute a well-formedness condition on traces applying at all syntactic levels of representation. The antecedent government condition applies at LF, as in most previous accounts of the ECP.

We concentrate in this paper on LF phenomena of the type discussed by May (1985). Due to space limitations, however, we are not able to provide a complete discussion of all the relevant facts which fall under the scope of the ECP. Our aim here is simply to provide the outline of such an analysis, hoping to be able to explore these issues further in future work.

1. QUANTIFIER SCOPE IN CONTEXTS OF WH-EXTRACTION IN SPANISH

Let us begin by considering further data which exhibits the contrast in (10).

The contrast shows up with several different types of transitive verbs, regardless of whether the object is human or not. It also shows up with quantifiers other than *cada*, 'every', such as numeral quantifiers. Occasionally we will use numeral quantifiers instead of *cada*.[4] Consider the following sentences.

(11) a. ¿Quién visitó cada ciudad (que Maria conoce)?
who visited every city that Maria knows

'Who visited every city (that Maria knows)'

b. ¿Quién acusó a tres delincuentes?
who accused three delinquents

'Who accused three delinquents?'

(12) a. ¿Qué ciudad visitó cada turista?
Which city visited every tourist

'Which city did every tourist visit?'

b. ¿A quién acusaron tres soplones?
whom accused three informers

'Who(m) did three informers accuse?'

The sentences in (11) do not allow a distributed reading for the quantifier in object position. That is, that quantifier cannot have scope over the subject wh-phrase in COMP. On the other hand, the sentences in (12) do allow such readings. The quantifiers in subject position in those sentences may be interpreted with scope over the object wh-phrase in COMP.

The contrast noted above for transitive verbs extends to (unergative) intransitives. Consider the following sentences:

(13) a. ¿Quién habló en cada conferencia de este año?
who spoke in every conference of this year

'Who spoke in every conference this year?'

b. ¿Quién durmió en cuatro suites de ese hotel?
who slept in four suites of that hotel

'Who slept in four suites of that hotel?'

(14) a ¿En qué conferencia habló cada professor?
in which conference spoke every professor

'In which conference did every professor speak?'

b. ¿En qué suite durmió cada invitado?
in which suite slept every guest

'In which suite did every guest sleep?'

Once again, the distributed reading is only available in the sentences in
(14). The sentences in (13), which involve the exraction of a wh-subject,
do not allow such a reading.

Consider next ergative constructions. One may wonder whether
ergative constructions, the subjects of which have D-structure VP-
internal positions, pattern with the cases discussed so far or not — in
the previous cases the trace of subject extraction is generally assumed
to be in VP-adjoined position (cf. Burzio 1981; Rizzi 1982; Jaeggli
1982).

(15) a. ¿Quién llegó   de   cada   ciudad que conoce Maria?
        who   arrived from every city   that knows Maria

        'Who arrived from every city that Maria knows?'

     b. ¿Qué metal existe   en tres   planetas del   sistema solar?
        which metal exists in three planets of+the system solar

        'Which metal exists in three planets of the solar system?'

(16) a. ¿De   qué   ciudad que conoce María llegó   cada
        from   which city   that knows M.   arrived every
        turista?
        tourist

        'From which city that M. knows did every tourist arrive?'

     b. ¿En qué   planetas del   sistema solar existen tres
        in which planets of+the system solar exist   three
        metales que   nos interesan?
        metals which us interest

        'In which planets of the solar system do three metals which
        interest us exist?'

As in the cases discussed so far, the sentences in (15) which involve the
extraction of a wh-subject do not allow a distributed reading for the
quantifier inside VP. On the other hand, the sentences in (16) do allow
a distributed reading for the quantifiers in subject position.[5]

Finally, consider sentences which involve extraction of an object. If
distributed readings are not available even in these cases, this would
indicate that quantifier phrases in object position are never allowed to
have scope over a wh-phrase in COMP. Note that all of the cases

considered so far where a quantifier phrase has scope over a wh-phrase involve quantifier phrases in subject position.
Consider then the following sentences.

(17) a. ¿A quién   entregó Maria cada   regalo?
       to whom handed Maria every gift

   'To whom did Maria give every gift?'

   b. ¿Qué   nota   le otorgó el professor   a   cada
      which grade gave   the professor to   every
      estudiante?
      student

   'What grade did the professor give every student?'

   c. ¿Sobre qué   habló   el   profesor con cada   estudiante?
      about what spoke the professor with every student

   'What did the professor speak about with every student?'

   d. ¿Cuándo salió   Juan con   cada   hija
      when   went-out J.   with every daughter
      del Sr. Martinez?
      of Mr. M.

   'When did Juan go out on a date with every daughter of Mr. Martinez?'

   e. ¿Desde cuándo existe   el hierro en cada   planeta del
      since when exists   the iron   in every planet of+the
      sistema solar?
      system solar

   'Since when does iron exist in every planet of the solar system?'

These sentences all involve extractions of different types of objects and a quantifier inside VP. All sentences allow wide scope readings, i.e. distributed readings, for the quantifiers inside VP. (The same point is made for English in May (1985)). It is only subject extraction which blocks a wide-scope reading for the quantifiers inside VP. Extraction of non-subjects do not have this property. It is precisely because of this type of evidence that it appears correct to attribute the noted asymmetry to the ECP. Otherwise we could simply stipulate that wh-elements in COMP always have wide scope over a non-subject quantifier. (In fact, this statement need not be a stipulation, but could be derived from other principles of grammar). But given the evidence presented in (17), such a statement would be empirically unsatisfactory. It would represent an incorrect generalization. Henceforth we will assume that these are ECP facts, and continue to explore the data in this direction.[6]

2. THE INADEQUACY OF THE CLASSICAL ECP

The Empty Category Principle may be stated as in (18):

(18)   A non-pronominal empty category must be properly governed.

where 'proper government' is defined as in (19):

(19) α properly governs β if α governs β and
         a. α is a lexical category (lexical government) or
         b. α is coindexed with β (antecedent government).[7]

These statements must be supplemented with the following auxiliary assumptions commonly made in the literature. First, [NP, IP] position (of a tensed clause) is never lexically governed. INFL (or AGR) does not count as a lexical governor as it is not a lexical category. Non-pronominal empty categories in subject position satisfy the ECP, then, only through antecedent government. A similar assumption is made concerning adjuncts. The assumption is straightforward if it is the case that adjuncts are external to VP, e.g. if they are under INFL'. Traces of adjuncts too, then, must meet the ECP via antecdent government, since they are never lexically governed. Second, antecedent government of a non-pronominal empty category in subject position is only available from the local Comp. A long-distance relation would not satisfy the local character of the 'government' relation. Third, and crucially, antecedent government is possible from the local Comp only if Comp is non-branching. A branching Comp does not allow antecedent government. Specifically, assume that Comp is a maximal projection. Then, a trace in subject, or adjunct, position is properly governed only if it is coindexed with Comp, as material inside Comp never governs out of

Comp, given its status as a maximal projection. Assume that Comp gets an index through the Comp indexing rule of Aoun, Hornstein and Sportiche (1981):

(20) $[_{Comp} \ldots X_i \ldots] \rightarrow [_{Comp} \ldots X_i \ldots]_i$

if Comp dominates only i-indexed elements. Other assumptions are needed in the standard account of the functioning of the Empty Category Principle but they need not concern us here. These assumptions include a specification of the level at which the ECP applies, and the level at which rule (20) applies. As we will ultimately reject this analysis, we present only those aspects which are relevant to our discussion.

Consider now how this theory accounts for the contrasts in (4) and (5), repeated here with the relevant structure supplied:

(4) a.   [[Who] (did) [you say [[t'] [t left early]]]]

   b.   [[Who] (did) [you say [[t'-that] [t left early]]]]

(5) a.   [[Why] (did) [you say [[t'] [Bill [left] t]]]]

   b.   [[Why] (did) [you wonder [[t'-when] [Bill [left] t]]]]

In (4a) and (5a), t is properly governed from the local Comp. In those sentences, Comp contains only t', hence rule (20) can apply and t will be coindexed with (i.e. antecedent governed by) Comp. In (4b) and (5b), on the other hand, Comp contains t' and another element which does not bear the same index. Hence, rule (20) cannot apply, and proper government will not obtain. Details omitted, this is the standard ECP analysis of *that-t* violations and adjunct extraction out of a wh-island.[8] Let us consider next how this analysis extends to the Spanish facts in (7)—(9).

In Spanish, it is possible to extract a subject over a lexical complementizer without violating the ECP.

(21) a. ¿Quién dijiste   que salió temprano?
         who   you+said that left   early

        'Who did you say left early?'

    b. ¿Quién dijiste   que conoce a Juan?
         who   you+said that knows   Juan

        'Who did you say knows Juan?'

(21) c. ¿Quién crees   que hablará?
         who   you+think that will+speak

'Who do you think will speak?'

Following an insight of Luigi Rizzi, previous analyses have assumed that an independent property of Spanish (and Italian) distinguishes these languages from English. These languages allow free inversion of the subject NP to post-verbal position. Subject extraction in these languages is always mediated by subject post-posing. Wh-extraction then proceeds from post-verbal position. A trace in that position is properly governed even in the presence of a filled Comp. Hence, *that-t* effects do not show up in Spanish (or Italian) in sentences like (21) because there is no ECP violation. The variable is left in a position of proper government in post-verbal position. The specific type of proper government involved has commonly been assumed to be *lexical government*. This must be the case as the conditions necessary for antecedent government to obtain (under rule (20)) are not present in the relevant structures. Lexical government obtains straightforwardly in sentences with ergative verbs, as in (21a), since the subjects of these sentences are generated in VP-internal position. In sentences with transitive verbs, or unergative intransitives, inverted position can be argued to be a VP-adjoined position, cf. Rizzi (1982). It has been assumed that this position too is lexically governed by the verb. This requires that we allow the head of a maximal projection to lexically govern a category adjoined to that maximal projection. Given these assumptions, subjects can be extracted 'long-distance' over a lexical complementizer in Spanish (and Italian).

Spanish patterns with English w.r.t. adjunct extraction. Adjunct extraction out of a wh-island violates the ECP, but adjunct extraction over a lexical complementizer is possible, as it is in English (cf. the sentences in (9)). The ECP violation in question follows naturally under the assumption that adjuncts in Spanish must be antecedent governed from the local Comp (but see note 7), and that the grammar of Spanish, like English, contains the Comp-indexing algorithm (20). Thus, adjunct extraction in Spanish receives the same analysis as adjunct extraction in English.

Finally, it should be pointed out that the theory of the ECP sketched above, which we have called the 'classical ECP', also accounts for the fact that the counterpart of a Superiority violation in English is grammatical in Spanish, as in (8) above. Once again, the trace of the subject left by the LF rule of wh-raising is in post-verbal position, where it is properly governed. The presence of an extra wh-element in Comp is immaterial, as no antecedent government is required.

Given the success of this theory in accounting for the contrasts discussed so far, it is worthwhile to ask if it also accounts for the facts described in section 1 concerning the scope of a quantifier in contexts of wh-extraction. Let us first consider what must be said in order to analyze the English facts described by May (1985) in terms of the Empty Category Principle.

The relevant facts are given (22):

(22) a. What did everyone buy for Max?

b. Who did you give every book to?

c. Who bought everything for Max?

In (22a, b) the quantifier can be interpreted as having scope over the wh-phrase in Comp. In (22c) the quantifier cannot have scope over the wh-phrase in Comp. For the quantifier to have scope over the wh-phrase in Comp it must adjoin to S, as in the following schematic representation:

(23) $[_{S'}[_{Comp}WH]\,[_{S}QP[_{S}\ldots]]]$

In cases of subject extraction, this will yield an LF representation as in (24):

(24) $[[_{Comp}who_1]\,[_{S}QP\,[_{S}\,t_1\,INFL\ldots]]]$

For this representation to violate the ECP, the trace in subject position must not be properly governed. If the trace of the wh-phrase is inside VP, where it is lexically governed by the Verb, as would be the case with extraction of an object wh-phrase, adjunction of the quantifier to S is immaterial. This is why (22a, b) admit of a wide scope reading for the quantifier. The trace of the subject, on the other hand, must fail antecedent government in a structure as in (24). These are the desired results.

Unfortunately, these results do not follow from the theory of the ECP sketched above. As Comp in (24) contains only one wh-phrase, rule (20) is free to apply. Then, Comp and the trace in subject position will be coindexed. This will allow for antecedent government. The trace in subject position in (24), then, is antecedent governed, and meets the ECP. Sentence (22c) is wrongly predicted to have a reading where the quantifier has scope over the wh-phrase.[9]

Before we turn to the Spanish facts, we digress briefly to fill in certain details which we have left open. May (1985) notes that sentence (22c) is merely unambiguous, not ungrammatical. It does not allow for a wide scope reading for the quantifier in object position. But the sentence is perfectly interpretable with a narrow scope reading for such a quantifier. May argues that it is not necessary to assume that LF movement always results in structures of adjunction to S. QR may result in structures in which a phrase is adjoined to categories other than S (as long as such movements and the structures resulting from them are consistent with other principles of grammar such as proper binding, the θ-Criterion, the ECP, etc.). Given this possibility, the LF representation of (22c) can be as in (25):

(25) $[\text{who}_1 \ [_\text{S} \ t_1 \ [_\text{VP} \ \text{everything}_2 \ [_\text{VP} \ \text{bought} \ t_2 \ \text{for Max}]]]]$

The analysis of Spanish subject extraction presented above follows Rizzi (1982) and Jaeggli (1982) in assuming that the trace of subject extraction is always in post-verbal position, either in VP-adjoined position (for transitives and unergative intransitives), or inside VP in a position analogous to the position of a direct object in a transitive structure (for ergative intransitives). In these positions, the traces meet the ECP via lexical government. These assumptions have a number of important consequences that lend them quite substantial support, among them the lack of a *that-t* effect in Spanish, the account of the Superiority facts mentioned earlier, as well as other consequences pointed out in Rizzi (1982), Jaeggli (1982), and elsewhere in the literature. A further piece of supporting evidence is provided by the following example from Torrego (1984).

(26)   [Quién [no   sabes   [cuánto   [pesa]]]]
         who   not you+know   how+much   weighs
    '*Who don't you know how much weighs?'

Note that the subject of the embedded clause is extracted from a wh-island. Cases of this type constitute very strong ECP violations in English (as the translation of (26), which we have starred, should make clear), while (26) is grammatical in Spanish. Under our assumptions, this is expected.[10] The trace of subject extraction is properly governed in its post-verbal position. Hence the subject wh-phrase is allowed to escape from a wh-island. Sentence (26) does not constitute a subjacency violation either, as Torrego (1984) demonstrates that in Spanish S(=IP) is not a bounding node for subjacency. All of this evidence, then, lends quite a lot of support to the original insight concerning post-verbal extraction.

The facts presented in section 1, on the other hand, present an obvious problem for these assumptions. If the trace of subject extraction is lexically governed by the verb, the presence of a quantifier adjoined to S in instances of subject extraction should have no effect on the well-formedness of those structures vis-à-vis the ECP. As an illustration, consider the structure in (27), a plausible LF-representation (details aside) for sentence (11a) with wide scope for the quantifier:

(27) $[Quién_1 [_S cada ciudad_2 [_S pro [_{VP}[_{VP} visitó \ t_2] \ t_1]]]]$

We are concerned here with the proper government status of t_1. Under the "classical" assumptions made above, it is lexically governed by the verb. The structure does not violate the ECP. Given this analysis, then, we cannot rely on the ECP in order to account for the lack of a wide-scope reading for the quantifiers in these cases. The same result obtains with unergative and ergative intransitive verbs. In fact, the situation is arguably worse with ergative intransitives. In such cases, the extraction site is the deep structure θ-position of the subject. Such a position corresponds exactly to the extraction site of a direct object; and we have seen that direct object extraction does not prevent a quantifier from having wide scope (cf. the sentences in (17)).

It seems impossible to avoid the conclusion that the standard treatment of subject extraction in Spanish makes completely the wrong prediction with respect to the facts presented in section 1. In a sense, then, we have a paradox here. On the one hand, the standard analysis is strongly supported by a well-known array of facts which it is impossible to dismiss. On the other hand, it completely fails to account for another array of facts which, it appears, should fall under the aegis of the Empty Category Principle.[11] Of course, it is always possible to claim that the quantifier scope facts should not be analyzed under the ECP. But as the asymmetry involved is so reminiscent of the central effects for which the ECP has been held responsible, we will adopt the working hypothe-

sis that this alternative should be avoided, or at worse, accepted only as
a last resort. The rest of this paper is devoted to this task.

3. THE STRUCTURE OF COMP, GOVERNMENT, AND BARRIERS

The structure assigned to Comp plays a crucial role in all theories of
the Empty Category Principle. In previous analyses, Comp was assumed to be a (maximal) projection sister to S (or IP). Chomsky (1986)
suggests an alternative analysis. He argues that the structure normally
assigned to maximal projections of lexical categories extends to Comp,
yielding a structure as in (28):

(28)

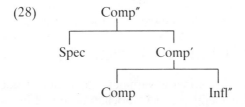

Under this theory, then, all categories, lexical (N, V, A, P) and non-
lexical (Infl, Comp) conform to X-bar theory. The structure in (28)
gives two positions under Comp″, a head position and a specifier
position. Under Emonds's Structure Preserving Hypothesis, it is reasonable to assume that the head position can only be occupied by an X°
category, and the specifier position by a maximal projection, X^{max}.[12]

The central notion in any theory of the Empty Category Principle is
the notion of government, which imposes a quite restrictive locality
condition.[13] The intuitive content of the notion is that an element
governs within its c-command domain those elements which are not
protected by a boundary of a particular type. The notion of c-command
which appears to be relevant is distinct from the notion of c-command
which is operative in binding theory. For the theory of government, the
relevant notion appears to ignore non-maximal projections. Following
Chomsky (1986), we assume the following definition of m-command
and government:

(29)   α m-commands β iff α does not dominate β and every γ
        that dominates α dominates β, where γ is restricted to
        maximal projections.

(30) α governs β iff α m-commands β and there is no γ, γ, a barrier for β, such that γ excludes α.

The definition of government in (30) makes reference to three concepts: m-command, exclusion, and barrier. We have already provided a definition for m-command in (29). Before we turn to the other two, consider adjunction structures as in (31):

(31) $\ldots w \ldots [_a \, x \, [_a \ldots y \ldots]]$

A question arises concerning whether the category α dominates x or not in such structures. May (1985) and Chomsky (1986) argue that in such cases, the category α consists of two segments, and that an element is dominated by a category consisting of two segments only if it is dominated by both segments of that category. Then, in (31), α does not dominate x, since one segment of α does not dominate x. Also, w and x m-command y, but y does not m-command either of those two categories. Note, in particular, that y does not m-command x, as there is a maximal projection which dominates y but does not dominate x, namely α.

Exclusion and barrierhood are defined in Chomsky (1986) as follows:

(32) α excludes y if no segment of α dominates y.

(33) γ is a barrier for β iff (i) or (ii):
        (i) γ immediately dominates δ, δ a blocking category for β, or
        (ii) γ is a blocking category for β, $\gamma \neq$ I'' (i.e. S)

(34) γ is a blocking category for β iff γ is not L-marked and γ dominates β.

The definition of blocking category involves the notion of L-marking, which is defined as follows:

(35) α L-marks β if and only if α is a lexical category that θ-governs β.

where 'θ-government' is understood as follows:

(36) α θ-governs β iff α is a zero level category that θ-marks β, and α, β are sisters.

Finally, 'proper government', the notion directly relevant to the ECP, may be construed as follows: α properly governs β iff α θ-governs β or α antecedent governs β, where antecedent government holds of a link (α, β) of a chain where α governs β.

The theory of government sketched above constitutes a reformulation of several concepts which enter into many of the crucial principles of several sub-components of the theory of grammar. It is natural to expect, then, that it will have a wide range of intricate consequences. We will focus primarily here on some of the consequences which concern the Empty Category Principle applying at LF, leaving aside many issues of great interest which fall outside the scope of our discussion.

4. STRUCTURES OF ADJUNCTION AND THE ECP AT LF

Let us return now to consider the facts discussed at the beginning of this paper concerning the scope properties of certain quantified expressions in contexts of wh-extraction. Recall that the English sentences discussed in May (1985) fall under the following generalization:

(37)   In contexts of subject extraction, a quantifier in complement position may not have wide scope over the subject wh-phrase.

Consider the LF representation of (1)b, repeated below, under the unavailable reading.

(1) b.   Who bought everything for Max?

(38) $[_{CP}\text{who}_i[_{C'}\text{C}\ [_{IP}\ \text{everything}_j[_{IP}\ t_i\ \text{bought}\ t_j]]]]$

We are concerned with the proper government status of the trace of *who* under the theory of government sketched above. It is antecedent-governed by *who* (via chain-government). It forms a link of a chain with *who*, and *who* governs it since I″, though a blocking category, is not a barrier. This representation, then meets the ECP as we have considered it so far. Something else must be involved if these contrasts are to follow from that condition. Given that we are dealing with an impossible (scopal) interpretation, the complicating factor must arise at LF.

Let us assume, then, that aside from antecedent-government, the ECP also imposes another condition at LF which is not met in the

structures in question. The condition in question involves a relation
between the head of Comp and the trace in subject position, hence a
condition between an $X°$ category and the specifier of the complement
of this category. We can account for the ungrammaticality of the
representation in (38) if we assume that this condition, which we will
call *head government*, is not met across a structure of adjunction.[14]
Thus, in a structure as in (39):

(39) $X° \ldots [_a \ w \ [_a \ y \ldots]]$

$X°$ does not head govern y. Let us make this assumption and explore
some of its consequences concerning the sentences in (1). First we will
consider consequences for processes which occur in the mapping from
S-structure to LF, essentially QR. Then, we turn to provide some
evidence that the head government relation is also invoked at S-structure, and that structures as in (39) also block head government at
S-structure, resulting in ungrammatical sentences.

First, as a direct consequence of this condition, it follows that (38)
will be ungrammatical since the head government requirement will not
be met for the trace in subject position. On the other hand, in cases of
object wh-extraction, we can assume that the traces of wh-movement
are head governed even if the quantifier adjoins to S, since those traces
are not head governed from Comp, but rather from the governing V.
Adjunction of the quantifier to S, then, will have no effect. Thus, this
possibility will be allowed, yielding a wide scope interpretation for the
quantifiers. The interpretation that is allowed for (1b), which has the
LF-representation in (25), repeated below:

(25)   [who$_1$ [$_{IP}$ t_1 [$_{VP}$ everything$_2$ [$_{VP}$ bought t_2 for Max]]]]

also presents no problem. It does not involve a structure of adjunction
to IP. This structure, then, satisfies both the antecedent government
requirement and the head government requirement. The central cases
discussed by May, then, would follow naturally given these assumptions.

Let us turn next to Superiority Condition violations. A central insight
of May's analysis was that the facts in (1) reflect the situation that
obtains in instances of violations of the Superiority Condition. A
natural question to ask at this point, then, is whether our analysis of the
facts in (1) also yields an analysis for Superiority violations. Consider

the standard examples which fall under the Superiority Condition in
English given in (6) and repeated below:

(6) a.   Who saw what?

    b.   *What did who see?

Assuming that wh-raising adjoins a wh-phrase to Spec of Comp containing another wh-element, the LF-representation of (6b) is as in (40):

(40) $[_{CP}[[\text{who}]_i[\text{what}]_j]_j$ $[_{C'}C$ $[_{IP}$ t_i INFL [saw t_j]]]]

Does the trace left by LF-raising of *who* meet the locality requirements
assumed so far? First let us consider whether it is antecedent-governed
or not. It is in a chain with *who*, and *who* governs it, as I″ is not a
barrier for t_i and *who* m-commands t_i. Thus, this trace is chain
governed. If we are to account for the ungrammaticality of this sentence
by appealing to the ECP, then, we cannot invoke the antecedent
government condition as defined in the framework given above in
section 3 (essentially, the *Barriers* framework). On the other hand, the
head government relation that we used to account for May's cases can
also serve to rule out structure (40). Let us now provide an explicit
definition of the head government relation:

(41) α head-governs β iff:
    i. α is an X°,
    ii. α canonically governs β, and
    iii. α is coindexed with β.

where 'canonical government' is understood in a directional sense. In
English, for example, canonical government amounts to government
from left to right. Consider now what head-governs an element in
subject position:

(42) $[_{CP}$ γ $[_{C'}[_C$ $\alpha]$ $[_{IP}$ β INFL VP]]]

Infl is not allowed to head govern β, since it does not canonically
govern β. The only zero level category which canonically governs β in
this structure is C, the head of Comp. β would be head governed, then,
if α were coindexed with β. Suppose that the head of Comp may
acquire an index through a process of agreement with the Specifier of
Comp position, a process which we will call Spec-Head Agreement (cf.
Chomsky 1986). If we assume that this relation is construed as a type

of feature sharing, then this agreement relation also enters into selection (for sentential complement types, for example) under the assumption that selection is uniformly a head-to-head relation, as in Chomsky (1986). Since selectional requirements in English are met at S-structure, we assume that this process of Spec-Head Agreement also occurs at S-structure. This process can be considered to be the analogue of the Comp-Indexing Algorithm of Aoun, Hornstein and Sportiche (1983). It can be formalized as follows:

(43) $[_{CP} [XP, +/-WH_i] [_{C'} [_c e] \ldots]] \Rightarrow$

$[_{CP} [XP, +/-WH_i] [_{C'} [_c [+/-WH_i] \ldots]]]$

Given the definition of head government in (43), the trace in subject position in the structure in (40) does not meet the head government requirement. In this structure, the head of Comp will be coindexed with *what*, which occupies the Spec of Comp position at S-structure. The trace in subject position, then, is not head governed. Superiority effects, then, are the result of a failure of head government.

Sentence (6a), repeated below, is grammatical, on the other hand, since all traces are head and antecedent-governed at LF. The trace of the subject is antecedent-governed by the wh-element in Comp and head governed by the head of Comp, with which it is coindexed. The trace of the object (after wh-raising) is head governed by the verb, and also antecedent-governed since it is θ-governed by the verb.[15]

Let us now consider the Spanish facts mentioned in section 1 involving the scope of a quantifier in contexts of wh-extraction. Spanish behaves like English with respect to those facts. How is this similarity to be accounted for?

The analysis based on Rizzi's original proposal for italian claims that subjects in Spanish are extracted from post-verbal position, where the trace left by Move α is properly governed. Sentence (44a), then, would be assigned the LF representation (44b) with the interpretation where the quantified direct object may be understood as having scope over the subject wh-phrase, an interpretation which we noted was unavailable in this case.

(44) a. ¿Quién vio a cada   estudiante?
          who   saw every student

       'Who saw every student?'

   b. $[_{CP}$ Quién$_i$ [vio $[_{IP}$ cada estudiante$_j$ $[_{IP}$ pro Infl $[_{VP}[_{VP}[_V e] t_j] t_i]]]]]$

If this representation is to be ruled out by the ECP we cannot allow the trace of subject extraction to satisfy the ECP in such structures. Under the standard assumption that traces in post-verbal position meet the ECP because they are lexically governed by the verb, such structures present an obvious problem.

Our proposal incorporates a suggestion made in Chomsky (1985) concerning expletive elements. For reasons which are independent of the issues that concern us here, Chomsky argues that "expletives are not permitted to appear in LF-representation." Chomsky suggests that an expletive x "can be eliminated in accordance with the condition on recoverability of deletion only if x is replaced by a coindexed element y, hence by movement of y to the position occupied by x, forming a chain (y, e)". Let us call this process *expletive substitution*.

Assuming a process of expletive substitution, the LF representation of (44a) is no longer (44b) but rather (45):

(45) $[_{CP}$ Quien$_i$ [vio $[_{IP}$ cada estudiante$_j$ $[_{IP}t_i$ Infl $[_{VP}$ $[_{V}e]$ $t_j]]]]]$

This representation is much closer to the LF representation of similar sentences in English. Expletive substitution has the effect of making Spanish and English very similar at the level of LF, at least with respect to the position of the subject. Notice, in particular, that the trace in subject position in (45) does not meet the head government requirement, just like traces in similar structures in English do not meet this requirement either. The adjunction of the quantifier phrase to IP blocks head government. Thus, this structure is ill-formed with respect to the head government requirement at LF, and the unavailable interpretation is correctly excluded. The structure in (45), then, yields the correct result with respect to the scope of the quantifier in instances of subject extraction. Object extraction, on the other hand, is unaffected by expletive substitution or adjunction of the quantifier to IP. This is exactly as required by the facts. In instances of object extraction, quantifiers are allowed to have scope over the wh-element in Comp.

Expletive substitution is a process which applies to all sentences containing expletive elements in an argument position. In Spanish it applies to all sentences with inverted subjects in VP adjoined position, and it also applies to sentences with ergative verbs. In the latter instance, movement originates from a θ-position internal to VP, with a resulting chain between [NP, IP] position and an internal position. Let us assume, now, that after expletive substitution, the variable is in [NP, IP] position. This element, then, must meet the ECP requirements of head government and antecedent-government. As before, adjunction will make head government impossible. Thus, even sentences with ergative intransitive verbs will show the effect observed above for transitive sentences, i.e. in the context of subject extraction a quantifier is not allowed to have scope over the wh-element in Comp. This analysis, then, naturally accounts for the facts regarding quantifier scope in contexts of subject extraction with transitive, unergative intransitive, and ergative verbs discussed in section 1 above.

Consider next the grammatical LF representation for (44a) after expletive substitution:

(46) $[_{CP}$ Quién$_i$ [vio $[_{IP}$ t_i Infl $[_{VP}$ cada estudiante$_j$ $[_{VP}[_V e]$ $t_j]]]]]$

Here *cada estudiante* does not have scope over *quién*, as it does not c-command (or govern) *quién*. But how is t_i head governed in this structure? Recall that head government requires government by a coindexed zero level category. What category is fulfilling this task in (46)? Note that the verb is in the head of Comp position in (46). Let us assume that the verb arrives into that position by first moving to Infl and then being raised with Infl to the head of Comp position. In Spanish, this process may occur in the syntax (in interrogatives) or at LF. A verb may move to the head of Comp position only if it attaches to Infl. Assuming this process then, the correct LF-representation for (44a) is not (46) but rather (47):

(47) $[_{CP}$ Quién$_i$ [[vio[Infl]] $[_{IP}$ t_i $[_I e]$ $[_{VP}$ cada estudiante$_j$ $[_{VP}[_V e]$ $t_j]]]]]$

If Infl is coindexed with the subject position and we assume that this coindexation is relevant, t_i is head governed by Infl in the head of Comp position once again. If a quantifier is adjoined to I″, though, the head government relation will be disturbed, and the sentence will be ruled out as before.

The trace in subject position in structures like (47) is head governed by Infl in the head of Comp position and it is antecedent governed by *quién* in the Spec of Comp position. Thus, the two conditions imposed by the ECP are satisfied, and the structure is grammatical. But it is well-known that in Spanish the antecedent (or the trace of the antecedent) of a subject trace does *not* have to occupy the local Comp. Cf. sentence (26) from Torrego (1984), repeated below for convenience:

(48)   [Quién [no sabes   [cuánto   [pesa]]]]
        who   not you+know how+much weighs

'Who don't you know how much weighs?'

where the subject *quién* has been extracted out of a wh-island. How does the trace of subject extraction meet the requirements imposed by the ECP in such structures? Let us consider the relevant LF representation, after expletive substitution and Infl raising have applied (irrelevant details omitted):

(49)   [Quién$_i$ [. . .[$_{CP}$ cuánto$_j$ [$_{C'}$ [pesa+Infl] [$_{IP}$ t_i [$_{I'}$ [$_I e$] [$_{VP}$ [$_V e$] t_j]]]]]]]]

Here t_i is head governed by the V+Infl combination in the head of Comp, as before. How is it antecedent governed? Its overt antecedent, *quién*, is too far away for chain-government to hold. This is what strongly rules out such sentences in English. In previous analyses it was claimed that such traces are lexically governed, assuming post-verbal extraction. But the process of expletive substitution, which we argued for above, no longer allows us to exploit this possibility straightforwardly.

Let us consider the following approach. Assume that in a structure like (49), the Verb+Infl combination *both* head governs and serves as the antecedent governor for t_i. This would permit long-distance extraction in such cases, without violating the ECP. Both conditions would be met by the governing Infl in the head of Comp position.

This idea accounts for all the facts discussed up to this point, but it also raises a problem. We argued above that long-distance subject extraction is allowed in Spanish only if the subject in question has been inverted first. In the absence of subject inversion, we do not want to permit long-distance extraction. (This is the original insight behind Rizzi's proposal, which we take to be essentially correct). The Italian *nessuno* facts point in this direction, as do certain wh-in-situ facts from Spanish, which we review next. Consider the following sentences:

(50) a.   ¿Quién dijiste   que compró qué?
           who   you-said that bought what

           'Who did you say bought what?'

   b.   ¿Qué dijiste   que compró quién?
          what you-said that bought who

          'What did you say that who bought?'

(50) c.   *¿Qué dijiste   que quién compró?
        what you-said that who bought

        'What did you say that who bought?'

   d.   ¿Qué dijiste   que Mario compró?
        what you-said that Mario bought

        'What did you say that Mario bought?'

In (50a), the wh-element in situ is in object position. It is wh-raised to the matrix Comp, occupied by *quién* at LF. Its trace meets both the antecedent-government requirement (since it is θ-governed by the verb) and the head government requirement. Consider now (50c). Note that this sentence should not be ruled out simply because Verb preposing did not apply. Verb preposing is not obligatory in these structures, as sentence (50d) shows. The object wh-element can move up to the matrix Comp in one step without violating Subjacency in Spanish (cf. Torrego 1984). The contrast between (50c) and (50d) shows quite clearly that the ungrammaticality of (50c) should be attributed to the fact that there is a wh-element in [NP, IP] position. In other words, (50c) is a Superiority Condition violation. The wh-element in situ is raised to the higher Comp by wh-raising and the trace of this movement violates the ECP. Such a trace will violate the ECP only if Infl raising, which raises Infl to the head of Comp position at LF, does *not* save this trace by providing a head and antecedent governor for this trace. Finally, in sentence (50b), the trace of *quién* left by wh-raising at LF also meets both requirements; it is both antecedent-governed and head governed by Infl.

Thus, we must ensure that Infl only antecedent-governs traces of subjects which have been extracted from inverted position in Spanish. We will assume that antecedent government from Infl is best viewed as an instance of θ-government. It is difficult to consider it an instance of chain-government, since no movement chain exists between Infl and subjects. Let us assume, then, that Infl serves as a θ-governor for certain traces in subject position, and that this is how such traces meet the antecedent government requirement imposed by the ECP. In line with the facts presented above, however, we can only allow Infl which has been raised to the head of Comp to serve as a θ-governor (and antecedent governor) for a trace in [NP, IP] position in certain cases, but not others. Only when the trace in [NP, IP] position is there due to

the process of expletive substitution, that is, when the original extraction site of the subject was the inverted subject position, can the Infl in
Comp function as an antecedent governor for that trace. Let us see how
we can execute this basic idea.

The definition of θ-government given above in (36), repeated below

(36) α θ-governs β iff α is a zero level category that θ-marks β,
         and α, β are sisters.

lists two requirements for θ-government: θ-marking and sisterhood.
Let us consider how these two requirements are met in the structures
that interest us. Let us assume, essentially following Safir (1985) that
subjects in Spanish can be θ-marked either in [NP, IP] position, or in
inverted position. However, there is a crucial difference between subjects which are θ-marked in [NP, IP] position and subjects which are
θ-marked in inverted position. To see this difference, consider the
following definition of sisterhood: α and β are sisters if they exclude
each other and they are dominated by the same lexical projections
(essentially the definition given in Chomsky 1986). A subject in [NP,
IP] position is a sister to VP, as it is excluded by VP. Hence, it may be
θ-marked by VP, just as it is in English. On the other hand, if the
subject has been inverted and adjoined to VP our definitions entail that
it cannot be θ-marked by VP, because it is no longer a sister to VP, as
it is not excluded by VP. On the other hand, it is a sister to Infl. An NP
subject in [NP, IP] position is a sister to VP, and can be θ-marked by
that category; while a subject in inverted position is not a sister to VP,
but it is a sister to Infl. In [NP, IP] position, then, we can assume that a
subject NP is θ-marked by VP. In inverted position, on the other hand,
a subject NP cannot be θ-marked by VP. Let us assume, rather, that it
is θ-marked by Infl (which, we assume, receives the relevant θ-role
from the VP).[16] Structurally, then, the following situations obtain. (The
elements which enter into θ-marking relations are shown in boldface
below):

(51) a.   [$_{IP}$ **NP** [$_{I'}$ Infl **VP**]]

     b.   [$_{IP}$ NP [$_{I'}$ **Infl**.[$_{VP}$ VP **NP**]]]

At this point the following question arises: why is is that Infl cannot
θ-mark the NP in [NP, IP] position in (51a)? Notice that if it did, we
would allow long-distance extraction out of that position directly. We
cannot claim that θ-government only holds to the right in Spanish, at

least not if θ-government is defined in terms of sisterhood and θ-marking. Sisterhood, as defined above, is not a directional concept, and neither is θ-marking, especially not in the case of subjects. Subjects must be capable of being θ-marked in [NP, IP] position, otherwise even simple sentences with pre-verbal subjects will be ruled out by the θ-Criterion. Let us assume then, that when a subject is in [NP, S] position, it is always θ-marked by VP, and never by Infl. This result would follow from the following principle:

(52)   A zero level category can only θ-mark to the right in Spanish.

Such a principle is needed independently for the grammar of Spanish, at least if we follow Stowell (1981) and many others in assuming that word-order facts follow from the directionality of Case assignment and θ-relations within the particular grammar of a given language. All other zero-level categories only θ-mark to the right in Spanish. Hence, (52) need not be stipulated only for purposes related to the ECP. We simply need to assume that (52) covers not only instances of θ-marking by lexical categories, but also θ-marking of the subject NP by Infl.

To summarize, the analysis presented in this paper involves the following claims:
1. the Empty Category Principle imposes a very general requirement of *head government*, which applies at all levels of representation, and in particular for the purposes which concern us in this paper, at LF;
2. the head government relation does not obtain across a structure of adjunction;
3. subject wh-extraction in Spanish proceeds from post-verbal position, but a process of expletive substitution replaces (at LF) the expletive in [NP, IP] position found in such structures with the variable left by extraction from post-verbal position. This variable in [NP, IP] position, then, is subject to the requirements imposed by the ECP, namely head government and antecedent government;
4. Infl may serve as a θ-governor (and antecedent-governor) for variables in [NP, IP] position after it has been raised to the head of Comp position, provided it θ-marks the subject NP. This is possible if the subject NP is θ-marked in inverted position.

This analysis accounts for the similarities and the differences that exist between English and Spanish in the area of data that has been considered here. Doubtless there remain a number of issues which have not been addressed here for lack of space. We believe that this analysis also provides an account of *that*-trace effects, as well as other ECP related phenomena which we do not discuss here.

APPENDIX: ON SOME PUTATIVE COUNTEREXAMPLES

There are a number of sentence types which appear to counterexemplify the basic claim made in section 1 concerning quantifier scope in contexts of wh-extraction. While we will not provide a complete analysis of these cases, it is useful to note them here together with the observation that there are important factors which distinguish these putative counterexamples from the clear cases discussed above.

First, if *cada* is read as 'each' instead of 'every', which is possible in the following sentence, then the distributive reading is possible.[17]

(53)   ¿Quién examinó a cada uno de los pacientes?
       who   examined each one of the patients

'Who examined each of the patients?'

The 'each' reading appears to focus the object NP, allowing it an interpretation parallel to *For each one of the patients, who examined him*. Note also that the object NP in this sentence has the structure of a partitive, namely *O uno de NP*. This is an important difference between this type of sentence and the sentences discussed in section 1. It appears to be the case that focussed partitives always have wide scope. The same is true of the following examples:

(54) a. ¿Quiénes examinaron a alguons de los pacientes?
        who(pl) examined   to some of the patients

'Who examined some of the patients?'

b. ¿Quién acusó a algunos de los sacerdotes?
   who   accused to some of the priests

'Who accused some of the priests?'

c. ¿Quiénes llegaron de algunas de las ciudates...?
   who(pl) arrived from some of the cities

'Who arrived from some of the cities (that Mary knows)?'

Note, furthermore, that in (54a, c) the subject wh-word is a plural. This also contributes (in ways which are not entirely clear to me) to allowing a distributive reading. We can account for these readings, following May (1985), on the assumption that these object NPs are adjoined not to IP, but to (the matrix) CP. From this position they will have scope broader than COMP without disturbing head government of the trace in subject position.

Another type of putative counterexample concerns instances of clitic doubling. Consider the following sentences:

(55) a. ¿Quién lo   examinó   a cada   paciente?
      who   him   examined to every   patient

    'Who examined every patient?'

   b. ¿Quién les   compró entradas a   algunos estudiantes?
      who   them   bought tickets   to some   students

    'Who bought tickets for some of the students?'

Here the quantified object NP can (and for many people, including myself, must) be understood as having wider scope than the wh-phrase in subject position. Once again, I would claim that in these instances, the object NPs are adjoined not to IP, but to CP, leaving behind an empty category which enters into a chain with the clitic, i.e. a *pro*. This is possible in those dialects which allow clitic doubling of this type (cf. Jaeggli (1986), for relevant discussion of clitic doubling structures). We can also rule out adjunction of the quantified NP to VP, which would yield a narrow scope interpretation which does not appear to be available in these cases, if we assume that from its VP-adjoined position, the quantified NP would locally A-bar bind the clitic (or the pro in argument position), and that this is not allowed.

There is clearly much more data that needs to be examined in connection with these facts. Space limitations do not allow us to go into these matters in detail here. Nevertheless, the basic outline of an account of these facts seems clear, allowing us to maintain the essential claim made in section 1.

ACKNOWLEDGEMENTS

I am indebted for helpful comments and discussion to Joseph Aoun, John Hawkins, Nina Hyams, Paula Kempchinsky, Robert May, Mario

Montalbetti, Carlos Otero, Mamoru Saito, Dominique Sportiche, Tim Stowell, Margarita Suñer, Esther Torrego, an anonymous reviewer, and audiences at the University of Texas at Austin, USC, UCLA, and Tsukuba University, where parts of this material were presented in classes and lectures. All errors remain my own.

NOTES

[1] Not all Superiority Condition violations are analyzable under the ECP. Ungrammatical sentences as in (i):

(i)   *What did you tell who(m) that Peter bought?

do not violate the ECP, yet they fall under the descriptive generalization of the Superiority Condition. See Pesetsky (1982) for discussion.

[2] The symbol '¿', used at the beginning of question in Spanish, is not to be confused with a mark of questionable grammaticality, for which we consistently use '?' at the beginning of a sentence.

[3] On the other hand, so-called 'psych-movement' verbs show different behavior. In the interest of brevity, we will not discuss them here. The interested reader should consult Jaeggli (1987) for a preliminary discussion of those facts. See also note 6.

[4] For reasons which we do not fully understand, some speakers of Spanish accept the quantifier *cada* only in subject position. (Obviously, this is not the case in the dialect studied in this paper). For such speakers, nevertheless, the contrasts observed in the text hold with complete regularity with other quantifiers in object position, such as numeral quantifiers. This is the reason why we occasionally use numeral quantifiers instead of *cada*, 'every'. It should be noted, furthermore, that Spanish *todo(s)*, functions differently from English *every*, in that it preferentially takes wide scope. For this reason we avoid using this quantifier. Additional facts which do not show the contrast mentioned in the text are discussed in the Appendix.

[5] The asymmetry, then, does not involve external vs. internal θ-positions. Rather, it appears to be a pure subject/object asymmetry, where 'subject' is understood in purely structural terms as the element that occupies the [Spec, IP] position.

[6] There is a type of verb which we have not considered above: 'psych-movement' verbs such as *gustar* 'to like' or (in one structure) *molestar* 'to bother'. These verbs take two arguments: a theme argument and an experiencer argument, and they agree in person and number with the theme argument. The experiencer argument is an indirect object at S-structure. Here judgments do not conform to what we have seen above. An object quantifier is allowed to have scope over a wh-phrase in Comp when the wh-phrase corresponds to a surface subject. The reader is referred to Jaeggli (1987) for discussion. Kim and Larson (1989) report similar facts for English 'psych' predicates. See also the Appendix, where some putative counterexamples to the claims made in this section are discussed.

[7] These definitions are taken from Lasnik and Saito (1984), which we will use as a basic framework for discussion throughout this paper. The ECP has been the focus of

much research in recent years. See the references cited in Lasnik and Saito (1984) and Chomksy (1986).

[8] Unaccounted for, given the assumptions sketched in the text, is why adjunct extraction does not show *that-t* effects. Cf.:

(i)   Why do you think that Bill left early.

An analysis along the lines sketched in the text can accommodate this fact if certain details which we have omitted are added. For complete details, see Lasnik and Saito (1985). See also Wahl (1988).

[9] It may be possible to achieve the desired result if we assume that adjunction of the quantifier disrupts the proper (antecedent) government relation because of an adjacency condition. We might stipulate that a proper governor must be adjacent to the empty category which needs to be properly governed. See Chomsky (1980) and Chomsky (1981, 272−273) for discussion relevant to such an adjacency condition on proper government. An altogether different approach is adopted in chapter 5 of May (1985), where crossing paths are held to be responsible for ECP effects, as in Pesetsky (1982). We assume below that adjunction disrupts the head government relation required by our version of the ECP. Long distance object extraction in Spanish argues against imposing an adjacency requirement on antecedent government.

[10] Torrego provides a slightly different analysis from the one in the text, assuming that the trace of the subject is properly governed in pre-verbal position by a preposed Verb. Regardless of the exact mechanism assumed, traces of subject extraction are lexically governed in either analysis.

[11] May (1985, chapter 2, footnote 10) points out that the Lasnik and Saito (1984) account of the ECP also runs into problems with the English data under discusson. In fact, aside from having to adopt an adjacency requirement on antecedent government, such an analysis runs into additional problems. May writes: "Lasnik and Saito (1984) state the ECP in such a fashion that once it comes to be satisfied for a given empty category, it remains so at all subsequent derivational levels. So, if the ECP is satisfied at S-structure, then nothing in the derivation to LF could change this. But this is precisely what we see happening in the derivation of (1b) [= *Who bought everything for Max*, OJ], which is consistent with ECP at S-structure but not at LF. Under Lasnik and Saito's formulation, then, this structure would be well-formed, and we would expect to find ambiguities where we do not." Similar remarks hold with respect to the Spanish data under discussion.

[12] The head of Comp position may be occupied by lexical complementizers, such as English *that, for,* and perhaps also *whether* and *if.* It is well-known that in Modern English a wh-phrase cannot coexist with another element in Comp at S-structure, e.g. *I wonder [who (*that) [John met t]],* etc. The structure in (28), however, allows for these sentences. Let us assume then, as in much previous work, that such sentences are disallowed by a version of the doubly-filled Comp filter suitably translated into this framework. We leave the technical details of this translation open.

[13] The following material concerning the notion of government and other auxiliary notions follows Chomsky (1986) quite closely. We point out where we diverge from the definitions given in that paper.

[14] This idea recalls a suggestion (attributed to Kyle Johnson) in Chomsky (1986) to the

effect that adjunction blocks θ-marking, although the principle we need is not reducible to this suggestion.
[15] The behavior of adjuncts in situ provides further support for the idea that only coindexed elements count as head governors at LF. The reader can check that the following familar contrasts follow directly from this idea. Sentences (ib, d), then are analyzed as a type of "Superiority" violation.

(i) a.   Who bought what?

b.   *Who bought the book why?

c.   What did Bill give to whom?

d.   *What did Bill give to Mary why?

[16] This view of subject θ-marking follows Safir (1985) in claiming that inverted subjects are θ-marked in their inverted position, and do not 'inherit' a θ-role from the element occupying [NP, S] position, but differs from Safir's treatment in that we assume that the direct θ-marker of the subject NP in inverted structures is Infl and not the VP.
[17] Several of the following sentences were pointed out by an anonymous reviewer.

REFERENCES

Aoun, J., Hornstein, N., and Sportiche, D.: 1981, 'Some Aspects of Wide Scope Quantification', *Journal of Linguistic Research* **1**, 69—95.
Burzio, L.: 1981, *Italian Syntax: A Government-Binding Approach*, Reidel, 1986.
Chomsky, N.: 1980, 'On Binding', *Linguistic Inquiry* **11**, 1—46.
Chomsky, N.: 1981, *Lectures on Government and Binding*. Foris Publications.
Chomsky, N.: 1982, *Some Concepts and Consequences of the Theory of Government and Binding*. MIT Press. Cambridge, MA.
Chomsky, N.: 1985, *Knowledge of Language: Its Nature, Origin and Use*. Praeger. New York, NY.
Chomsky, N.: 1986, *Barriers*. MIT Press, Cambridge, MA.
Jaeggli, O.: 1982, *Topics in Romance Syntax*. Foris Publications.
Jaeggli, O.: 1987, 'Quantification and Wh-Questions in Spanish', in: Montreuil, J-P. and D. Birdsong (eds.), *Advances in Romance Linguistics* (the Proceedings of the 14th Linguistic Symposium on Romance Languages, University of Texas at Austin, Texas). Foris Publications.
Kim, H. and Larson, R.: 1989, 'Scope Interpretation and the Syntax of Psych-Verbs', *Linguistic Inquiry* **20**, 681—688.
Lasnik, H. and Saito, M.: 1984, 'On the Nature of Proper Government', *Linguistic Inquiry* **15**, 235—289.
May, R.: 1985, *Logical Form: Its Structure and Derivation*. MIT Press, Cambridge, MA.
Pesetsky, D.: 1982, *Paths and Categories*. Unpublished Ph.D. dissertation. MIT. Cambridge, MA.
Rizzi, L.: 1982, *Issues in Italian Syntax*. Foris Publications.
Stowell, T.: 1981, *Origins of Phrase Structure*. Unpublished Ph.D. dissertation. MIT. Cambridge, MA.

Stowell, T.: 1986, 'Null Antecedents and Proper Government', in: S. Berman *et al.* (eds.), *Proceedings of NELS 16*, GLSA, Amherst, MA.

Stowell, T.: 1987, '*As* Clauses', ms., UCLA, CA.

Torrego, E.: 1984, 'On Inversion in Spanish and Some of its Effects', *Linguistic Inquiry* **15**, 103—129.

Wahl, A.: 1988, 'Two Types of Locality', *Linguistic Inquiry* **18**, 537—578.

KATALIN É. KISS

LOGICAL STRUCTURE IN SYNTACTIC STRUCTURE:
THE CASE OF HUNGARIAN

1. INTRODUCTION

According to standard assumptions of generative theory, operators are subject to the following universal principle of scope interpretation:

(1)   An operator c-commands its scope.[1]

Sentences are checked for principle (1) when they enter the semantic interpretive component of grammar. Principle (1) is either satisfied in syntax already: at D-structure, by base-generation, or at S-structure, as a result of Move WH; or is only met at LF, the abstract level of representation directly feeding into semantic interpretation. In English, for instance, non-variable-binding operators, e.g. the negative particle, *only*, *even*, or such scope-bearing elements as adverbials of time, place, etc., are assigned to positions from which they c-command their scope at D-structure already (e.g., sentence adverbials are hanging from the S node, c-commanding the material in S, while predicate adverbials are generated hanging from the VP node, c-commanding the material in the VP.) Variable-binding operators, on the other hand, get into positions from which they c-command their scope at S-structure or at LF. A single WH-operator per sentence is preposed into an A'-position c-commanding S in the transformational component of syntax, by a substitution transformation. Quantified phrases, WH-phrases not pre-posed in syntax, and the focus are moved into positions where they satisfy principle (1) only in the LF component, by adjunction.

This distribution of facts is obviously neither invariant across languages, as a necessary consequence of some universal principle, nor is an accidental, ad hoc phenomenon of English, but is the result of the interplay of various components of English grammar. Namely, non-variable-binding operators can be base-generated in observance of principle (1), because, not being either complements or specifiers of a head, or heads of complements and specifiers, they are not affected by constraints imposed on English phrase structure by X'-theory, government theory, case theory, or theta theory. The fact that in syntax only

111

one variable-binding operator per sentence can be preposed into an
A′-position c-commanding S; i.e., the fact that substitution has a single
A′-position available as its target, and operator adjunction is forbidden,
is related in Szabolcsi (1983b) to the configurational character of
English. Indeed, if in a language grammatical functions are encoded in
phrase structure configurations, the possibilities for the reorganization
of phrase structure are necessarily limited, since the demolition of
phrase structure beyond a certain point would endanger the interpretation of the sentence.

This explanation predicts that in a so-called non-configurational
language, where the configurations of major sentence constituents are
exempt from encoding information on grammatical functions, more —
or perhaps all — of the operator-preposing transformations can take
place visibly, in syntax. In any case, no principle or constraint of
Universal Grammar is known to block this possibility.

The purpose of this paper is to show that the theoretical possibility
of performing all operator preposing transformations triggered by
principle (1) in syntax is realized at least in one language: in Hungarian.
In the Hungarian sentence principle (1) is fully observed at S-structure
already; i.e., the S-structure and LF representations of a sentence are
non-distinct with respect to quantifier placement. In other words,
principle (1) functions in Hungarian as a well-formedness condition on
S-structure, which, together with a small number of auxiliary hypotheses, e.g., the constraint in (2):

(2)   An operator precedes its scope.

correctly predicts all and only the grammatical permutations of the
major constituents of the Hungarian sentence, also predicting the
semantic differences of the various permutations. (Constraint (2) is
presumably not universal; as will be shown, exceptionally it can also be
overridden in Hungarian; nevertheless, it appears to represent the
perceptually unmarked option.) Recapitulating our claim to be defended below:

(3)   Principle (1) is met in the S-structure of the Hungarian
        sentence.

The paper is organized as follows: Section 2 presents the D-structure
of the Hungarian sentence. Sections 3 and 4 describe the substitution

rules of Focusing, and Topicalization, respectively. Section 5 deals with negation. The topic of section 6 is Quantifier-Raising, the syntactic equivalent of the English adjunction rule operating in LF. Section 7 analyzes operators in Left Dislocation, while section 8 introduces a stylistic rule affecting operators.

2. D-STRUCTURE

As I argued elsewhere (most recently in Kiss (1987a) and (1987b)), in the Hungarian sentence all the arguments of the V, including the subject, are generated under V′, in an arbitrary order, as right sisters of the V. The VP also contains an empty specifier position, which is filled by substitution. At S-structure this is the locus of the focus operator. The VP is preceded and c-commanded by an A′-position to be substituted by a constitutent or set of constitutents which assume a topic role in it. The topic and the VP, dominated by S, are in a predication relation. In embedded sentences, the initial position is occupied by a complementizer. That is:

(4)

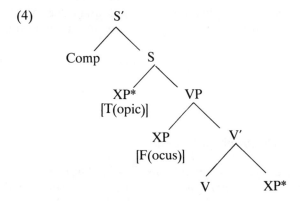

Quantified phrases, as will be made clear in section 6, have no base-generated landing site, but are adjoined to VP.

The claim that of the base-generated empty A′-positions, the focus slot is inside the VP, while the topic slot is immediately dominated by the S node is supported, among others, by the operation of the Nuclear Stress Rule, and by the placement of adverbials.

The Nuclear Stress Rule, the direction of which in Hungarian is opposition to that in English, treats the sentence part beginning with the focus as one phrase, putting the heaviest primary stress on the phrase-initial focus. In sentences containing QPs adjoined in front of the focus, the heaviest one of primary stresses falls on the leftmost QP.

That the leftmust major constituent dominated by VP always receive a primary stress is ensured by the following rule:

(5)   Assign [1 stress] to the first major category dominated by a VP node.

(That is, the focus, or in case the focus slot is empty, the V is a target of obligatory primary stress assignment. If QP-adjunction to the VP creates a new VP node, the QP immediately dominated by it also obligatorily receives a primary stress. The primary stresses assigned by rule (5), often crucial to the structural and semantic interpretation of the sentence, will be marked in the examples below by the symbol ′.)

The topic, on the other hand, is usually unstressed, and when it does receive a pitch accent, its stress is never stronger than the stress of the QP or focus immediately following it — i.e., the operation of the Nuclear Stress Rule shows the topic not to form a phrasal category with the VP. Consider, for instance, the stress values in the following sentence:

(6)   0/1   1   2   0   3
        [$_S$ Jánost$_i$ [$_{VP}$ mindegyikönk$_j$ [$_{VP}$ fel$_k$ [$_{V'}$ hívta telefonon
        John-acc   each-of-us-nom   up   called by-phone
        $e_i \, e_j \, e_k$]]]]^2
        'John was called by phone by each of us.'

The labelling of the node immediately dominating the focus as VP, and the node immediately dominating the topic as S is motivated, among others, by the position of predicate adverbials and sentence adverbials. It is reasonable to assume that predicate adverbials are daughters of the VP node, while sentence adverbials are daughters of S. This is what we find in the proposed structure: predicate adverbials appear either adjoined to VP, or in the specifier position of VP — as in (7) (for detials, see section 6), while sentence adverbials stand in the sentence part immediately dominated by S, either after or before the topic — as in (8) (see also section 4).

(7) a.   [$_S$ János$_i$ [$_{VP}$ 'szépen   [$_{V'}$ zongorázik   e$_i$]]]
          John   beautifully   plays-the-piano
          'John plays the piano beautifully.'

cf. b.   *[$_S$ Szépen János$_i$ [$_{VP}$[$_{V'}$ zongorázik e$_i$]]]

(8) a.   [$_S$ Szerencsére Jánost$_i$ [$_{VP}$ 'otthon$_j$ [$_{V'}$ találtam e$_i$ e$_j$]]]
          luckily   John-acc   at-home   found-I
          'Luckily, I found John at home.'

cf. b.   *[$_S$ Jánost$_i$ [$_{VP}$ 'szerencsére [$_{V'}$ találtam otthon e$_i$]]][3]

The Hungarian phrase structure argued for above is unorthodox to the extent that S is not a projection, but is an exocentric category: the realization of prediction relation. Nevertheless, the hypothesized structure is not unprecedented in recent generative literature — cf. e.g., Williams (1982), or Chung and McCloskey (1987).

3. FOCUSING

3.1.

The preposing of a maximal projection from V' into the specifier position of the VP has a "focusing" effect. That is, the preposed constituent assumes a meaning component described as 'exhaustive listing' (cf. Szabolcsi (1981)), or as 'identification by exclusion' (Kenesei (1964)), and also assumes primary stress (cf. rule (S)), "eradicating" the stress of the subsequent V at the same time, too (see Kalman *et al.* (1986)). E.g.

(9) a.   [$_S$[$_{VP}$ 'János$_i$ [$_{V'}$ kisérte   haza   Marit   e$_i$]]]
          John-nom   escorted   home   Mary-acc
          'It was John who escorted Mary home.'

    b.   [$_S$[$_{VP}$ 'Marit$_i$ [$_{V'}$ kisérte   János   haza e$_i$]]]
          Mary-acc   escorted   John-nom   home
          'It was Mary who John escorted home.'

As the English glosses indicate, the scope of the focus operator extends over the VP, its c-command domain — as required by principle (1). Thus a constitutent in T is outside the domain of focusing — cf.

(10)   [János$_i$ ['Marit$_j$ [kisérte haza e_i e_j]]]
        John-nom   Mary-acc   escorted home

'As for John, it was Mary who he escorted home.'

The focus cannot be separated from the V by an intervening constituent, which is explained in Horvath (1985) as follows: in the type of grammar represented by Hungarian FOCUS is a syntactic feature inherent to the lexical category V, which can be assigned by the V to other categories under the general locality condition on feature assignment, including the requirements of government and adjacency.

An X° constituent subcategorized by the V, i.e., a bare N, Adj or Adv semantically incorporated into the V, often also forming a lexical unit with it (e.g., *levelet olvas* 'letter-reads', *moziba megy* 'to-cinema-goes', *beteg volt* 'sick was', *el ment* 'away went') is not interpreted in F as a "focus", i.e., as expressing exhaustive listing or identification by exclusion. Because of its semantic dependence it expresses the prominence of the X° + V unit as a whole; but even so, its preposing into F does not assign the X° + V unit focus role in the above sense, since 'identification by exclusion' normally cannot be interpreted on Vs.[4] Cf.

(11)   [$_S$ János$_i$ [$_{VP}$ 'haza$_j$ [$_{V'}$ kisérte   Marit e_i e_j]]]
        John   home   escorted   Mary-acc

'John escorted Mary home.'

While the filling of the F slot is, in general, optional, in sentences including an incorporated constitutent F cannot remain empty; if it is not occupied by a "genuine" focus (i.e., an XP), the incorporated constituent must go into it.

3.2. Questions

In questions the specifier position of the VP, i.e., position F, is filled by the interrogative phrase. The preposing of the interrogative phrase into F is obligatory, i.e., Hungarian has no echo-question — as required by principles (1) and (2). Cf.

(12) a.   [$_S$[$_{VP}$ 'Kit$_i$ [$_{V'}$ kisért   haza   János e_i?]]]
            whom   escorted home   John-nom

'Who did John escort home?'

cf. b.   *[$_S$[$_{VP}$ Haza$_t$ [$_{V'}$ kisért János kit e_i?]]]

As predicted by principle (1), a phrase in T is outside the scope of interrogation:

(13)   [$_S$ János$_i$ [$_{VP}$ 'kit$_j$ [$_{V'}$ kisért   haza e_i e_j?]]]
         John-nom   whom   escorted   home

    'As for John, who did he escort home?'

The fact that the landing site of the interrogative phrase is the F slot instead of some other A'-position c-commanding the VP is a consequence of an independently motivated principle of WH-interpretation, formulated in Horvath (1981, 1985) as follows:

(14)   *The FOCUS Constraint on the Wh-Q Operator*
    A non-echo question interpretation can be derived only if the Wh-Q operator bears the feature FOCUS at LF.[5]

                          (Horvath 1985, 118)

As follows from principles (1) and (2), no interrogative phrase can remain in its base-generated position in multiple questions, either. What happens in multiple questions is that one of the interrogative phrases is preposed into F, while the rest of them are iteratively adjoined to the VP node immediately dominating F. Naturally, each interrogative phrase takes scope over the sentence part it c-commands and precedes, i.e., the left-to-right order of interrogative phrases also represents their scope order. Cf.

(15) a.   [$_S$[$_{VP}$ 'Ki$_i$ [$_{VP}$ 'mit$_j$ [$_{VP}$ javasolt e_i e_j?]]]]
         who   what-acc   proposed

    'Who proposed what?'
    [Tell me for each person what he proposed.]

    b.   [$_S$[$_{VP}$ 'Mit$_i$ [$_{VP}$ 'ki$_j$ [$_{V'}$ javasolt e_i e_j?]]]][6]
          what-acc   who   proposed

    'Who proposed what?'
    [Tell me for each item who proposed it.]

(15a) and (15b) only have what Higginbotham and May (1981) call a 'bijective' interpretation; i.e., they express the presupposition that more than one individual proposed more than one thing, and the individuals and the things proposed form pairs. The relation between an element of the set of individuals, and an element of the set of things proposed is not necessarily biunique. Pair-formation starts from the set mentioned first; each element in this set is expected to be linked to one or more element of the set mentioned next. E.g. in the case of (15a), links of the following types are presupposed:

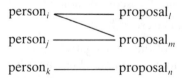

In answering (15b), on the other hand, the following types of links can be formed:

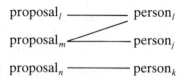

The interpretation of the left-hand side interrogative operator ('take each element of the relevant domain one by one') basically corresponds to the interpretation of the universal quantifier *each* — cf. the glosses in (15a) and (15b). This operator also behaves syntactically as a universal quantifier; it undergoes exactly the same adjunction to VP (to be described in section 6) as universally quantified phrases do.

The interpretation of one of the two interrogative phrases as a universal quantifier has roughly the same effect semantically as the operation of Absorption has in English. In English multiple questions the two WH-phrases are analyzed as being unified into a single operator which binds two variables — see Higginbotham and May (1981). Since, however, the Hungarian way of deriving a paired interpretation involves two operators asymmetrically c-commanding each other, i.e., entering into an asymmetric scope relation with each other, pair formation in Hungarian has a direction — as a result of which e.g. (15a) and (15b) are semantically non-equivalent. The English way of deriving a paired interpretation, on the other hand, involves a single operator, the two components of which perhaps do not enter into a scope relation with each other at all, or if they do, it will be a symmetric scope relation, since the two WH-phrases mutually c-command each other. Consequently, English multiple questions cannot express the subtle semantic difference e.g. between (15a) and (15b).

In multiple questions the interrogative phrase with the widest scope is to be interpreted as [+specific]. Therefore, e.g. a NP containing the [-specific] *milyen* 'what' cannot occur as the leftmost one of the interrogative phrases:

(16) a. $[_S[_{VP}$ 'Ki$_i$ $[_{VP}$ 'milyen ajándékot$_j$ $[_{V'}$ kapott $e_i e_j?]]]]$
who   what   present-acc   received

'Who received what present?'

cf. b. *$[_S[_{VP}$ 'Milyen ajándékot$_i$ $[_{VP}$ ki$_j$ $[_{V'}$ kapott $e_i e_j?]]]]$

If *milyen* is replaced by its [+specific] counterpart, the sentence will be grammatical no matter which interrogative phrase stands first:

(17) $[_S[_{VP}$ 'Melyik ajándékot$_i$ $[_{VP}$ 'ki$_j$ $[_{V'}$ kapta $e_i e_j?]]]]$[7]
which   present-acc   who   received

'Who received which present?'

The interrogative adverbs *hogyan* 'how' and *miért* 'why' can presumably only occur in the F position of multiple questions because they resist a [+specific] interpretation.[8]

4. *Topicalization*

Topicalization, a substitution rule, preposes one or more maximal projection into the A'-position c-commanding and preceding the VP, dominated by S. The arguments preposed into T are associated with a flat, even intonation contour typically not involving any primary stresses, and with a topic interpretation. The semantic-communicative function of the topic is to present an object and/or a person, or a set of objects and/or persons that, or whose relation, the VP will state something about. E.g.

(18) a. $[_S$ János$_i$ $[_{VP}$ 'a   lemezt$_j$ $[_{V'}$ adta Marinak $e_i e_j]]]$
John-nom   the   record-acc   gave Mary-dat

'John gave Mary THE RECORD.'

b. $[_S$ Marinak$_i$ $[_{VP}$ 'János$_j$ $[_{V'}$ adta a   lemezt $e_i e_j]]]$
Mary-dat   John-nom   gave the record-acc

'Mary was given the record BY JOHN.'

(18) c. [$_s$ A lemezt$_i$ [$_{VP}$ 'Marinak$_j$ [$_{V'}$ adta János $e_i e_j$]]]
          the record-acc   Mary-dat   gave John-nom

'The record was given by John TO MARY.'

In sentences in which more than one argument has been topicalized, it is the relation of the topicalized arguments that is "commented upon". Such sentences give the impression of involving "absorption" in the sense of Higginbotham and May (1981), i.e., a single topic binding more than one empty argument position. E.g.

(19)   [$_s$ A lemezt$_i$ Marinak$_j$ [$_{VP}$ 'János$_k$ [$_{V'}$ adta $e_i e_j e_k$]]]
        the record-acc Mary-dat   John-nom gave

'The record, Mary was given BY JOHN.'

As follows from principle (1), the topic is outside the scope of the operators dominated by the VP or by a segment of the VP — i.e., it is outside the scope of the focus, the interrogative operator, the quantified phrases etc. That the topic is not subordinated to any operator following it is especially clear if, e.g., the topicalized argument contains a numeral, or if it is represented by an indefinite, or a *vala-*('some-') pronoun. (These are the types of quantificational elements that can occur in T position.) Consider the glosses of the following sentences:

(20)   [$_s$ Két regényt$_i$ [$_{VP}$ 'mindenki$_j$ [$_{VP}$ 'el$_k$
        two novel-acc   everybody-nom   (pref.)
       [$_{V'}$ olvasott $e_i e_j e_k$]]]]^9
        read

'There are two novels which everybody read.'

(21)   [$_s$ Egy regényt$_i$ [$_{VP}$ 'mindenki$_j$ [$_{VP}$ el$_k$
        a   novel-acc   everybody-nom   (pref.)
       [$_{V'}$ olvasott $e_i e_j e_k$]]]]
        read

'There is a novel which everybody read.'

(22)   [$_s$ Valaki$_i$ [$_{VP}$ 'mindenkinek$_j$ [$_{VP}$ szólt $e_i e_j$]]]
        everybody-nom   everybody-dat informed

'There is somebody who informed everybody.'

In accordance with the fact that the role of a topic is to foreground

an element of the universe about which the VP will predicate something, Topicalization assigns a name-like status to all NPs affected by it,
including quantified NPs — that is why, e.g., indefinites only have a
specific interpretation in T; and that is why topicalized NPs cannot be
subordinated to any logical operation.

The name-like status of topicalized constituents is also indicated by
the fact that in the case of multiple topicalization they do not enter into
any scope relation with each other — e.g.,

(23) $[_S$ Két rendör$_i$ három autóst$_j$ $[_{VP}$ 'ezer
        two two policemen-nom three   driver-acc   thousand
        forintra$_k$ $[_{V'}$ büntetett $e_i e_j e_k]]]$
        forint-to   fined

'There were two policemen, and there were three drivers
such that former fined the latter a thousand forints.'

Sentence adverbials are also located in the position immediately
dominated by S, as sisters of the topicalized arguments, ordered
arbitrarily with respect to them and to each other. They are presumably
base-generated in that position. As scope-bearing elements with maximally wide scope, they are certainly forced by principles (1) and (2)
into a position immediately dominated by S. E.g.,

(24) $[_S$ Tegnap   János$_i$ az   egyetemen $[_{VP}$ 'meg$_j$
        yesterday John-nom the university-on   (pref.)
        $[_{V'}$ ismerkedett   egy lánnyal $e_i e_j]]]$
        got-acquainted a   girl-with

'Yesterday, at the university, John got acquainted with a girl.'

(25) $[_S$ Tegnap   János$_i$ meglepetésemre $[_{VP}$ 'meg$_j$
        yesterday John-nom to-my-surprise   (pref.)
        $[_{V'}$ ismerkedett   egy lánnyal $e_i e_j]]]$
        got-acquainted a   girl-with

'Yesterday John, to my surprise, got acquainted with a girl.'

5. *Negation*

The position and interpretation of the negative particle is determined
by principles (1) and (2). Namely, the negative particle can be adjoined

either to V', or the VP. In the former case, giving the impression of 'sentence negation', the scope of negation extends over V', the propositional component of the sentence, but it does not extend over the focus and the topic:

(26) a. [$_S$ János$_i$ [$_{VP}$[$_{V'}$ 'nem [$_V$ szereti a   bort   e$_i$]]]]
         John   not   likes the wine-acc

'As for John, he does not like wine.'

   b. [$_S$ János$_i$ [$_{VP}$ a   'bort$_j$ [$_{V'}$ nem [$_V$ szereti e$_i$ e$_j$]]]]
       John-nom   the   wine-acc   not   likes

'As for John, it is wine that he does not like.'

When the negative particle is adjoined to the VP, it also includes the focus in its scope, only excluding the topic. Such sentences create the impression of constituent negation:

(27) [$_S$ János$_i$ [$_{VP}$ 'nem [$_{VP}$ a   bort$_j$ [$_{V'}$ itta   meg e$_i$ e$_j$]]]]
      John-nom   not   the wine-acc   drank up

'As for John, it was not the wine that he drank.'

In sentences (26a) and (27), in which the negative particle is followed by a constituent subject to primary stress assignment, the distribution of primary stresses is not correctly predicted by the stress assignment rule in (5). Namely, the negative particle, a non-major category, unexpectedly receives primary stress, while the major category following it, to be assigned primary stress by rule (5), remains unstressed. We can account for this phenomenon if we assume that in negative sentences the negative particle is phonologically cliticized to, and is semantically incorporated into the category following it. That is, patterns (26a, b), interpreted as instances of 'sentence negation', contain instead of a negative particle with scope over V', a negative V with scope over the arguments in V'. (This would also explain why the negative particle intruding between the V and the focus does not violate the adjacency requirement on FOCUS assignment by the V). Similarly, (27), interpreted as an instance of 'constituent negation', contains, instead of a negative operator with scope over the VP, a negative focus with scope over V'.

The cliticization of the negative particle to the major constituent following it is blocked when the negated V' or VP is set into contrast with the corresponding part of a positive sentence — obviously because in this case negation can by no means be interpreted merely on the constituent immediately following the negative particle. E.g.,

(28) a. [$_S$ János$_i$ [$_{VP}$ nem [$_{VP}$ 'meg$_j$ [$_{V'}$ itta   a   bort e_i e_j]]]]
         John-nom   not   up   drank the wine-acc
         hanem [$_S$[$_{VP}$ 'ki$_k$ [$_{V'}$ borította e_k]]]
         but   out   poured-he-it

         'As for John, he did not drink the wine, but he poured it out.'

   b. [$_S$ János$_i$ [$_{VP}$ nem [$_{VP}$ a   'bort$_j$ [$_{V'}$ itta   meg e_i e_j]]]]
       John-nom   not   the wine-acc   drank   up
       hanem [$_S$[$_{VP}$ a   'pezsgövel$_k$ [$_{V'}$ koccintott e_k]]]
       but   the champagne-with   clinked-glasses

       'As for John, it was not the wine that he drank, but it was the champagne that he clinked glasses with.'

6. QUANTIFICATION

6.1. *Q-Raising*

Quantified phrases, among them phrases containing a universal quantifier (e.g., *mindenki* 'everybody', *mindig* 'always', *senki* 'nobody', *soha* 'never'), phrases modified by *is* 'also', phrases containing a positive quantifier such as *sok* 'many', positive adverbials of degree, manner, and frequency (e.g., *nagyon* 'very much', *szépen* 'beautifully', *gyakran* 'often', etc.) are adjoined to VP. Unlike Focusing, which is substitution into the single base generated position of SpecVP, Q-Raising, an adjunction rule, can be performed iteratively if necessary. That is, while the sentence can contain at most one focus, it can contain any number of Q-raised phrases. (While both the focused constituent and the Q-raised constituents will be immediately dominated by a VP node and will bear primary stress (see rule (5)), the Q-raised constitutents, not only dominated by a VP node but also dominating a VP, will naturally not trigger a focus interpretation.)

The Q-Raising rule assumed is the syntactic equivalent of the Q-Raising rule proposed in May (1977, 1985), an LF rule assigning scope to quantifiers, e.g., in English. The realization of Q-Raising in the syntax component of Hungarian grammar is in accordance with our claim that principle (1) operates in Hungarian as a well-formedness condition on S-structure.

As predicted by principle (1), in the output of Q-Raising each operator takes scope over the sentence part it c-commands, and is included in the scope of the operators it is c-commanded by. Consider, e.g., the structure and interpretation of the following sentence:

(29)   [s János_i   [vp 'többször is_j   [vp 'mindent_k
         John-nom   several-times   everything-acc
         [vp 'világosan_l [vp 'el_m   [v' magyarázott $e_i\, e_j\, e_k\, e_l\, e_m$]]]]]]
         clearly   (pref.)   explained

'As for John, on several occasions he explained everything clearly.'

(In the English glosses, the surface order of the operators is intended to represent their scope order, as well.)

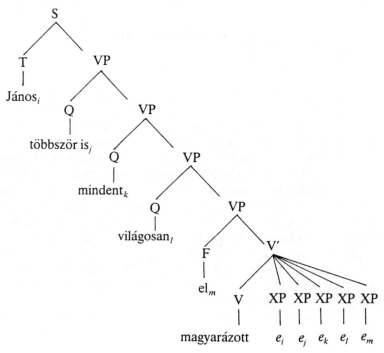

The interpretation of the quantified phrases in (29) is determined by principle (1) — which predicts that their scope order is the equivalent of their surface order; while their stressing is determined by rule (5) — which predicts that each of them, as well as the constituent in F, bears a primary stress.

If the QPs in the D-structure of (29) undergo Q-Raising in a different order, i.e., if the surface order and hierarchy of the operators changes, the interpretation of the sentence will also change in a well-defined way — precisely as it is predicted to change by principle (1). E.g.,

(30) a. $[_S$ János$_i$ $[_{VP}$ 'mindent$_j$ $[_{VP}$ 'többször is$_k$
       John-nom   everything-acc   several-times
      $[_{VP}$ 'világosan$_l$ $[_{VP}$ 'el$_m$ $[_{V'}$ magyarázott $e_i\,e_j\,e_k\,e_l\,e_m]]]]]]$
      clearly   (pref.)   explained

     'As for John, everything was several times explained by him clearly.'

b. $[_S[_{VP}$ 'Többször is$_i$ $[_{VP}$ 'mindent$_j$ $[_{VP}$ 'János$_k$
     several-times   everything-acc   John-nom
     $[_{V'}$ magyarázott el   világosan $e_i\,e_j\,e_k]]]]]$
     explained   (pref.) clearly

     'On several occasions, it was true of everything that it was John who explained it clearly.'

If a quantified phrase is intended to have narrower scope than the focus, then condition (2), requiring that an operator precede its domain, gets into conflict with the adjacency condition on FOCUS assignment (cf., Horvath 1985, 321—132; and section 3.1 above). It is the adjacency condition which gets the upper hand; i.e., the immediately preverbal position of the focus is maintained, and the operator to be included in its scope is left in argument position. This is what happened to the adverb *világosan* 'clearly' in (30b). Here is a further example:

(31) $[_S[_{VP}$ 'János$_i$ $[_{V'}$ látott mindent $e_i]]]$
     John-nom   saw everything-acc

     'It was John who saw everything.'

(31) does observe principle (1), since the QP in V' c-commands every element of V', its domain. (On the other hand, (31) violates the

Condition on Quantifier Binding of May (1977), according to which every quantified phrase must properly bind a variable, since *mindent* is in argument position. Nevertheless, since (31) observes principle (1), it contains all the information that is needed to its scope interpretation; i.e., no invisible Q-Raising in LF needs to be assumed.)

Condition (2) is also lifted when a QP has narrower scope than a sentence negating particle. E.g.,

(32) $[_S[_{VP}[_{V'}$ 'Nem $[_{V'}$ volt ott   mindenki]]]]
                    not   was there everybody

'Not everybody was there.'

If the hypothesis we raised in connection with (27) can be maintained, i.e., the sentence negating particle is phonologically cliticized to, and semantically incorporated into the V, then it also explains why the negative particle cannot be separated from the V by a QP adjoined to V', i.e., why the QP in the scope of *nem* must remain in V'.

In sentences in which the F slot is filled by an interrogative phrase, Q-Raising is blocked. E.g.,

(33) a. *$[_S[_{VP}$ 'Mindenki$_i$ $[_{VP}$ 'kivel$_j$ $[_{V'}$ beszélt $e_i\,e_j$?]]]]$[10]
                  everybody   who-with   spoke

'With whom did everybody speak?'

b. *$[_S[_{VP}$ 'János is$_i$ $[_{VP}$ 'kivel$_j$ $[_{V'}$ beszélt $e_i\,e_j$?]]]]$
            John also   who-with   spoke

'With whom did also John speak?'

In questions, the only possibility for the placement of a QP is to leave it — unstressed — in V', where it is included in the scope of the interrogative operator. E.g.,

(34) a. $[_S[_{VP}$ 'Kivel$_i$ $[_{V'}$ beszélt mindenki e_i?]]]$

'Who is the (single) person with whom everybody spoke?'

b. $[_S[_{VP}$ 'Kivel$_i$ $[_{V'}$ beszélt János is e_i?]]]$

'Who is the person with whom also John spoke?'

The ungrammaticality of (33a, b) is given the following explanation in Szabolcsi (1983a): questions are sets, and not propositions, i.e., truth-value denoting expressions; therefore, operators, e.g., quantifiers, cannot be applied to them.

If Szabolcsi is right, then we would expect to find no questions with a wide scope QP in any language. In English, however, sentences containing both an interrogative phrase and a QP are reported to be ambiguous with respect to relative scope; i.e., they are said to have an interpretation (albeit a marked one) in which the QP takes scope over the interrogative phrase. E.g.,

(35)   What did everybody order?

(In *Who ordered everything?* the interrogative phrase in subject position has no narrow scope interpretation, which is attributed to the Empty Category Principle — cf. May (1985)).

The two interpretations of (35) are derived in the framework of May (1985) by adjoining the QP to the S node at LF:

(35′)   [What$_i$ did [$_S$ everybody$_j$ [$_S$ e_j order e_i?]]]

The scope interpretation of operators is claimed to be determined by the so-called Scope Principle, according to which operators mutually c-commanding each other are free to take any relative scope. The Scope Principle employs the government definition of Aoun and Sportiche (1983), according to which

(36) α governs β = $_{def}$ α c-commands β and β c-commands α, and there are no maximal projection boundaries between α and β.

(37) α c-commands β = $_{def}$ every maximal projection dominating β dominates α, and β does not dominate α.

In (35′) the interrogative phrase and the QP mutually govern each other (the segment of S intervening between them does not count as a maximal projection), consequently the sentence is ambiguous with respect to their relative scope.

In fact, the LF of (35) does not necessarily contradict the claim of Szabolcsi (1983a) that questions cannot undergo quantification; after all, in (35′) it is the universally quantified proposition to which the interrogative operator is applied, and not the other way round; merely this order of operations yields a semantically ambiguous output — owing to the interaction of the Scope Principle and Aoun and Sportich's notion of government.

The Hungarian equivalent of (35) is not ambiguous because in Hungarian scope interpretation is based on the stricter Reinhart-type notion of c-command (Reinhart 1976; see footnote 1). Of course, the assumption that the structural notion determining operator scope interpretation has to be parametrized is not very appealing; it is not clear how a child acquiring his mother tongue can figure out which variant of the notion of c-command underlies operator scope interpretation in the sentences he hears. Perhaps it would be worth-while to attempt to base operator scope interpretation on Reinhart's definition of c-command across languages (in English, too, as is done in May (1977)). In this case, of course, the marked interpretation of (35) could only be derived by some auxiliary hypothesis.

6.2. *The Focusing of Quantified Phrases*

Universally quantified phrases, phrases quantified by is 'also', as well as adverbials expressing totality, maximal degree, or maximal frequency, can only be assigned scope through Q-Raising, i.e., through adjunction to VP. They cannot be topicalized — presumably because they can by no means assume a 'name' status; and they cannot be focused — presumably because the specific meaning of 'identified by exclusion' they would assume in F position is incompatible with universal quantification.

The impossibility of the focusing of universally quantified phrases is the easiest to test in the case of verbs subcategorizing for an incorporated constitutent, e.g., for a prefix. The unmarked surface position of incorporated constituents is F (see also section 3.1):

(38) $[_S[_{VP}$ 'Meg$_i$ $[_{V'}$ érkezett egy vendég $e_i]]]$
         (pref)   arrived   a   guest

'A guest arrived.'

An incorporated constituent can be kept out of F only by a focused XP:

(39) a. *$[_S[_{VP}[_{V'}$ 'Érkezett meg egy vendég$]]]$

     b. $[_S[_{VP}$ Egy 'vendég$_i$ $[_{V'}$ érkezett meg $e_i]]]$

'It was a guest who arrived.'

Unlike, e.g., the focused NP in (39b), a universally quantified XP does not keep the incorporated constituent out of F; i.e., in the presence of an incorporated constituent a universally quantified phrase cannot be adjacent to the V. Compare with (39):

(40) a. $[_S[_{VP}$ 'Mindenki$_i$ $[_{VP}$ 'meg $[_{V'}$ érkezett $e_i]]]$
  everybody   (pref.)   arrived

  'Everybody arrived.'

  b. *$[_S[_{VP}$ 'Mindenki$_i$ $[_{V'}$ érkezett meg $e_i]]]$

Negated universally quantified phrases, however, behave differently: they can stand in F. E.g.,

(41) $[_S[_{VP}$ 'Nem $[_{VP}$ mindenki$_i$ $[_{V'}$ ment el $e_i]]]]$
  not   everybody   went away

  'Not everybody left.'

Quantified phrases containing a negative quantifier like *kevés* 'few', as well as negative adverbials of degree, manner, and frequency, e.g., *kicsit* 'little', *rosszul* 'badly', *ritkán* 'seldom', cannot undergo either Q-Raising, or Topicalization; they can only land in F from among the A'-positions. E.g.,

(42) a. $[_S$ János$_i$ $[_{VP}$ 'késŏn$_j$ $[_{V'}$ hívott   fel
  John   late   called-me up
  telefonon $e_i e_j]]]$
  telephone-on

  'As for John, it was late when he called me up by phone'

cf. b. *$[_S$ János$_i$ $[_{VP}$ 'késŏn$_j$ $[_{VP}$ 'fel$_k$ $[_{V'}$ hívott telefonon $e_i e_j e_k]]]]$

  c. *$[_S$ Késŏn$_i$ János$_j$ $[_{VP}$ 'fel$_k$ $[_{V'}$ hívott telefonon $e_i e_j e_k]]]$

Perhaps QPs of this type are understood as involving covert negation, and are restricted to the F position as negated constituents. This explanation, unfortunately, cannot account for the fact that such negatively quantified phrases can also remain in V' when included in the scope of focus or sentence negation — see (43) — even though overtly negated constituents can in no circumstances show up in V'.

(43) $[_S[_{VP}$ 'János$_i$ $[_{V'}$ hívott   fel késŏn telefonon $e_i]]]$
  John   called-me up late

  'It was John who called me up late by phone.'

Non-universal, positive QPs, among them adverbials expressing a non-maximal, positive degree, frequency, or manner, can undergo either Q-Raising or Focusing. Positively quantified NPs that allow a name-like (i.e., topic) interpretation, and positive adverbials that can be understood as sentence adverbials can also be moved into a position immediately dominated by S. If focused or topicalized, naturally, they not only assume a particular scope, but also assume the sematic-communicative properties of the focus or topic. Compare, for instance, the position and the interpretation of *sok új szót* 'may new words' in (44a), where it has undergone Q-Raising, in (44b), where it is focus, involving 'identification by exclusion', and in (44c), where it is a [+specific] topic.

(44) a. [$_S$ János$_i$ ebböl az angol regényböl$_j$ [$_{VP}$ 'sok
        John-nom this   the English novel-from   many
        új   szót$_k$ [$_{VP}$ 'meg$_i$ [$_{V'}$ tanult e_i e_j e_k e_l]]]]
        new word-acc   (pref.)   learnt

   'As for John, from this English novel he learnt many new words.'

   b. [$_S$ János$_i$ ebböl az angol regényböl$_j$ [$_{VP}$ 'sok új szót$_k$ [$_{V'}$ tanult meg e_i e_j e_k]]]

   'As for John, from this English novel, it was many new words that he learnt.'

   c. [$_S$ Sok új szót$_i$ [$_{VP}$ 'ebböl az angol regényböl$_j$ [$_{V'}$ tanult meg János e_i e_j]]]

   'There are many new words which it was from this English novel that John Learnt.'

6.3. *QPs in the NP*

Principles (1) and (2), which require that an operator c-command and precede its domain, together with our claim that they are checked at S-structure in Hungarian, make the following predictions for QPs occupying the complement or specifier position of a NP:

(i)   A QP in the specifier position of a NP cannot have narrower scope than the head.

(ii)   A QP in the complement position of a NP cannot have wider scope than the head.

Let us check if these predictions are borne out. As for (i), consider example (45), containing a NP with a quantified genitive specifier and a quantified head.

(45)   [Minden családtag   két fényképe] jól   sikerüit.
        every   family-member two photo-his well came-out

        'Every family-member's two photos came out well.'

Theoretically, example (45) can be associated with the following two interpretations:

(45) a.   Two photos showing all the family-members came out well.

    b.   Two photos of each family-member came out well.

In fact, the (a) reading of (45) is absent; *minden családtag* cannot be interpreted as being within the scope of *két fényképe*, since *két fényképe* does not precede *minden családtag*; on the contrary, *minden családtag* precedes *két fényképe* in violation of principle (2). (45) is also marginal if it is associated with the (b) reading, in which *minden családtag* has wider scope than *két fényképe*, obviously because *minden családtag* is to be assigned sentential scope; it, however, does not c-command the proposition — as is clear from the tree structure of (45):

(45′)

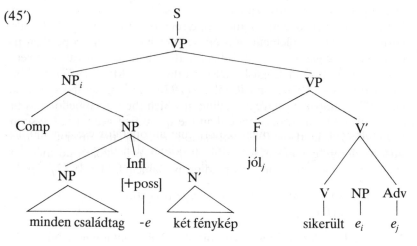

The inner structure of NP_i, containing a [+/−possessive] Infl node, the [+poss] value of which cooccurs with Agr, as well as a Comp functioning as an escape hatch, is justified in Szabolcsi (1983b).

The (b) reading of (45), involving a wide scope universal quantifier, can be rendered in a fully grammatical form if the genitive specifier is raised out of the NP by a genitive raising rule (which is optional if no quantification is involved — see Szabolcsi (1983b)), and is attached to the matrix S node, where it undergoes Q-Raising proper, arriving at a position c-commanding the proposition. That is:

(46) a. $[_S[_{VP}$ 'Minden családtagnak$_i$ $[_{VP}$ 'jól$_j$ $[_{V'}$ sikerült
            every   family-member-dat   well   came-out
        $[_{NP} e_i$ két fényképe] $e_j]]]]$
            two photo-his

'In the case of every family-member, two photos of him came out well.'

   b. $[_S[_{VP}$ 'Minden családtagnak$_i$ $[_{VP}[_{NP} e_i$ 'két fényképe]$_j$
            every   family-member-dat   two photo-his
        $[_{V'}$ sikerült   jól e_i' $e_j]]]]$
            came-out well

'In the came of every family-member, it was two photos of him that came out well.'

(When passing through the Comp slot of the NP, the genitive specifier picks up a -nak/nek dative suffix.)

Prediction (ii) concerning the scope relation of QPs in the NP is also borne out: the complement of a NP cannot have wider scope than the head, i.e., Hungarian does not display the phenomenon called inverse linking, described in English, among others, by May (1977), Gabbay and Moravcsik (1974), and Reinhart (1976). In English, NPs containing a PP complement have a reading in which the QP embedded as the object of the P has wider scope than the quantified head, i.e., the scope order of QPs in the NP is understood as being the inverse of their surface hierarchy and surface order. If the NP is in subject position, the inverse reading is often the only reading available (cf. May 1977). E.g.,

(47)   Every entrance to some large downtown store was smashed in the riot.

Although Hungarian does have complex NPs containing a NP or PP complement on the right branch — see (48), the "doubly" quantified NP in the subject position of (47) cannot be rendered by a similar Hungarian construction. Cf.,

(48)　　A   bejárat   a   boltba   megrongálódott   a
　　　　the   entrance   the   store-to   was-damaged   the
　　　　zavargások   során.
　　　　riots   during

　　　　'The entrance to the store was damaged during the riot.'

(49)　　*Minden   bejárat   több   boltba   megrongálódott   a
　　　　every   entrance   several   store-to   was-damaged   the
　　　　zavargások   során.
　　　　riots   during

　　　　'Every entrance to several stores was damaged during the riot.'

(49) is ungrammatical because of violating principles (1) and (2). Namely, *több boltba* 'to several stores' neither c-commands nor precedes the domain over which it is intended to take scope. The intended meaning of (49) can be expressed if *több boltba* is turned into a genitive specifier, c-commanding and preceding the universally quantified head:

(50)　　?[Több   bolt   minden   bejárata]   megrongálódott   a
　　　　several   store's   every   entrance   was-damaged   the
　　　　zavargások   során.
　　　　riots   during

　　　　'Every entrance of several stores was damaged during the riots.'

(50) also has a more fully grammatical variant, in which the QP *több bolt* 'several stores' has undergone genitive raising, as a result of which both QPs c-command the proposition:

(51)　　$[_S[_{VP}$ 'Több   boltnak$_i$ $[_{VP}[_{NP}$ e_i 'minden   bejárata]$_j$
　　　　　　several   store-dat   every   entrance-its
　　　　$[_{VP}$ 'meg$_k$ $[_{V'}$ rongálódott   a   zavargások   során
　　　　　　(pref.)   was-damaged   the   riots   during
　　　　$e'_i e_j e_k$]]]]]

　　　　'Every entrance of several stores was damaged during the riots.'

In English, a QP in the complement position of a NP_i is capable of binding a coargument of NP_i, without c-commanding it at S-structure. This phenomenon is considered, e.g., in May (1985) as direct evidence for the existence of LF as a level of representation distinct from S-structure. Consider the following sentence:

(52)   Somebody from every city despises it.

A condition of the bound variable interpretation of a pronominal is that it be in the c-command domain of the quantifier binding it. This condition is not met in the S-structure of (52); however, it is met in its LF representation:

(53)

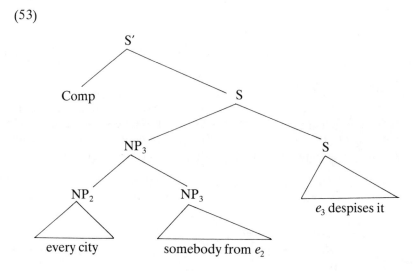

The c-command definition of Aoun and Sportiche (1983) states that α c-commands β if α does not dominate β, and the first maximal projection dominating β also dominates α. In (53), the first maximal projection dominating *every city* is S′ (the segments of NP_3 and S intervening between them do not count as maximal projections). Since S′ also dominates the pronoun *it*, *it* is in the c-command domain of the QP *every city*, i.e., binding is possible.

If our claim that the S-structure and LF representations of the Hungarian sentence are non-distinct with respect to the position of operators is tenable, then in the Hungarian equivalent of (52) the pronoun cannot have a bound variable interpretation. This prediction is borne out:

(54) a. *$[_{NP}$ Valaki $[_{NP}$ minden városból$_i]]$ utálja   pro/azt$_i$.
       somebody   every   city-from   despises it.
'Somebody from every city despises it.'

   b. *Minden városból$_i$ utálja   pro/azt$_i$ valaki.
      every   city-from despises it   somebody
'From every city, somebody despises it.'

(54a) is ungrammatical because *minden városból* cannot take scope over *valaki* — neither c-commanding, nor preceding it. In (54b) this problem has been eliminated, as the universally quantified phrase has been extraposed from *valaki*, then it has undergone Q-Raising, as a result of which it has assumed scope over the VP:

(54) b.'*$[_S[_{VP}$ 'Minden városból$_i$ $[_{VP}[_{V'}$ 'utálja   pro/azt$_i$
         every   city-from   despises it-acc
        valaki $e_i]]]]$
        somebody-nom

In (54b) *minden* cannot bind the pronominal because trace e_i of *minden városból* and the pronominal mutually c-command each other within their governing categories; i.e., Binding Principles B and C force them to have disjoint reference.

7. LEFT DISLOCATION

Our claim put forth in (3), according to which the Hungarian sentence observes principles (1) and (2) at S-structure, is apparently undermined by the sentence type illustrated in (55)—(57). (The symbol following the initial constituent of the examples will mean that the constituent is to be pronounced with a rising intonation.)

(55)   Mindenki/ 'nem hitt   nekem.
        everybody   not   believed   me
'Not everybody believed me.'

(56)   Mindenkit/   csak 'János   ismer.
        everybody-acc only John-nom   knows
        'It is only John who knows everybody.'

(57)   Gyakran/   'két férfival   vacsorázik együtt.
        often   two   man-with   dines-she   together
        'It is two men she often dines out with [with one at a time].'

In (55)—(57) the initial QP has two unexpected properties: on the one
hand, it is pronounced with a rising intonation as an independent
phonological phrase; and, on the other hand, it has narrow scope with
respect to a subsequent operator. The two properties are interdepen-
dent: if the initial QP is pronounced as a topic, a QP adjoined to VP, or
as a focus, it either assumes a wide scope interpretation, or it cannot be
interpreted at all. E.g. (55) becomes ungrammatical if *mindenki* is
pronounced as a QP adjoined to VP:

(58)   *$[_S[_{VP}$ 'Mindenki$_i$ $[_{VP}[_{V'}$ 'nem $[_V$ hitt   nekem e_i]]]]]
         everybody   not   believed me

(58) is out since the universal quantifier c-commands, and takes scope
over a negative particle; however, as Hausser (1976) claims, a universal
quantifier of the *every* type has inherently narrower scope than negation.

In the case of (56)—(57), the lack of rising intonation on the initial
quantifier changes the scope relations to the opposite. While in (56)
mindenki has narrower scope than the focus, in (59) it includes the
focus in its scope:

(59) $[_S[_{VP}$ 'Mindenkit$_i$ $[_{VP}$ csak 'János$_j$ $[_{V'}$ ismer $e_i e_j$]]]]
         everybody-acc   only John-nom   knows
        'It is true of everybody that only John knows him.'

While in (57) *két férfival* 'with two men' includes *gyakran* 'often' in its
scope, in (60) *gyakran* takes scope over *két férfival*:

(60) $[_S$ Gyakran $[_{VP}$ 'két férfival$_i$ $[_{V'}$ vacsorázik együtt e_i]]]
         often   two man-with   dines-she together
        'On many occasions, it is two men that she dines out with.'

The narrow scope reading of a QP pronounced with a rising intonation is obligatory. If the sentence contains no other operator to which the QP could be subordinated, the sentence is ungrammatical:

(61)   *Mindenki/ 'megszerette Jánost.
         everybody got-to-like   John-acc
         'Everybody got to like John.'

We propose the following analysis for (55)—(57): the initial QP is in Left Dislocation, outside S', the maximal freely recursive category in Hungarian, and it is coindexed with an empty category in V'. It is pronounced as an independent phonological phrase precisely because the boundaries of a phonological phrase cannot extend over S'. The maximal domain of sentential operations, e.g., movement and interpretive rules (among them scope interpretation) is S' — consequently the A'-chain constituted by the NP in Left Dislocation and the empty category coindexed with it can only be represented in sentential processes by the latter, empty element.[11]

This analysis also correctly predicts the ungrammaticality of (58). In (58), the representative of the universal quantifier in scope interpretation is the empty subject in V':

(61')   *[$_E$ Mindenki$_i$/ [$_S$[$_{VP}$ 'meg$_j$ [$_{V'}$ szerette   Jánost e_i e_j]]]]
         everybody   (pref.)   got-to-like John-acc

(61) is ungrammatical because the universally quantified phrase represented by e_i fails to precede its domain, i.e., it violates principle (2). In examples (55)—(57), the empty category standing for the initial QP is exempted from satisfying principle (2) because in (55) it is included in the scope of a sentence negating particle, while in (56)—(57) it is included in the scope of the focus, in which cases the adjacency requirement between the negative particle and the V, and between the focus and the V, respectively, blocks principle (2). That is, examples (55)—(57) are equivalent to the following grammatical sentences for the purposes of scope interpretation:

(62)   [$_S$[$_{VP}$[$_V$ 'Nem [$_{V'}$ hitt   nekem mindenki]]]]
         not   believed me   everybody
         'Not everybody believed me.'

(63)   [$_S$[$_{VP}$ Csak 'János$_i$ [$_{V'}$ ismer   mindenkit e_i]]]
         only John-nom   knows everybody-acc
         'It is only John who knows everybody.'

(64)   [$_S$[$_{VP}$ 'Két férvival$_i$ [$_{V'}$ vacsorázik gyakran együtt e_i]]]
        two man-with   dines-she often   together

'It is two men she often dines out with.'

(61), however, has no such grammatical equivalent; (61) also violates principle (2) if e_i is substituted by the universally quantified phrase:

(65)   *[$_S$[$_{VP}$ 'Meg$_i$ [$_{V'}$ szerette mindenki   Jánost e_i]]][12]
        (pref.)   liked   everybody-nom John-acc

'Everybody got to like John.'

Summarizing our discussion of QPs in sentence-initial position, pronounced with a rising intonation: the analysis of such QPs as constituents in Left Dislocation correctly accounts both for their apparently irregular phonological behaviour, and for their apparently irregular scope interpretation; i.e., our claim that principles (1) and (2) function in Hungarian as well-formedness conditions on the S-structure of the sentence does not have to be given up.

8. A SCRAMBLING RULE

With the construction involving Left Dislocation eliminated as a potential problem for our claim in (3), there is a single Hungarian sentence type left in the case of which it is not obvious how principles (1) and (2) are observed at S-structure. Namely, QPs which are available for Q-Raising, e.g., universally quantified phrases, can show up, instead of in a position adjoined to VP, in V', where they are assigned the same scope (extending over the VP) and the same primary stress that they would receive in the position adjoined to VP. E.g.,

(66)   [$_S$[$_{VP}$[$_{V'}$ 'Ismerek 'minden vendéget]]]
        know-I   every   guest-acc

'I know every guest.'

(67)   [$_S$ Mária$_i$ [$_{VP}$ 'két lányt$_j$ [$_{V'}$ mutatott   be
        Mary-nom   two girl-acc   introduced (pref.)
        'mindenkinek e_i e_j]]]
        everybody-to

'As for Mary, in the case of each person, it was two girls that she introduced to that person.'

The scope of the universal quantifier extends over the VP both in (66) and in (67), i.e., the QP behaves scopewise as if it had undergone Q-Raising. That is, the interpretation of e.g. (67) is identical to that of (68):

(68)   [$_S$ Mária$_i$ [$_{VP}$ 'mindenkinek$_j$ [$_{VP}$ 'két lányt$_k$
          Mary-nom   everybody-dat   two girl-acc
       [$_{V'}$ mutatott   be $e_i\,e_j\,e_k$]]]]
          introduced (pref.)

       'As for Mary, in the case of each person, it was two girls that she introduced to that person.'

In fact, (67) appears to be a stylistically somewhat marked variant of (68).

The wide scope interpretation of *mindenkinek* in (67) is conditional upon primary stress being assigned to it. If *mindenkinek* is unstressed, it is interpreted as having narrower scope than the focus. Cf.,

(69)   [$_S$ Mária$_i$ [$_{VP}$ 'két lányt$_j$ [$_{V'}$ mutatott   be
          Mary-nom   two girl-acc   introduced (pref.)
       mindenkinek $e_i\,e_j$]]]
       everybody-to

       'As for Mary, it was two girls that she introduced to everybody [the same two girls].'

QPs which can stand in the position immediately dominated by S with a maximally wide scope reading, e.g., sentence adverbials, can marginally also show up in V', retaining their wide scope:

(70)   [$_S$[$_{VP}$ 'Mindenki$_i$ [$_{VP}$[$_{V'}$ 'tudott szerencsére a
              everybody   knew fortunately the
       dologról e_i]]]]
       matter-about

       'Fortunately, everybody knew of the matter.'

In (70) *szerencsére*, though located in V', takes scope over the whole sentence, also including the universal quantifier adjoined to the VP in its scope.

The principles of scope interpretation formulated in (1) and (2), if checked at S-structure, cannot account for the scope reading of (66), (67), and (70). The stress pattern of (66), and (67) cannot be predicted, either, by the rule of stress assignment proposed in (5). Consequently, either the claim that principles (1) and (2) are observed at S-structure has to be given up, or some rule or constraint has to be identified whose effect neutralizes the effects of principles (1) and (2).

Let us provisionally assume that in Hungarian principle (1) is not always observed at S-structure, after all; i.e., LF as a level of representation structurally distinct from S-structure cannot be dispensed with. Focusing always takes place in syntax; Q-Raising, however, can either be performed in syntax, or, invisibly, in LF.

This assumption can correctly account for the wide scope reading of the S-internal QPs in (66), (67), and (70); however, it cannot account for the primary stress assigned to the wide scope QPs in (66)—(67). The problem is that in the current version of generative theory, the phonological form — the component where stress assignment presumably takes place — does not directly feed into logical form and semantic interpretation. Cf.,

(71)

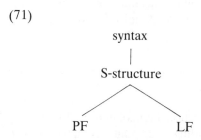

If we want to express that the wide scope interpretation of a V'-internal QP is conditional upon primary stress being assigned to the QP, we have to assume a rule of primary stress assignment operating in syntax. That is, we have to claim that primary stress can be assigned in two radically different ways: either in PF, obligatorily, to a certain position, or in syntax, optionally, to a certain type of category (namely, to a QP which is available for Q-Raising). In this framework, the scope assigning rule operating in LF could not be formulated in an elegant way, either. It would have to obligatorily adjoin to the VP QPs available for syntactic Q-Raising if they bear primary stress, and optionally attach to S QPs available for Topicalization or for base generation under S.

An alternative solution would be to employ the treatment of English VP-internal wide-scope quantifiers proposed in Huang (1982). Huang hypothesizes the following universal principle:

(72)   If a quantificational or logical expression A c-commands another quantificational or logical expression B at S-structure, then A also c-commands B at LF.

English examples in which a VP-internal quantified phrase has wider scope than the quantified phrase in subject position, e.g., (73) in one of its readings, apparently violate this principle.

(73)   Somebody loves everybody.

Huang claims that if *everybody* has wider scope than *somebody*, then *everybody* has been dislocated vacuously into a position c-commanding S. If this analysis were applied to S-internal QPs in Hungarian, then it would wrongly predict that a wide scope quantified phrase in S is always in final position. In fact, an S-internal wide scope QP can stand anywhere in S; it can also precede narrow scope quantified phrases which obviously have not undergone right dislocation. E.g.,

(74)   [$_S$ A vállalatnál$_i$ [$_{VP}$[$_{V'}$ 'beszél 'mindenki
        the company-at   speaks   everybody-nom
        2—3 nyelvet e_i]]]
        2—3 language-acc

        'At the company, everybody speaks 2—3 languages.'

This solution would run into the same problem with primary stress assignment as the hypothesis involving the LF movement of wide scope QPs in V', discussed above. So as to account for the fact that the right dislocation of a QP available for syntactic Q-Raising goes together with primary stress assignment to the QP, while the right dislocation of a QP available for Topicalization, or base-generation in a position immediately dominated by S, involves no primary stress assignment, we could assume that QPs can be located in an A'-position either on the left or on the right-hand side of V'; i.e., principle (2), requiring that a quantifier precede its domain would have to be given up. Thus, Q-Raising and Topicalization would have two possible landing sites, as follows:

(75)

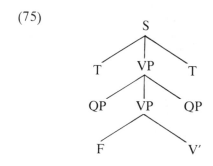

Then the stress rule in (5) would correctly predict that a wide scope universal QP whether in preverbal or postverbal positon always receives primary stress, while, e.g., a wide scope sentence adverbial — whether in preverbal or postverbal position — is always unstressed.

The structure hypothesized in (75), however, also makes wrong predictions; e.g., in sentences containing two postverbal QPs bearing primary stresses, it predicts the QP on the right-hand side to have wider scope. This prediction is not borne out: the two QPs can be in any scope relation (though perhaps the reading in which the left-hand side QP has wider scope is more preferred.) E.g.,

(76) János 'találkozott 'többször   is   'mindenkivel.
      John   met   several-times also everybody-with

   a. 'As for John, on several occasions he met everybody.'
   b. 'As for John, he met everybody several times.'

Because of the problems either of the potential solutions outlined above raise, we propose a different analysis for wide scope quantifiers in V'. We claim that in Hungarian principle (1) must be observed uniformly at S-structure, but there is an optional stylistic rule operating in PF which can scramble back a QP c-commanding the VP into a postverbal position. This rule could be formulated as follows:

(77)   *QP Postposing*
       Postpose a QP c-commanding the VP.

That rule (74) can postpose a QP only into a postverbal position presumably does not have to be stated in the formulation of the rule. A stylistic rule must not change the meaning of the sentence — after all, it does not feed into semantic interpretation — consequently, it cannot move material into another operator position, where it would alter scope relations.

In this framework, sentences containing a wide scope quantified phrase in V', e.g., those in (66), (67), and (70), have the QP in a preverbal A'-position at the level of S-structure. The surface structures in (66), (67), and (70), for instance, have been derived from the following S-structures:

(78) $[_S[_{VP}$ 'Minden vendéget$_i$ $[_{VP}[_{V'}$ 'ismerek $e_i]]]]$
              every guest-acc   know-I

        'I know every guest.'

(79) $[_S$ Mária$_i$ $[_{VP}$ 'mindenkinek$_j$ $[_{VP}$ 'két lányt$_k$
            Mary-nom   everybody-dat   two girl-acc
        $[_{V'}$ mutatott be $e_i\, e_j\, e_k]]]]$
            introduced (pref.)

        'As for Mary, everybody was introduced two girls by her.'

(80) $[_S$ Szerencsére $[_{VP}$ 'mindenki$_i$ $[_{VP}[_{V'}$ 'tudott a
            fortunately   everybody   knew the
        dologról $e_i]]]]$
        matter-about

        'Fortunately, everybody knew about the matter.'

Since it is the S-structures in (78)–(80) that undergo stress assignment, it follows that the universal QPs in (78) and (79) will bear primary stresses, while the sentence adverbial in (80) will be unstressed. Similarly, since it is the S-structures in (78)–(80) that undergo semantic interpretation, it follows that the universal QPs in (78)–(79) are interpreted as taking scope over the VP they c-command, while the sentence adverbial in (80) has a maximally wide scope — in accordance with principle (1).

9. CONCLUSION

Although the Hungarian data we analyzed, showing that in the Hungarian sentence all operators c-command their scope, i.e., scope relations are disambiguated at S-structure already, suggest that S-structure and Logical Form are nondistinct in Hungarian, at the same time they can also be interpreted as indirect evidence for the existence of Logical Form in Universal Grammar. What the Hungarian data prove is that Focusing and Q-Raising are not mere artifacts stipulated in order to solve problems of scope interpretation and binding, but are operations in Universal Grammar with a potentially "visible" output. (Whether or not a language opts for performing Focusing and Q-Raising palpably is obviously related to the fact whether or not S-structure hierarchy in the language is exempted from expressing grammatical functions.)

NOTES

[1] We assume the c-command definition of Reinhart (1976), according to which α c-commands β if α does not dominate β, nor β α, and the first branching node dominating α also dominates β.

[2] As will be pointed out below, the constituent in the specifier of the VP "eradicates" the stress of the subsequent V — in the terminology of Kálmán et al. (1986).

[3] The constituent order in (8b) is also ungrammatical if *szerencsére* receives no stress, and the obligatory primary stress assigned by rule (5) to the first major constituent of the VP falls on the V, since the constitutent *otthon* 'at home', semantically incorporated into the V, can be kept out of the specifier position of the VP only by another focused constituent (see Kiss 1987a).

[4] Farkas (1986), Ackerman and Komlósy (1983), Ackerman (1984), Kenesei (1984), and Szabolcsi (1986) treat the incorporated constituent + V sequence as a unit dominated by V'. In the approach emerging from their work, the propositional component of the Hungarian sentence begins with V'. The focus position precedes the propositional component. The complementary distribution of the focus and the incorporated constituent in preverbal position is ensured by a principle which requires the adjacency of the focus and the V, forcing an intruding X° to be postponed. In my view, a more attractive version of their approach would be to regard the incorporated constituent + V unit a bare V, as proposed in Baker (1985). A treatment of the incorporated constituent along these lines would not affect the findings presented in this paper.

[5] The interrogative phrase *miért* 'why' apparently can also do without the feature FOCUS; it can also be adjoined to the VP, including a focus in its domain:

(i) $[_S[_{VP}$ 'Miért$_i$ $[_{VP}$ 'János$_j$ $[_{V'}$ ment el e_i e_j?]]]]
         why   John   went away

'Why was it John who left?'

Apparently *why*, unlike the rest of the interrogative phrases, can include a focus and the proposition subordinated to it in its scope across languages — see the English equivalent of (i).

⁶ In multiple questions containing both [+human] and [−human] interrogative phrases, the [+human] [−human] order (e.g., the order in (15a)) sounds more neutral than the [−human] [+human] order. Cf. also the neutral (i), and the marked (ii):

(i)   [s[vp 'Kit_i   [vp 'mi_j   [v' érdekel   e_i e_j?]]]]
         whom   what   interests
         'Who does what interest?'

(ii)   ?[s[vp 'Mi_i   [vp 'kit_j   [v' érdekel   e_i e_j?]]]]
         what   whom   interests
         'What interests whom?'

⁷ Multiple questions in which the quantificational domains of the interrogative constituents are identical, i.e., in which the Disjoint Reference Condition excludes the possibility of a bijective interpretation (cf. Higginbotham and May 1981), have a rare, marked form, the structure of which is not clear. Cf., e.g.,

(i)   A regényber ki   öl   meg   kit?
         the novel-in   who kills (pref.) whom
         'Who kills whom in the novel?'

Notice that multiple questions in which the Disjoint Reference Condition is not at work do not allow this pattern:

(ii)   *Ki   javasolt   mit?
         who   proposed   what-acc
         'Who proposed what?'

In (i) kit 'whom' has all the semantic and phonological properties of focus — therefore, it might appear to be appropriate to locate it under the same VP node that dominates the focus proper, as follows:

(iii)

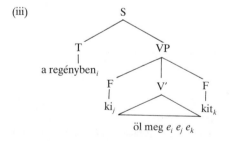

If (iii) is correct, then the constraint in (2), requiring that an operator precede its domain, is a mere tendency in Hungarian. Indeed, we shall also see other cases in which condition (2) is lifted, being blocked by an interfering principle. Perhaps (i) sounds marked precisely because it violates condition (2).

In (16a, b) the V kap has the -ott past sg. 3rd person indefinite object suffix, while in (17) it has the -ta past sg. 3rd person definite object suffix.

[8] The QPs immediately dominated by S are not intended to be pronounced with a rising intonation. A rising intonation contour is indicative of Left Dislocation, which will be discussed in section 7.

[9] The sections about negation and Q-Raising employ the empirical generalizations of Hunyadi (1981, 1982).

[10] See note 8.

[11] A Left Dislocation construction, dominated by E(xpression), is marginally also possible embedded under the complementizer *hogy* 'that', therefore *hogy* has to be allowed to subcategorize either for S, or, in the marked case, for E.

[12] *Mindenki* is intended to be pronounced unstressed. QPs in V' bearing primary stress will be discussed in section 8. (65) can also be saved if the V has an extra heavy stress, and expresses 'assertion', i.e., the denial of a previous denial. Assertive sentences are attributed in Kiss (1987a) an invisible modal operator in F.

REFERENCES

Abraham, W. and de Mey, S. (eds.): 1986, *Topic, Focus, and Configurationality*, John Benjamins, Amsterdam.

Ackerman, F.: 1984, 'Verbal Modifiers as Argument Taking Predicates: Complex Verbs in Hungarian', *Groninger Arbeiten zur Germanistischen Linguistik* **25**, 3—71.

Ackerman, F. and Komlósy, A.: 1983, 'Néhány lépés a magyar szórend megértése felé', ms., Linguistic Institute of the Hungarian Academy of Sciences, Budapest.

Barker, M.: 1985, 'Incorporation: A Theory of Grammatical Function Changing', Ph.D. dissertation, MIT, Cambridge, MA.

Farkas, D.: 1986, 'Focus in Hungarian', *Natural Language and Linguistic Theory* **4**, 77—97.

Gabbay, D. and Moravcsik, J.: 1974, 'Branching Quantifiers, English and Montague Grammar', *Theoretical Linguistics* **1.1**.

Higginbotham, J. and May, R.: 1981, 'Questions, Quantifiers and Crossing', *The Linguistic Review* **1**, 41—80.

Horvath, J.: 1981, 'Aspects of Hungarian Syntax and the Theory of Grammar', Ph.D. dissertation, UCLA, CA.

Horvath, J.: 1985, *Focus in the Theory of Grammar and the Syntax of Hungarian*, Foris, Dordrecht, The Netherlands.

Huang, J.: 1982, 'Logical Relations in Chinese, and the Theory of Grammar', Ph.D. dissertation, MIT, Cambridge, MA.

Hunyadi, L.: 1981, 'A nyelvi polaritás kifejezése a magyarban', dissertation for the candidate's degree, Kossuth Lajos University, Debrecen.

Hunyadi, L.: 1982, 'Remarks on the Syntax and Semantics of Topic and Focus in Hungarian', *Acta Linguistica Academiae Scientiarum Hungaricae* **31**, 107—136.

Kálmán, L. *et al.*: 1986, 'Hocus, Focus, and Verb Types in Hungarian Infinitive Constructions', in: Abraham and Mey (eds.), 129—142.

Kenesei, I.: 1989, 'Logikus-e a magyar szórend?', *Általános Nyelvészeti Tanulmányok* **XVII**, 105—152.

Kiss, K.: 1986, 'The Order and Scope of Operators in the Hungarian Sentence', in: Abraham and Mey (eds.), 181—214.

Kiss, K.: 1987a, 'Configurationality in Hungarian', *Studies in Natural Language and Linguistic Theory*, Reidel, Dordrecht, and Akadémiai Kiadó, Budapest.

Kiss, K.: 1987b, 'Eliminating the Configurationality Parameter' unpublished, Linguistic Institute of the Hungarian Academy of Sciences, Budapest.

Kiss, K.: 1987c, 'Még egyszer a magyar mondat hangsúlyozásáról és intonációjáról', *Nyelvtudományi Közlemények* (to appear).

May, R.: 1977, 'The Grammar of Quantification', Ph.D. dissertation, MIT, Cambridge, MA.

May, R.: 1983, *Logical Form Its Structure and Derivation*, MIT Press, Cambridge, MA.

Reinhart, T.: 1976, 'The Syntactic Domain of Anaphora', Ph.D. dissertation, MIT, Cambridge, MA.

Szabolcsi, A.: 1981, 'The Semantics of Topic-Focus Articulation', in: J. Groenendijk *et al.* (eds.), *Formal Methods in the Study of Language*, Matematisch Centrum, Amsterdam.

Szabolcsi, A.: 1983a, 'Focussing Properties, or the Trap of First Order', *Theoretical Linguistics* **10**, 2.

Szabolcsi, A.: 1983b, 'The Possessor that Ran Away from Home', *The Linguistic Review* **3**, 89—102.

Szabolcsi, A.: 1986, 'From the Definiteness Effect to Lexical Integrity', in: W. Abraham and S. de Mey (eds.), 321—348.

Williams, E.: 1982, 'The NP Cycle', *Linguistic Inquiry* **13**, 277—295.

GIUSEPPE LONGOBARDI

IN DEFENSE OF THE CORRESPONDENCE
HYPOTHESIS: ISLAND EFFECTS AND PARASITIC
CONSTRUCTIONS IN LOGICAL FORM

0. INTRODUCTION

It has often been proposed since at least Chomsky (1976), May (1977) that the assignment of scope to various quantified expressions is performed by LF rules (that is rules mapping S-structures onto Logical Forms), essentially similar to syntactic movement rules.[1] Such rules (e.g., May's QR) are assumed to create operator-variable structures akin to the wh quantifier-trace relations yielded by the usual wh-movement. A remarkable advantage of this approach is that the scope of the quantifier moved in LF to an A'-position is thus identified with its c-domain in such a position (cf. our discussion in Longobardi 1985a, among others) exactly as the scope of an interrogative operator moved to the Spec of a Comp by wh-movement in the syntax (cf. Chomsky 1977) usually corresponds to its S-structure c-domain (that is to the CP headed by such a Comp).[2] Logical Forms so created also display the interesting, and *a priori* not necessary, property of looking quite similar to operator-variable formulae traditionally used by modern logicians to represent quantificational structure. Obvious empirical arguments to substantiate this hypothesis are represented by cases in which the two proposed rules, i.e., overt wh-movement and quantifier movement in LF, seem to be constrained by the same principles.

In the present article we want to provide what seems to us the most direct and persuasive evidence supporting the general approach in question or at least, more abstractly, the embedded claim of a strong parallelism between syntactic movement and scope interpretation.[3]

The hypothesis that the government and bounding conditions constraining overt wh-movement do apply to a large extent also to scope assignment processes will be referred to as the "Correspondence Hypothesis" (henceforth CH).

Rather than as a detailed empirical hypothesis, the latter will be conceived of as a research strategy or a heuristic expectation: on the

149

grounds of some new evidence this paper will argue in favor of its validity, partially denied in recent work (cf. Huang 1982; Lasnik and Saito 1984).

In successive work (cf. Longobardi forthcoming) we will try to reconcile the assumptions of the Correspondence Hypothesis with the original contrary evidence provided by Huang (1982).

1. ON NON-EVIDENCE FOR LF MOVEMENT

It is necessary, at this point, to make an important distinction: there have already been mentioned sometimes in the literature two constraints which turn out to apply both to overt wh-movement and to the rule of scope assignment for quantifiers. In fact the Specificity Condition (cf. Huang 1982 among others) rules out both (1) and the assignment of sentential scope to *every* in (2):

(1)   *Who did you like this portait of e?

(2)   I liked this portrait of every student

Similarly, what we called the Scope Condition in Longobardi (1985a) (May's 1977 Proper Binding Condition) rules out both sentence (3), i.e., a case of improper movement (lowering of a wh-phrase toward a more embedded Comp), and the reading of (4) in which *Noone* has scope only over the subordinate clause:

(3)   *I asked e_i [who$_i$ Mary liked him]

(4)   Noone thinks that Mary likes him

However, the existence of these constraints is not completely satisfying as an argument for the parallelism between overt movement and the supposed LF movement, since the same conditions extend also to elements which are usually not considered traces of movement rules or assumed to give rise to operators in LF, like, e.g., bound pronouns:

(5)   *Noone$_i$ thinks that you like this portrait of him$_i$

(6)   *His$_i$ mother knows the woman that everyone$_i$ likes most

Namely, it seems that the Specificity Condition and the Scope Condition apply to any element which essentially ends up understood as a bound variable, i.e. as a non-uniquely referential NP (cf. also Haïk 1984).

In order to show convincingly that movement rules of the usual sort do exist in LF and form structures with operators binding variables, it is necessary to isolate properties singling out together just quantifiers and overt traces; in other words, we must look for constraints which might be thought of as applying not to rules interpreting something as a variable but to rules actually *creating* an operator (in A'-position) and a variable (in A-position) out of a bare quantifier in A-position at S-structure.

Evidence for one such constraint was brought by Kayne (1982), who pointed out that the rule assigning wide scope to the French negative quantifier *personne* "nobody" displays the same subject-object asymmetry, typical of wh-movement, which is commonly traced back to Chomsky's (1981) ECP:

(7) a. Je n'exige que la   police arrête personne
         I require that the police arrest nobody

    b. *Je n'exige que personne soit arrêté   par le   police
         I require that nobody   be arrested by the police

(8) a. Qui exige-t-il   que la police arrête e?
         Who does he require that the police arrest?

    b. *Qui exige-t-il oue e soit arrêté   par la police?
         Who does he require that be arrested by the police?

According to Kayne, a similar contrast arises in English with a quantified expression like *not a single*,[1] which is able to get wide scope over the matrix clause from the embedded object position, given an appropriate context, but not from subject position:

(9) a. In all these years she's required that they write not a single term paper

    b. In all these years she's required that not a single term paper be submitted to the committee

Kayne's contrasts are of interest because they do not extend to pronouns when they are interpreted as bound variables. In fact a bound pronoun may always occur in the preverbal subject position of a tensed sentence both in French and in English as well as in other languages:

(10)   Personne$_i$ ne croyait qu'il$_i$ allait être arrêté

        'Nobody believed that he was going to be arrested'.

(11)   Not a single student$_i$ believed he$_i$ would pass the examination

Therefore, it appears that Kayne was actually able to identify a constraint applying exactly to overt traces and to wide scope quantifiers: such a fact strongly supports the hypothesis that the logical form of (7b), derived by a movement rule, is something like (12) and is thus ruled out by whatever reason disallows the preverbal trace of (8b), probably the ECP or any principle which the ECP derives from:

(12)   [Personne [je n'exige que *e* soit arrêté par la police]

In the course of this article we will try to deepen the analysis of the corresponding negative quantifiers in Italian started by Rizzi (1982) and we will provide new evidence for the existence of a close parallelism between overt wh-movement and rules assigning scope to certain quantifiers, showing that the latter are not constrained only by ECP but also by other conditions obeyed by the former.

2. UNBOUNDED QUANTIFIERS AND CONDITIONS ON MOVEMENT

We will begin, in this section, to point out the existemce of certain kinds of quantified expressions whose scope assignment rules closely resemble syntactic wh-movement in two respects (see also Hornstein 1984):

(13) a. they appear to be potentially unbounded

     b. they display typical ECP-like asymmetries

The quantified phrases under discussion whose behavior is the most clear in Italian fall into two major classes:

(14)   Negative phrases such as *nessuno*, "*nobody, anybody*", *niente*, "nothing, anything", *nessun(o)+N̄*", "no, any + N̄" *neanche* (*neppure, nemmeno*) + XP, *né XP né XP* "neither XP nor XP" (of this class *nessuno* or *niente* will be taken as representatives in most examples).[4, 5]

(15)   Phrases of the form *solo* (*soltanto, solamente*) + *XP* "only XP",whose quantified character, briefly discussed also in Longobardi (1985a), after a long tradition started by Geach (1962), results from their logical equivalence with expressions of the form *nobody* (or *nothing*) *but XP*.[6]

The salient property of quantified expressions belonging to one of these classes is that they are especially easy to interpret as having scope wider than the minimal clause dominating them at S-structure:

(16)   Non pretendo   che   tu   dica niente
        I do not require   that   you   say anything

(17)   E' veramente necessario che io parli soltanto con Gianni

        'It is really necessary that I speak only with Gianni'.

thus, in (16), *niente* has scope over the whole sentence, as is required by the presence of *non* on the matrix verb. Descriptively speaking, such a morpheme, placed on the inflected verb of a clause, acts as a surface scope marker for negative phrases when they occur in certain positions in the sentence.[7]

Similarly, in (17), at least with a pause between the quantified PP and the verb governing it, *soltanto con Gianni* may be understood as having scope over the matrix sentence, although such an interpretation is not obligatory as in the previous case, owing to the absence of any overt scope marker.

The scope of such phrases is, in principle, unbounded, given appropriate conditions:[8] in the following sentences root scope seems again to be possible for both quantifiers (obligatory for *nessuno*, just because of the position of *non*):

(18)   Non credo che lui pensi che io desideri vedere nessuno

        'I do not believe that he thinks that I wish to see anyone'

(19)   E' davvero indispensabile che lui creda che io desideri vedere soltanto Gianni

        'It is truly indispensable that he believe that I wish to see only Gianni'

Furthermore in (19) any intermediate sentential scope appears to be available for the *only* phrase.

That the rule assigning scope to such quantified expressions is an LF movement rule is suggested by their displaying the usual ECP effects, i.e., the same impossibility of wide scope from preverbal subject position discovered by Kayne for sentences like (7b) above. For negative quantifiers this fact had been pointed out by Rizzi (1982) with respect to the equivalents of (7b):

(20) a. Non pretendo che nessuno sia arrestato

      'I do not require that nobody be arrested'

    b. No credo che niente possa spaventare Gianni

      'I do not believe that nothing may frighten Gianni'

But it had gone unnoticed that the same phenomenon reappears with *only* phrases as well:

(21) a. E' proprio necessario che ci venga a trovare solo Gianni

      'It is really necessary that come to visit us only Gianni (i.e. "the others must not/need not come")

    b. E' proprio necessario che solo Gianni ci venga a trovare

      'It is really necessary that only Gianni come to visit us ("the others must not/*need not come")

(21a) is ambiguous between a wide scope reading over the entire sentence and a narrow scope over the embedded clause, but only the latter is acceptable in (21b). Similarly, while (22a) is perfectly normal with the scope of *solo Gianni* over the matrix, strongly imposed by the environment for reasons of semantic naturalness, (22b) sounds remarkably awkward, due precisely to the lack of such a reading:

(22) a. Ormai, bisogna che ci telefoni solo Gianni, prima di poter cominciare

      'Now, it is necessary that call us up only Gianni, before being able to start'

    b. Ormai, bisogna che solo Gianni ci telefoni, prima di poter cominciare

      'Now it is necessary that only Gianni call us up before being able to start'

The LF representation of, say, (21b) in thus likely to resemble (23), which clearly stands in violation of the ECP:

(23)   [solo Gianni [è necessario che *e* ci venga a trovare]].[9]

If the rule assigning scope to these two classes of quantifiers is an apparently unbounded and ECP-governed movement rule akin to wh-movement the next natural question which arises is whether it obeys the usual island constraints, thus contradicting Huang's (1982) idea that the Bounding principles do not concern the syntax of LF.
Consider the following sentences:

(24) a.   Non approverei che tu gli consentissi di vedere nessuno

       'I would not approve that you allow him to see anybody'

    b. *Non approverei la tua proposta di vedere nessuno

       'I would not approve your proposal of seeing anybody'

(25) a.   Non credo che sia possible che ci consenta di fare niente

       'I do not believe that it is possible that he allows us to do anything'

    b. *Non credo alla possibilità che ci consenta di fare niente

       'I do not believe the possibility that he allows us to do anything'

These constrasts point out that the scope rule for negative items seems to respect the CNPC and to parallel exactly the long known paradigm of overt extraction:

(26) a.   Quale ragazzo approvi che io gli consenta di vedere?

       'Which boy do you approve that I allow him to see?

    b. *Quale ragazzo approvi la mia proposta di vedere?

       'Which boy do you approve my proposal of seeing?'

(27) a.   Che cosa credi che sia possible che ci consenta di fare?

       'What do you believe that it is possible that he allows us to do?'

    b. *Che cosa credi alla possibilità che ci consenta di fare?

       'What do you believe the possibility that he allows us to do?'

Also scope assignment out of a relative clause is generally impossible, even in the case of heads which should not yield violations of the Specificity Condition or in that of free relatives:

(28) a. *Non cercavo una ragazza che fosse amica di nessuno

'I did not look for a girl who was friend with anybody'

b. *Non ho incontrato chi potrebbe fare niente

'I did not meet who might do anything'

A very similar pattern is provided by the other class of quantifiers:

(29) a. A questo punto, approverei che tu gli consentissi di parlare solo con Gianni

'At this point, I would approve that you allow him to speak only with Gianni'

b. A questo punto, approverei la tua proposta di parlare solo con Gianni

'At this point, I would approve your proposal of speaking only with Gianni'

(30) a. Dubito veramente che sia possibie assumere soltanto Gianni

'I really doubt that it is possible to hire only Gianni

b. Dubito veramente della possibilità di assumere soltanto Gianni

'I really doubt about the possibility of hiring only Gianni'

Matrix scope assignment appears to be considerably more natural in the (a) examples than in the (b) ones, where it seems as unacceptable as in the following:

(31) a. Cercavo una persona che si occupasse solo di lei

'I looked for a person who would take care only of her'

b. Non ho incontrato chi potrebbe fare solo ouesto

'I did not meet who might do only this'

Another well-known type of island constraint is the Coordinate Structure Constraint (cf. Ross 1967).

This condition as well can be shown to apply to the rule assigning scope to the quantified phrases under discussion (or to its output):

(32) a. *Non pretendo che tu dica questo o chiami nessuno

'I do not require that you say this or call anyone'

b. *Non pretendo che tu dica niente o chiami Mario

'I do not require that you say anything or call Mario'

(33) a. E' necessario che tu rispetti Maria o che ami solo Gianni

'It is necessary that you respect Maria or that you love only Gianni'

b. E' necessario assumere Maria e licenziare solo Gianni

'It is necessary to hire Maria and to fire only Gianni'

Wide scope is impossible in both (32) and (33), with the usual results in acceptability. The data in (24)—(33) all seem to strongly suggest that island effects of the usual sort show up to constrain the rules assigning scope to certain kinds of quantified phrases. In this connection, it is interesting to remark, that the same constraints are also obeyed by *nessuno* type phrases when they are understood not as negative quantifiers, but as *interrogative* polarity items (cf. note 7), whose scope appears to be defined by a fronted wh-question morpheme or by *se* "whether" or even by no overt marker when the root sentence is a yes/no question: cf., in fact, the following:

(31) a.   Credi probabile che ci proponga di fare nulla di positivo?

'Do you believe it likely that he will propose us to do anything positive?

b.   *Credi possibile una proposta di fare nulla di positivo?

'Do you believe likely a proposal of doing anything positive?'

(32) a.   ?*Pretendi che io dica questo o chiami nessuno?

'Do you require what I say this or call anyone?'

b.   ?*Pretendi che io dica niente o chiami Mario?

'Do you require that I say anything or call Mario?'

The pattern of behavior that we have exemplified in this section naturally leads us to extend the investigation to the functioning of scope rules with respect to the two major island conditions subsumed under Huang's (1982) CED and under our revisions of Kayne's (1983) Connectedness Condition (CC) (Longobardi 1983, 1985b, 1986): the Subject Condition and the Adjunct Condition. This will be our task in the next section.

3. CED EFFECTS

The effects of the Subject Condition proper, with negative quantifiers, are plainly much subtler than the ones we have just reviewed even for the least liberal speakers:

(36) a. Non è stata invitata la moglie di nessuno

'Was not invited the wife of anyone'

b. ?La moglie di nessuno è stata invitata

'The wife of no one was invited'

(37) a. A tali richieste non risponderà affermativamente la moglie di nessuno degli ostaggi

'To such requests will not answer in the affirmative the wife of any of the hostages'

b. ?La moglie di nessuno degli ostaggi risponderà affermativa-mente a tali richieste

'The wife of none of the hostages will answer in the affirmative to such requests.[10]'

On the other hand, by testing the effects of the Subject Condition with the other class of quantifiers in question, a preliminary difficulty arises: in fact XP introducers such as *solo*, or *anche* "also", *perfino* "even" etc. can never occur between a P and a NP, and only marginally appear between a head N and its PP complement.

(38) a.   *Il ritratto di solo Gianni

'The portrait of only Gianni'

b.   (?)Il ritratto solo di Gianni

'The portrait of only Gianni'

However it seems that here an asymmetry comparable to those of the preceding section appears in (39):

(39) a. (?)Non è stato ancora richiesto l'intervento solo della polizia

'(There) has not yet been requested the intervention only of the police'

   b. (?)L'intervento solo della polizia non è stato ancora richiesto

'The intervention only of the police has not yet been requested'

(39a) seems to be judged ambiguous, with the *only PP* having either sentential scope or scope internal to the NP: in the first case, it might be naturally followed in a discourse by something like (40):

(40)   However, the intervention of *everybody else* (doctors, fire brigade, etc.) has already been requested

Instead the NP-internal scope reading may be paraphrased by:

(41)   However, the intervention of the police *along with some-body else* has already been requested.

In this reading, the meaning of *solo della polizia* is close to that of the phrase *of the police alone*. Now, (39b), displays a strong tendency to favor, if any, this latter reading. If this is correct, such a preference could be explained by the Subject Condition preventing the *only PP* from reaching a position of sentential scope outside the subject NP. In section 5 we provide, in turn, an explanation for the lack of clear contrast in the case of (36)—(37).

Clear asymmetries always arise, instead, when we consider the subcase of the Subject Condition which is named Sentential Subject Constraint (Ross 1967); here in fact the contrasts are always rather sharp:

(42) a.   Non sarà possibile chiamare nessuno

'It will not be possible to call anyone'

   b. ?*Chiamare nessuno sarà possible

'To call no one will be possible'

(43) a.   Non è necessario che tu faccia niente

'It is not necessary that you do anything'

b.   *Che tu faccia niente è necessario

'That you do nothing is necessary'

The effects of the Sentential Subject Constraint prevent the negative phrase in the (b) examples from being assigned wide scope over the matrix sentence. On the other side the assignment of narrow scope over the embedded subject clause (a possible reading for the corresponding English glosses) is forbidden because no *non* occurs on the verb of such a clause: hence the ungrammaticality of the two Italian examples. In fact, the insertion of *non* on the embedded verb makes the two sentences perfect with the narrow scope reading:

(44) a.   Non chiamare nessuno sarà possible

b.   Che tu non faccia niente è necessario

As expected, in the examples with *only* phrases, the Sentential Subject Constraint does not produce overt ungrammaticality, but again it rules out the matrix scope reading in the (b) examples, whereas the (a) sentences are obviously ambiguous:

(45) a.   Sarà possible chiamare soltanto Gianni

'It will be possible to call only Gianni'

b.   Chiamare soltanto Gianni sarà possible

'To call only Gianni will be possible'

(46) a.   E' necessario che tu faccia solo questo

'It is necessary that you do only this'

b.   Che tu faccia solo questo è necessario

'That you do only this is necessary'

Let us consider now the Adjunct Condition, which, descriptively speaking, prevents overt extraction out of adverbial clauses: in Huang (1982) and Longobardi (1983, 1986) it has been argued that it patterns like the Subject Condition and the Sentential Subject Constraint and that all of these descriptive principles fall together under the CED

(Huang) or a reformulated CC (Longobardi). The obvious expectation of such theories is that whatever process will obey, say, the Sentential Subject Constraint, will also observe at least the sentential part of the Adjunct Condition (as for the non sentential part cf. again section 6 below). In fact, this prediction is fulfilled by the scope-assigning rule we are discussing, both when the adverbial clause occurs preverbally and when it occurs postverbally (what was said in fn. 10 about the appearance of *non* in the two cases extends to the following examples as well):

(47) a. *Non fa il suo dovere per aiutare nessuno

     'He does not do his duty in order to help anyone'

   b. *Per ottenere nulla ha fatto il suo dovere

     'In order to obtain nothing has he done his duty'

   c. *Non ho scoperto la verità indagando su nessuno

     'I did not discover the truth by investigating anyone'

   d. *Prima di ricevere nessuno ha preparato la sua torta di mele

     'Before receiving noone has he prepared his apple pie'

In (47) narrow scope of the quantifier is always impossible, again because *non* does not appear on the embedded verb, but matrix scope, while semantically easily conceivable, seems to be ruled out by the Adjunct Condition. Equally impossible is the matrix scope reading for *only* phrases:

(48) a. Fa il suo dovere per aiutare solo Maria

     'He does his duty in order to help only Maria'

   b. Per evitare solo questo ha fatto il suo dovere

     'In order to avoid only this has he done his duty'

   c. Sarei felice se incontrassi solo Maria

     'I would be happy if I met only Maria'

   d. Se incontrassi solo Maria sarei felice

     'If I met only Maria I would be happy'

Examples of this sort are easily multiplied. We assume that the ones provided are sufficient to substantiate the claim that LF rules assigning scope to the quantified phrases under discussion do observe island constraints.[11]

In the assumed framework, the main consequence of this inquiry is obviously the following: if the rule assigning scope to negative and *only* phrases is a movement rule in LF and obeys (or its output does) the CNPC, the CED and the Coordinate Structure Constraint, then these constraints are to be properties of the LF component as well, contrary to the conclusion arrived at in Huang (1982).[12]

4. PARASITIC CONSTRUCTIONS

In sections 2 and 3 we have provided some new arguments in favor of the theory of a strict parallelism between overt movement rules and the process of assigning scope to certain quantifiers. One plausible conclusion we have suggested is that such potentially "unbounded" quantifiers move in LF to their scope position, subject to the same bounding constraints as syntactically moved wh-phrases. In this section and in the next one we will provide an even more striking argument for assimilating the relation between the argument position and the scope domain of a quantifier to that between a moved wh-phrase and the associated gap(s). Recall in fact that in two basic cases, widely discussed in the literature, a fronted wh-phrase can be associated with more than one empty A-position: parasitic gap constructions and so-called ATB constructions in coordinate structures. In both cases, otherwise effective islands can be violated.

Virtually all the constraints on movement so far reviewed, in fact, have been argued to display, with respect to overt wh-gaps, a typical diagnostic behavior whose properties, after the earliest fundamental works on multiple gaps (Taraldsen 1981; Engdahl 1981 and subsequent works; Chomsky 1982; Pesetsky 1982), have emerged through a number of further analyses of the phenomenon (Kayne 1983; Longobardi 1985a, b; Chomsky 1986):

(49) a. They are observed by single (non parasitic) empty categories

   b. They are freely violated by some parasitic empty categories

   c. They are observed again by other parasitic empty categories, whose licensing gap is not "properly" located.

"Not properly located" of (49c) is a complex theoretical notion which in most cases means "separated from the parasitic one by more than one island", i.e. there must not exist more than one island configuration containing the parasitic gap but not containing the antecedent and the licensing gap. This condition on the structural "distance" between the licensing and the parasitic element has been tentatively explained by Kayne (1983) with his Connectedness Condition, which applies to sets of categories sharing a common antecedent, and by Chomsky (1986b) through the notion of "chain compositionality". In this article we are not primarily interested in the elaboration or evaluation of such proposals, but rather we will use the properties in (49) as a heuristics to uncover properties of scope assignment. Only informally will we refer to the licensing effect of a licit element with respect to a "local enough" parasitic one as the 'connectedness effect', in the obvious pretheoretical sense of the term. The intricate array of acceptable and unacceptable structures yielded by the "connectedness effect," if reproducible for unmoved quantifiers, may provide a very strong argument for the parallelism between overt movement and scope assignment. In order to show that this is the case let us recall that a kind of parasitic effect with wh-phrases *in situ* has been reduced by Kayne to his CC (1983). He has shown that when two wh-phrases display the "paired" interpretation yielded by Higginbotham and May's (1981) Absorption rule, one of them can "license" the other under "connectedness", permitting it to appear in an improperly governed position, i.e. remedying even an ECP violation. Such a violation, which distinguishes (50a) from (50b), can in fact be weakened by adding a licensing wh-phrase *in situ* in a governed position, as in (50c):[13]

(50) a. I'd like to know who hid it where

b. *I'd like to know where who hid it (Kayne's 1983 (34a))

c. ?I'd like to know where who hid what (*ibid.* (34b))

This is not surprising, actually, if interpretively Absorption produces a unique operator out of the two original ones, so that the two variables, though distinct, are in a sense bound by an antecedent which counts as 'common' for the CC purposes.

An essentially similar phenomenon shows up in a clearer way with Italian negative phrases: we will explore it in detail and show that it displays all the basic properties of overt parasitic and ATB constructions.

Recall that the violation of the Sentential Subject Constraint or of the Adjunct Condition in assigning scope to negative phrases yielded serious ungrammaticality in most cases; but notice now that such unacceptable status tends to disappear almost completely when a second negative quantifier occurs along with that inside the island:

(51) a. (?)Chiamare nessuno servirà a niente, ormai

      'To call nobody will do any good, now'

    b. Salvare nessuno ha mai richiesto niente di così pericoloso

      'To rescue nobody has ever required anything so dangerous'

    c. ?Il progetto di invitare nessun altro linguista aveva mai trovato tanta opposizione nella commissione

      'The plan to invite no other linguist had ever met so much opposition in the board'

    d. Non fa niente per aiutare nessuno

      'He doesn't do anything in order to help anyone'

    e. (?)Non ho scoperto niente indagando su nessuno

      'I didn't discover anything by investigating anyone'

    f. Per ottenere nulla ha mai fatto niente di simile

      'In order to obtain nothing has he ever done anything like that'

    g. Prima di ricevere nessuno avrebbe preparato niente di simile, in passato

      'Before receiving no one would he have prepared anything similar, in the past.[14]

(52) a. *Chiamare nessuno servirà a Gianni, ormai

      'To call nobody will profit Gianni, now'

    b. ?*Salvare nessuno lo ha richiesto

      'To rescue nobody required it'

(52) c.   *Il progetto di invitare nessun altro linguista aveva già trovato l'opposizione della commissione

'The plan to invite no other linguist had already met the opposition of the board'

d.   *Non fa questo lavoro per aiutare nessuno

'He doesn't do this work in order to help anyone'

e.   *Non ho scoperto la tua assenza indagando su nessuno

'I didn't discover your absence by investigating anyone'

f.   *Per ottenere nulla ha fatto questo lavoro

'In order to obtain nothing has he done this work'

g.   ?*Prima di ricevere nessuno avrebbe preparato il suo discorso, in passato

'Before receiving no one would he have prepared his speech, in the past'[15]

In all the sentences in (51), which contrast quasi-minimally with (52) and with most of the ungrammatical examples of (42) and (47), the potentially offending negative quantifier appears to be licensed by the addition of a second one, like *niente* (or *niente* and *mai* together).[16] As is often the case with overt parasitic gaps, the embedding of the parasitic element inside a finite sentence is less acceptable, but certainly not always impossible:

(53) a.   ?Che tu inviti nessuno servirà più a niente, ormai

'That you invite anyone will do any good, now'

b.   ??Non ha mai fatto nulla perché tu potessi parlare con nessuno

'He never did anything so that you could speak with any of us'

It is also important to remark that the same licensing role can also be played by normal negative polarity items (cf. fns 7 and 11) and by indefinite phrases which are not inherently negative but may assume the status of polarity items when in the scope of a negative operator, in this case the parasitic quantifier itself:

(54)
$$
\text{Salvare nessuno aveva richiesto} \begin{cases} \text{alcunché di così} \\ \text{complesso} \\ \text{tanto sforzo} \end{cases}
$$

in passato

$$
\text{To rescue no one had required} \begin{cases} \text{anything so complex} \\ \text{so much effort} \end{cases}
$$

in the past

Tanto sforzo "so much effort" is likely to be understood here as a negative polarity item on *nessuno*, thus licensing the matrix scope of the latter.

In order to be sure that the behavior of such negative operators can really be assimilated to that of overt parasitic gaps it is necessary to check whether it displays the third essential property of the diagnostic criteria which we have presented in (49): so far we have seen, first, that negative phrase scope obeys the usual island conditions and, second, that potential violations can be circumvented by the proper insertion of a licensing item of the same sort as the parasitic one. Now, under the CH we may expect that a violation cannot be successfully avoided if the licensing phrase is improperly located, e.g., too high in the tree, as in the corresponding cases with overt parasitic gaps. This prediction is straightforwardly borne out:

(55) a. *Partire per incontrare nessuno servirà a niente

'To leave in order to meet no one will do any good'

b. *Non fa niente per scoprire la verità indagando su nessuno

'He doesn't do anything in order to discover the truth by investigating anyone'

c. *Prima di vestirsi per ricevere nessuno aveva mai riflettuto così a lungo sulle scelte da compiere

'Before dressing in order to receive no one had he ever reflected so long on the choices to be made'

in these examples a negative phrase is embedded within two islands and the licensing phrase may rescue only the violation of the less embedded one, exactly as in the examples with overt parasitic gaps discussed above; notice also that the ungrammaticality of (55) cannot be simply attributed to the depth of embedding, since the latter does not affect the status of (56), where the parasitic quantifier is embedded within a single island:

(56) a. Cercare di incontrare nessuno servirà a niente

      'To try to meet no one will do any good'

    b. Non fa mai niente per convincerla ad invitare nessuno

      'He never does anything in order to persuade her to invite anyone'

    c. Prima di decidere di ricevere nessuno ha mai riflettuto così a lungo sulle scelte da compiere

      'Before deciding to receive no one has he ever reflected so long on the choices to be made'

In sentences (56) the licensing of the parasitic quantifer is perfectly possible and confirms once again the correctness of the CH. We must now raise the question why the licensing of a negative quantifier by another one is possible at all.

We know that the possibility of licensing under "connect edness" presupposes the existence of a sort of unique antecedent for the licensing and the parasitic element. We have already seen that such a situation may arise for quantifiers *in situ* in the case of English multiple questions, due to the absorption operation which creates at LF a single operator out of two or more distinct wh-phrases.[17] Our task will then be to show that the same happens with multiple negation. In such a case we cannot apply the classical test of paired answers, of course, yet the meaning itself of multiple negation suggests an "absorbed" interpretation. Consider in fact a simple case:

(57)   Nessuno ha mai detto niente

    'Nobody has ever said anything'

As suggested by the English gloss, the meaning of (57) is roughly represented by a logical translation like (58):

(58)   not ($\exists x$, x a person, $\exists y$, y a thing, $\exists z$, z a time) such that x said y in z

The three negative operators do not negate each other: only one negation is understood in the sentence, with scope over three existential quantifiers: in other words, we can say that the two post-auxiliary negative quantifiers act as polarity items triggered by the first one. This is exactly the interpretation which obtains for the negative quantifiers in the parasitic constructions of (51) through (54).[18]

Now, consider that in (58) the whole expression formed by the negation plus the operators in brackets can be plausibly taken as a unique antecedent.

A clear similarity between English multiple questions and the multiple negation construction under discussion lies, furthermore, in the fact that also the latter displays the typical behavior of polarity phenomena: as in English multiple questions the fronted wh-phrase licenses the one *in situ*, here the preverbal negative quantifier (more precisely, the negative quantifier preceding the inflected verb or auxiliary, i.e. the head I of IP) licenses the other(s), which otherwise, in the absence of *non* or of an interrogative context, would be ungrammatical (cf. fn. 7.):

(59)   *Ho mai dett niente

       'I have ever said anything'

(60) a.   Non ho mai detto niente

       'I not have ever said anything'

    b.   Hai mai detto niente?

       'Have you ever said anything?'

We will assume therefore that to sentence (51a), e.g., there corresponds an LF representation such as (61):

(61) $\left[_{IP} nessuno_i \left[_{IP} niente_j \left[_{IP} chiamare\ e_i\ servirà\ a\ e_j \right] \right] \right]$ [19]

In this structure *nessuno* and *niente* undergo an absorption process (to ultimately give rise to a reading similar to that informally represented by formulae like (58) and can be considered a unique antecedent for the two differently indexed traces:

(62) $[_{IP}$(nessuno$_i$ niente$_j$) $[_{IP}$chiamare e_i servirà a $e_j]]$

Now (62) must plainly be accepted by the conditions on movement as much as the most usual instances of parasitic gaps, e.g. (63):

(63)   ?A person who for us to approach e might even flatter e . . .

The same applies to all other examples in (51) and (53)—(54), which have each a closely parallel structure involving overt multiple gaps.[20]

Different is the case of *only XP* phrases. The latter in fact never need any effect of licensing (cf. (64a)) and when they occur multiply in the same sentence they do not display any absorbed interpretation:

(64) a.   Ho visto solo Gianni

'I saw only Gianni'

b.   Solo Gianni ha amato solo Maria per tutta la vita

'Only Gianni has loved only Maria for the whole of his life'

In fact, if the meaning of *only NP* can be represented as *no one (or nothing) except NP* as suggested before (cf. section 2), i.e., as *not $\exists x$, x $\neq$ NP*, it is clear that the interpretation of (64b) is a double negation as in (65a) and not a single one as in (65b):

(65) a.   Not ($\exists x$, $x \neq$ Gianni) such that not ($\exists y$, $y \neq$ Maria) such that x loved y . . .

b.   Not ($\exists x$, $x \neq$ Gianni, $\exists y$, $y \neq$ Maria) such that x loved y
    . . .

Using other terms of ordinary language, (64b) means that "everybody apart from Gianni has loved someone else in addition to Maria".[21]

For these reasons we can expect that there will be nothing like a unique antecedent relevant for the "connectedness" effect in the case of *only*-phrases, hence no parasitic constructions. The prediction is correct:

(66) a.   Chiamare solo Gianni infastidirà solo Maria

'To call only Gianni will bother only Maria'

b.   Fa solo il suo dovere per aiutare solo Gianni

'He does only his duty in order to help only Gianni'

In fact, in (66) *only Gianni* embedded in both examples within an island can never be assigned scope over the matrix sentence.

Turning back now to negative quantifiers, their distribution parallels that of overt multiple gaps also in another construction: the so-called Across-the-Board (ATB; cf. Williams 1978) violations of the CSC. As is known, in the case of overt empty categories with a unique antecedent the presence of a gap in each of the coordinated constituents is often sufficient to circumvent a CSC violation:

(67) a. *Chi pretendi che io inviti *e* o che Maria ti presenti Gianni?

   'Who do you require that I invite *e* or that Maria introduce Gianni to you?'

   b. *Chi pretendi che io inviti Gianni o che Maria ti presenti *e*?

   'Who do you require that I invite Gianni or that Maria introduce *e* to you?'

   c. Chi pretendi che io inviti *e* o che Maria ti presenti *e*?

   'Who do you require that I invite *e* or that Maria introduce *e* to you?'

The same phenomenon reappears with the now usual pair of negative phrases, giving rise to grammatical sentences like (68), in contrast to those of (34)—(35):

(68) a. Non pretendo che tu dica niente o che chiami nessuno

   'I do not require that you say anything or that you call anyone'

   b. Vuoi che io faccia niente o che chiami nessuno?

   'Do you want me to do anything or to call anyone?'

In sum, the whole pattern of parasitic and ATB constructions in LF displays a parallelism with that of overt multiple gaps which cannot reasonably be imputed to chance and, thus, supports in the strongest possible way the claim that the same bounding conditions constrain both syntactic movement and scope assignment.

5. SCOPE AND LEXICAL CATEGORIES

In this section we will try to reconcile the Correspondence Hypothesis with an apparent exception to the parallelism between syntactic movement and scope assignment.

We have already noticed in section 3 that the "non-sentential" part of the Subject Condition seems to be very weakly observed by negative phrases, if at all. We have thus contrasts like the following:

(69) a.   (?)La presenza di nessuno lo spaventerebbe

'The presence of noone would frighten him'

b.   *Che fosse presente nessuno lo spaventerebbe

'For noone to be present would frighten him'

This fact is not isolated: in fact, we anticipated that negative phrases seem to fully observe only the "sentential" cases of other constraints as well, e.g., the Adjunct Condition:

(70) a.   Non voglio partire dopo nessuno

'I do not want to leave after anyone'

b.   Non potrai partire dopo l'arrivo di nessuno

'You cannot leave after the arrival of anyone'

c.   *Non potrai partire dopo che sarà arrivato nessuno

'You cannot leave after anyone will have arrived'

(71) a.   Dopo nessuno voglio partire!

'After noone do I want to leave!'

b.   ?Dopo l'arrivo di nessuno potrai partire!

'After the arrival of noone can you leave!'

c.   *Dopo che sarà arrivato nessuno potrai partire!

'After noone will have arrived can you leave!'

Consider, now negative quantifiers embedded within post-verbal NPs:

(72) a. Non aspetterò l'arrivo della lettera di nessuno

'I will not wait for the arrival of the letter of anyone'

b. Non abbiamo trovato gli indizi relativi a nessuno degli imputati in questione

'We have not found the clues relative to any of the defendants in question'

c. Non ho indagato i tuoi rapporti con nessuno degli imputati

'I have not investigated your relationships with any of the defendants'

(73) a. *Maria, di cui non aspetterò l'arrivo della lettera . . .

'Maria, of whom I will not wait for the arrival of the letter . . .'

b. *A quale degli imputati avete trovato gli indizi relativi?

'To which of the defendants did you find the clues relative?'

c. *Con molti degli imputati ho indagato i tuoi rapporti

'With many of the defendants I have investigated your relationships'

In (72a, b and c) we have grammatical LF violations of the NP Constraint, which are all impossible, in Italian, with the corresponding overt cases of the same (descriptive) condition (73a, b, and c); the sentential CNPC cases are instead observed by negative phrases, as shown in section 3 and below:

(74) *Non accetterò la proposta di aspettare la lettera di nessuno

'I will not accept the proposal to wait for the letter of anyone'

Furthermore, even a subcategorized PP is normally an absolute island for overt movement in Italian, but not for the assignment of scope to a negative quantifier:

(75) a. Non ho assistito alla deposizione di nessuno

'I was not present at the testimony of anyone'

b. *Mario, di cui ho assistito alla deposizione . . .

'Mario, of whom I was present at the testimony . . .'

The facts just reviewed seem at first sight to cast some serious doubts on the claim that the syntactic islands hold in LF, i.e., on the CH. A more careful consideration suggests however that the process assigning wide scope to the quantifiers in question may perhaps have nothing to do with the supposed LF movement, thus more generally with island constraints.

Notice, first of all, that negative and *only* phrases are likely to be unique in the class of non-wh quantifiers in showing properties of scope unboundedness. In fact most quantifiers are normally unable at all to attain wide scope over a higher predicate and its arguments, as often noticed in the literature (cf. May 1977; Haïk 1984; Hornstein 1984). Such is certainly the case for monotone increasing quantifiers, in the sense of Barwise and Cooper (1981), like, e.g., *every* (in Italian *ogni*):

(76)   E' sufficiente che si presenti ogni invitato, per mettere in pericolo la stabilità dell'edificio

'It is sufficient that every guest shows up to jeopardize the stability of the building'   .

(76) can only have the meaning expressed in (77a), not that of (77b), i.e., "every guest" may assume the matrix predicate "is sufficient" in its scope;

(77) a.   It is sufficient that the guests all show up to jeopardize . . .

     b.   Every guest (i.e., a guest whosoever) is such that his showing up would be sufficient to jeopardize . . .

This fact might suggest that such quantifiers are assigned scope in a way which differs, at least partially, from syntactic wh-movement, whose most salient property in languages like Italian or English appears to be precisely unboundedness.[22] It is plausible, then, to hypothesize that the scope of such quantifiers, whether it is assigned by QR or not, must coincide with the minimal Complete Functional Complex (in the sense of Chomsky 1986a) to which they belong. This restriction straightforwardly excludes a matrix predicate from the possible scope of the embedded quantifier in a sentence such as (76): the notion of CFC, in addition to being a semantically relatively well-defined notion, is also independently established in the vocabulary of another module of grammatical theory, the Binding principles (cf. Chomsky 1986a; Giorgi 1987).[23]

Let us, then, propose the Minimal Scope Principle (78):

(78)
$$\text{MSP: the scope of a} \left\{ \begin{array}{l} \text{-Neg} \\ \text{-wh} \end{array} \right\} \text{operator}$$

cannot exceed the least CFC containing it

However, again, a non-sentential domain, even if it constitutes a CFC, like an NP, does not represent an island, so that (79), unlike (76), is ambiguous, roughly in the same sense as specified by (77):

(79)   Può metterlo in imbarazzo la presenza di ogni ragazza

         'May embarrass him the presence of every girl'

Ogni ragazza may apparently take scope just over its NP or over the whole sentence. Such ambiguity is also clear with a preverbal nominal subject (in which case a direct movement analysis of the wide scope reading would violate the Subject Condition as well), whereas the closely corresponding sentential case is obviously unambiguous in favor of the narrow scope reading:

(80) a.   La presenza di ogni ragazza può metterlo in imbarazzo

           'The presence of every girl may embarrass him'

     b.   Che sia presente ogni ragazza può metterlo in imbarazzo

           'For every girl to show up may embarrass him'

Notice, further, that the wide scope reading of a quantifier embedded in a non-sentential argument may show up with respect not only to a matrix predicate but also to a matrix quantifiable NP:

(81) a.   L'annuncio della morte di ogni soldato gettava nel lutto due famiglie (p. es. quella del soldato e quella di sua moglie)

           'The announcement of the death of every soldier threw into mourning two families (i.e., the soldier's and his wife's)'

     b.   L'annuncio che era morto ogni soldato $\left\{ \begin{array}{l} \text{?? gettava} \\ \text{gettò} \end{array} \right\}$ nel lutto due famiglie

           'The announcement that every soldier had died threw into mourning two families'

In (81a) the two families are easily "multiplied" by the embedded "every"; in (81b), where wide scope of "every" is impossible, the two families are rigidly designated and the use of the imperfective (iterative) past tense sounds inappropriate to the situation, where the subject NP refers just to a single, definite announcement.[24]

Notice, also, that in (81a) the subject NP "the announcement of the death of every soldier" seems to be roughly equivalent to "every announcement of the death of a soldier", i.e., the universally quantified character of the head noun *soldier* induced by the specifier *every*, seems to be able to percolate up to the head noun *announcement*.

On the grounds precisely of this interpretive equivalence let us suggest that wide scope in (79), (80a) and (81a) is only apparent or, better, indirectly acquired through upward percolation of a [+Q] (i.e., quantified, in a sense specified for each different operator) feature: it is the whole subject NP which would then count as the quantified one, i.e., would be locally assigned scope in agreement with the restriction of such a process to its CFC.

As (76), (80b) and (81b) indicate, the feature percolation must be so restricted as to exclude the intervention of a "sentential" constituent like IP or CP; a reasonable generalization might make reference to the contrast between lexical and non lexical heads, since we have evidence that at least one of the two non lexical heads, i.e., I or C, must be unable to receive or transmit the feature [+Q] and that, instead, at least three of the lexical ones are able to do so: in fact (79), (80a) and (81a) have already shown that Ns and Ps must be able to perform the required percolation; (82) shows that this must be true also for As:

(82)   Le notizie relative alla morte di ogni soldato venivano raccolte da due ufficiali

'The news relative to the death of every soldier was collected by two officers'

In fact wide scope is perfectly possible also in this case. We will thus formulate the percolation convention as in (83):

(83)   If a lexical head α governs a lexical head β bearing a feature [+Q], then α may inherit the feature [+Q] from β.

The symbol Q ranges, of course, over a wide number of quantificational possibilities: bare plurals, universals, existentials, cardinals, WH etc.

In some cases the feature [+Q] is an intrinstic component of the morphological or lexical nature of the original head N: such is the case of plural morphology (in the distributive reading) or of items like Italian *niente* ("nothing"), English *who* or *what*.

In the other cases the feature [+Q] seems to be an intrinsic property of the Specifier of N and we can assume that the head assumes it through the agreement with its Spec.

If, among the quantifiers identified under the feature [+Q] we include also negative phrases, as we have already implicitly assumed, mentioning *niente*, the embarassing cases of island violations on the part of such quantifiers all disappear as exceptions to the application of the bounding principles in LF.

The grammatical sentences of the paradigm (69)—(75) are all cases where, owing to a succession of lexical heads and to the recursive application of (83), the feature [+negative Q] may be eventually inherited by a constituent not properly included in the island structure. The process is, in an obvious sense, analogous to the application of a pied-piping convention for syntactic Wh-movement.

(83) is in fact an extension of a sort of "logical" pied-piping convention already proposed by Kayne (1983, section 8); as such it is able, like Kayne's original, to deal with the following interpretative contrast in English:

(84) a.   John regretted nobody's departure

b.   John regretted nobody's having left early

(Kayne (1983)'s (53)—(54))

In (84a), wide scope of the genitive negative phrase is possible (actually obligatory, perhaps for the reasons given in Fiengo and Higginbotham 1981), in (84b), it is impossible, according to Kayne (1983).

Under the CH these contrasts are unexpected, given that overt extraction of both kinds of genitives appears sharply impossible (with or without the stranding of the particle *'s*, as noticed by Kayne):

(85) a. *Nobody's do I regret departure

b. *Nobody do I regret's departure

c. *Nobody's do I regret having left early

d. *Nobody do I regret's having left early

One conceivable theoretical approach to these data is presented in Longobardi (1987a).

Anyway, what counts here is the lack of such a uniform paradigm in the process of scope assignment, exemplified by (84); suppose that, as is natural, the morpheme *-ing* is a non-lexical head (let us say a form of I with some nominal features, a specification probably shared also by Romance infinitives), unlike the lexical N *departure*.

Only this latter will then be able to inherit the feature [+Q], so that its maximal projection will count as a negative quantifier and can be assigned scope over the clause of the predicate *regret*.

The subject of the non-lexical morpheme cannot instead exploit convention (83) and its scope will be blocked within its gerundive clause.

This analysis independently confirms, then, the existence of a convention like (83) and the irrelevance of the paradigm (69)—(75) as exceptions to the hypothesis that the bounding principles apply in LF as well.

6. *ONLY* PHRASES AND AGREEMENT

In section 3 we had noticed that the asymmetries expected as effects of the Subject Condition do show up in the case of *only*-phrase; now the impossibility of wide (sentential) scope for *only* in (86) (analogous to (39b) above) suggests, then, that convention (83) is inapplicable with this kind of quantifiers:

(86) (?)La presenza solo della polizia mi sorprese

'The presence only of the police surprised me'

in fact the formulation of (83) is already able to exclude cases like (86) from its scope of application: notice that (83) makes explicit reference to head-to-head feature percolation and that the [+Q] feature has been taken to be either intrinsic to a lexical head or acquirable through agreement with its specifier. Now in the case of the usual *only* phrases the feature +Q does not originate in the head or in the specifier, but in the adverbial element *only* for its correspondents in the other languages), which is not a specifier (it shows no distributional interaction with the elements of the internal structure of the XP to which it is fixed and, even in languages with more overt agreement realization than English, does not agree with the head. So, the +Q feature never shows up on any head in this case.

The kind of pied-piping effect yielded by (83) can only be performed, in the case of (86), by overtly preposing the word for "only" to
the whole subject NP but letting it focus on the genitive complement
alone (not on the head noun):

(87)   Solo la presenza della polizia mi sorprese

        'Only the presence of the police surprised me'

In this sense we can conclude that *only*-prefixation is the means of
overtly marking the quantified nature of a phrase, i.e., in cases such as
(87), of making explicit the process implicitly performed by (83),
through percolation, with normal quantifiers.[25]

The correctness of formulation (83) and of the related assumptions
about the [+Q] feature and the role of agreement seems independently
confirmed by the following considerations: there exists, in Italian, an
adjectival variant of the adverb *solo* (*soltanto, solamente*), i.e., of the
item which corresponds to *only*; such an adjective is regularly inflected
for gender and number (*solo/ -a/ -i/ -e/*) and is also the normal translation for English "alone". The adjective *solo* may obviously occur as part
of an NP: it often appears in the Spec position between a determiner
and the head noun and always agrees with this latter; (83) predicts, in
this case, that since agreement should be able to transmit the head the
[+Q] feature induced by *solo*, such a feature can percolate to a higher
N rendering sentences corresponding to (86) ambiguous; this is actually
the case:

(88) a.   La presenza di due sole persone potrebbe mettere in
           imbarazzo il nostro conferenziere

           'The presence of only two persons might embarrass our
           lecturer'

    b. (?)La presenza solo di due persone potrebbe mettere in
           imbarazzo il nostro conferenziere

           'The presence only of two persons might embarrass our
           lecturer'

in fact (88a) is, in principle perfectly ambiguous between NP-internal
and sentential scope of the genitive argument, while (88b), in addition
to being, as usual, less readily acceptable, displays just the narrow scope
reading.

At a stylistically higher level it is possible for adjectival *solo* to occur between a definite determiner and a proper name, reproducing again the same contrast as in (88):

(89) a.   La presenza del solo Gianni potrebbe creare difficoltà

'The presence of only Gianni might raise difficulties'

b.   (?)La presenza solo di Gianni potrebbe creare difficoltà

'The presence only of Gianni might raise difficulties'

Sentences like those in (88) and (89) provide, thus straightforward support for the proposed approach based on convention (83).

On the other side, recall also that, among the mentioned overt negatives, there are some items which, unlike *nessuno* or *niente*, function as syntactic prefixes like the adverbial *solo* and not as heads or adjectival specifiers: cf. *neppure* "not even" (and its variants) and *né . . . né* "neither . . . nor" (see section 3 and note 18). As predicted by (83) their scopal behavior parallels that of adverbial *solo* rather than that of *nessuno* or of adjectival *solo*.

Consider now what happens to a postverbal subject NP: here the Subject Condition is obviously irrelevant, so that wide scope of *only*-phrases becomes more generally possible, as noticed in section 3 and the interpretive contrasts of (88)—(89) tend to disappear:

(90) a.   E' raccomandabile la presenza di due sole persone

'Is advisable the presence of only two persons'

b.   (?)E' raccomandabile la presenza solo di due persone

'Is advisable the presence only of two persons'

(91) a.   E' richiesta la presenza del solo Gianni

'Is required the presence of the only Gianni'

b.   (?)E' richiesta la presenza solo di Gianni

'Is required the presence only of Gianni'

However, it is well known that not all wh-extractions of arguments of a head noun are possible in Italian: Cinque (1980), and others after him, have shown that in the Romance languages, apart from marked cases of extraposition and reanalysis, only genitive arguments (i.e., arguments introduced by a preposition like Italian *di*) may be extracted from an NP and, further, that even among genitive arguments only those which can independently move to the Spec of the NP (to be realized there as possessives) are extractable. To derive such a generalization in a principled way, in Longobardi (1987a) we argued, on independent grounds, that nouns are non-structural governors, in Kayne's (1983) sense i.e., insufficient governors for non-local movement; this assumption prevents wh-extraction of any phrase governed by N. In this framework, we explain the systematic exceptions noted by Cinque hypothesizing that subject phrases which one move to the Spec of an NP, are accessible, in such a position, to an external structural governor, i.e., the verb selecting the whole NP, which then allows for their unbounded movement. Anyway, whatever its theoretical explanation, the generalization discovered by Cinque may be expected, under the CH, to display some effects on scope assignment as well.

Although the judgments on the relevant facts are delicate, and the structures are never perfect, the impression is that even in this case the Correspondence Hypothesis tends to be confirmed; consider first, in fact, the subcase of non-genitive arguments of N:

(92) a. (?)Ha suscitato scalpore il tuo accenno solo a due colleghi

'Your reference only to two colleagues has surprised'

b. (?)Ho aperto per errore un messaggio solo per Maria

'I opened by mistake a message only for Maria'

(92) c. (?)Io disapproverei una lettera solo al presidente

'I would disapprove a letter only to the president'

d. (?)Ho trovato un trattato di pace solo con i Montefeltro, tra i vecchi documenti dell'archivio

'I found a peace treaty only with the Montefeltros, among the old documents of the archive'

these PPs, which are clearly unextractable by syntactic movement, also very strongly favor the NP-internal scope reading, if any, thus giving support to the CH.

Consider now the case of a genitive non-subject argument; here the facts are even more delicate, since most genitive arguments can, at various levels of marginality, be extraposed from the NP, nullifying thus the effects of Cinque's generalization, at least in the case of constructions, like these with *only*, which are already slightly marginal; it seems, however, that in cases which are more resistant to extraposition the expected subject-object asymmetry with respect to wide scope eventually arises:

(93) a. (?)Abbiamo appurato la conoscenza di Gianni solo dell'inglese

      'We ascertained Gianni's knowledge only of English'

    b. (?)Abbiamo appurato la conoscenza dell'inglese solo di Gianni

      'We ascertained the knowledge of English only of Gianni'

Our judgement is that sentential scope of *only* tends to be rather marked in the case of the "objective" genitive of (93a), but perfectly available (perhaps favored) for the now "subjective" genitive phrase in question in (93b).

Other two island effects mentioned above reappear with the scope processes of *only*-phrases; the first is the islandhood in Romance of simple PPs, even subcategorized, which gives rise to a scope contrast like (94):

(94) a. (?)Abbiamo manifestato contro l'allontanamento solo del ministro della Difesa

      'We demonstrated against the removal only of the Defense minister'

    b. (?)Abbiamo contestato l'allontanamento solo del ministro della Difesa

      'We contested the removal only of the Defense minister'

Again, wide scope is much more readily possibile in (b) than in (a). The second case in question is that in which the *only*-phrase is embedded within more than one NP, another position wherefrom wide scope assignment is at best marginal:

(95) (?)E′ stata confermata la notizia della presenza solo del
     ministro della Difesa

    'The news of the presence only of the Defense minister was
     confirmed.[26]

The interpretations of these examples seem thus to confirm the validity
of the CH and to reinforce our reliance on the interaction of an
independent mechanism (i.e., the lexical pied-piping convention) to
explain away the apparent island violations of negative phrases in
(82)—(87).

More generally, the evidence presented throughout the paper appears to provide indisputable support to the idea that scope assignment
shares many fundamental properties with syntactic movement. If, then,
scope is really assigned to quantifiers *in situ* by invisible LF movement
rules, like May's QR, the facts discussed here immediately fall under
the natural hypothesis that the same bounding conditions constrain
movement through all components. From this perspective what becomes theoretically surprising and worthy of investigation is now that
wh-phrases *in situ* in many languages do not seem to obey island
constraints (Huang 1982; Lasnik and Saito 1984).

Moreover, although the hypothesis itself of the existence of LF
movement is less conclusively established by the data of this article, yet
it turns out to be most immediately compatible with all of them, while
some of its conceivable alternatives are less so and can probably be
discarded on the grounds of the evidence here contained: for instance,
the parallel behavior of overt negatives and *only* phrases seems to
undermine van Riemsdijk and Williams' (1982) proposal (cf. also
Williams 1986) to treat Kayne's *ne . . . personne* ECP facts (or their
Italian correspondents with *non*) in terms of syntactic extraction of *ne*
(*non*) at S-structure.[27]

At the very least, it appears that such results confirm the heuristic
value of the approach and point out the range of far-reaching consequences that the analysis of the phenomena falling under the Correspondence Hypothesis may uncover.

ACKNOWLEDGEMENTS

I am especially indebted to G. Cinque, P. Cole, R. Kayne, B. Schein and two anonymous referees for their comments on the original drafts of this article, dating back from December 1984 and June 1986, and to D. Delfitto, A. Giorgi and J. Higginbotham for several discussions about the main topics involved.

NOTES

[1] Cf. e.g. May (1977; 1985), Higginbotham (1980a), Aoun, Hornstein and Sportiche (1980), Huang (1982), Hornstein (1984), Pesetsky (1985).

[2] Throughout the paper we assume the X'-theory and the theory of landing sites for movement rules proposed in Chomsky (1986b).

[3] Although we will not discuss the issue in detail, it must be clear in fact that two distinct ways to explain the correspondence between wh-movement and scope assignment are conceivable: along the lines of May (1977), it can be imagined that scope is assigned by an abstract movement rule creating a level of LF and obeying the regular conditions on movement. Alternatively it is possible to assume that scope is assigned to quantifiers *in situ* via some other device and that island constraints are conditions on scope assignment itself and are observed by overt wh-movement precisely because the latter is always a scope assigning rule. In the latter approach the argument in favor of a distinct LF level is, of course, much less compelling, as e.g., in Kayne's (1983) framework; distinguishing between thetwo alternatives is hard and anyway goes far beyond the space limits of this work. Just to give an idea of one possible kind of evidence which should be brought to bear on the question, consider, for instance, the following line of reasoning: if it can be conclusively shown that other instances of movement are not scope-assigning rules (e.g. NP-movement or V-movement) but obey the same constraints as wh-movement (ECP, island conditions), this may turn out as an argument in favor of the first approach. Some further remarks on this problem, will be made in note 27.

[4] We assume that the interpretation of items like *nessuno* and *niente* (or their English correspondents) is adequately represented by a double structure: a simple negative operator and an existential quantifier, something like "not ∃."

An alternative option would be to consider negative quantifiers as single operators directly assigning zero values to their variable, exactly as, say, *three men* has a variable ranging over 3 individuals.

A positive consequence of representing negatives as "not ∃" is that, supposing a tendential biuniqueness between quantified formulae and their lexicalizaton in natural languages, we may explain the lack in many languages of structures *not some . . .* (on the model of *not all . . .*), whose "place" is occupied precisely by the negative NPs in question.

[5] In the light of the results achieved in Giorgi and Longobardi (1987), it appears that the projection of N following a quantified specifier like *nessun(o)*, here traditionally labeled N', must rather be defined as N^{max-1}.

[6] As we say in the text *only*-phrases are essentially implicit negatives, representable by means of formulae "not ∃" plus an "inequality" restriction introduced by " ≠ ".

Consider, in fact, that the difference between (1a) and (1b) can be represented as in (2):

(1) a.   No young person can go there

   b.   Only young people can go there

(2) a.   not $\exists x$, $x =$ "young person", such that x can go there

   b.   not $\exists x$, $x \neq$ "young people", such that x can go there

A question which may arise with *only*-phrases is whether, e.g., (2b) is sufficient as a representation of the meaning of (1b) or we should conjoin it to a clause of the form of (3):

(3)   (and) Young people can go there

actually, it appears that the most accurate representation of the *asserted* meaning consists of (2b) alone; in fact placing (1b) under negation affects only the meaning expressed in (2b), and does not negate (3) at all, as is easy to check:

(4)   It is not the case that only young people can go there

therefore (3) can be, at most, part of the presuppositions of (1b).

The semantic import of such presuppositions must not, however, be understimated: consider, for instance, that the intuitive meaning of (5) can be, in analogy to that of sentences with *only*, easily represented as in (6):

(5)   Also John came here

(6)   John came here and $\exists x$, $x \neq$ John such that x came here

Now the usual negation test shows that here the situation is reversed and that the asserted meaning is only the first, non quantified, part of the conjunction in (6); cf.,

(7)   It is not the case that also John came here

the second, quantified, conjunct of (6) is unaffected by the negation in (7) and thus is to be considered only a presupposition of sentence (5).

However this conjunct is particularly important since it is just for it that (5) differs semantically from the simpler (8):

(8)   John came here

Finally it is noteworthy that, playing around with the symbols and quantified formulae used to represent the asserted meanings and the presuppositions of *only*- and *also*-phrases, the interpretation of a variety of at least 8 quantified expressions could be represented: as a matter of fact many languages we are familiar with (probably most or all or them) lexicalize only another one of such potential quantifying prefixes, i.e. English *neither* and its correspondents (interpretable as follows: "neither John P" = John not P and $\exists x$, $x \neq$ John, such that x not P, for P an arbitrary predicate). Consider in fact the following chart:

(9)

	Semantic formula	Informal interpretation	Specific lexicalization
a.	John P and $\exists x$, $x \neq$ John, such that x P	John P and someone else P	"also John"
b.	John P and $\exists x$, $x \neq$ John, such that x not P	John P and someone else not P	none
c.	John P and not $\exists x$, $x \neq$ John such that x P	John P and noone else P	"only John"
d.	John P and not $\exists x$, $x \neq$ John such that x not P	John P and everyone else P	none
e.	John not P and $\exists x$, $x \neq$ John such that x P	John not P but someone else P	none
f.	John not P and $\exists x$, $x \neq$ John such that x not P	John not P and someone else not P	"neither John"
g.	John not P and not $\exists x$, $x \neq$ John such that x P	John not P and noone else P	none
h.	John not P and not $\exists x$, $x \neq$ John such that x not P	John not P but everyone else P	none

Now, the nonexistence of simple specific lexicalizations for (9d) and (g) can, perhaps, be related to the logical equivalence of the corresponding formulae with those of the simple *everyone* and *noone*, respectively; but the other gaps are more mysterious: even assuming that the formula in (h) may be expressed by *everyone but John*, the gaps of (b) and (e) still call for an explanation (and the whole paradigm is in need, of course, of a wider typological investigation). On similar topics see also Horn (1969) and Cushing (1978).

[7] Two important distinctions must be made in order to clarify the behavior of Italian negative items with respect to their scope markers: the first distinction concerns occurrences of negative quantifiers with sentential scope vs. others, e.g., occurrences of negative quantifiers with scope over an NP.

Among the former we must then operate the second distinction, that between negatives occurring at S-structure before the head of the IP which constitutes their scope and negatives occurring after it.

Such an I position is visibly represented by the auxiliary verb, if present, or, otherwise, by the main verb (probably raised to I: see Pollock 1988) of the clause in question.

Thus we will conventionally call the two positional classes "preverbal" and "postverbal" negative quantifiers, keeping in mind the qualification that the relevant I position is that heading the sentence over which they have scope, hence not necessarily their own clause.

Negative quantifiers preceding it are independent of the presence of other negative expressions and display, alone, a full negative meaning, essentially like English *no*-forms:

(1) a.   Nessuno è venuto
          'Noone has come'

   b.   A nessuno ho parlato
          'To noone have I talked'

   c.   (?)La lettera di nessuno è arrivata in tempo
          'The letter of noone arrived on time'

   d.   Mai ho detto questo!
          'Never did I say this!'

Negative items occurring after the head of their sentential scope domain, instead, display a behavior more similar to that of English polarity *any*-forms, i.e. in the standard language they need be licensed by *non* or by another negative quantifier occurring before the head in question and assume the scope of the latter, which, thus, functions as a scope marker.

(2) a.   *E' venuto nessuno
          'Has come anyone'

   b.   *Ho parlato a nessuno
          'I have talked to anyone'

   c.   *E' arrivata in tempo la lettera di nessuno
          'Has arrived on time the letter of anyone'

   d.   *Ho mai detto questo
          'I have ever said this'

(3) a.   Non è venuto nessuno
          'Has not come anyone'

   b.   Nessuno ha detto niente
          'Noone has said anything'

   c.   Nessuno mi ha chiesto di fare niente
          'Noone has asked me to do anything'

   d.   Nessuno ha mai detto questo
          'Noone has ever said this'

In such a post-head position, furthermore, Italian negative items do not have an independent negative meaning, but simply share the negation of their licensing element, so that the examples (3) are never interpretable as double negations, exactly as their English glosses. (For this property cf. section 4).

This observation is reinforced by the fact that, like *any*, post-head *nessuno, niente, mai* may also be licensed by an interrogative context and function, then roughly as non-specific existentials (cf. also section 2):

(4) a.   E' venuto nessuno?

'Has anyone come?'

b.   Chi ha mai detto niente?

'Who has ever said anything?'

the analogy with *any* must not, however, be overestimated: *any*-phrases, in fact, do not show the clear island effects which constitute the bulk of the argumentation of this article and which may directly motivate an LF movement analysis.

As for negative items with non-sentential scope, hey behave always as independent negative quantifiers (i.e., like English *no*-phrases and usually take NP as their scope domain:

(5)   La presenza di nessuno potrebbe metterla in imbarazzo

'The presence of noone could embarass her'

(5) is, in principle, ambiguous between a wide (sentential) scope of *nessuno* (for which cf. section 6) and a more marked NP-scope reading, in which the subject NP is roughly equivalent to "the absence of everyone".

In neither reading is *non* required or possible.

[8] In addition to the island constraints which form the main topic for this paper, the assignment of scope to the quantifiers under discussion also observes the condition that they can have wide scope only out of non-indicative clauses (where non-indicative encompasses subjunctive, infinitive and conditional moods and also certain instances of future tense embedded under verbs usually governing subjunctive).

This restriction will be devoted less attention here (cf. for some examples, note 17). For the use of subjunctive in Italian cf. also Giorgi (1984).

[9] Narrow scope over its own clause is instead always possible for any subject quantifier. The ECP may perhaps be satisfied through LF adjunction of the quantified NP to IP and, thus, local binding of the trace (see Kayne 1982; Rizzi 1982). Alternatively, it is possible that movement is not obligatorily required for the assignment of narrow scope, at least for subjects, whose c-domain at S-structures already coincides with their scope IP.

[10] With respect to such examples one point is worth clarifying: the careful reader will have noticed that in the (a) examples of (36)—(37) *non* is present on the verb, while it disappears in the (b) cases. This fact, far from playing any role in the decreased acceptability of (36b) and (37b), is a consequence of the independent requirement that, essentially, *non* be present with post-verbal negative phrases and absent otherwise (for which cf. note 7). This informal traditional statement on the distribution of *non* needs further refinement but is sufficient for our purposes here. For now let us just point out that not only would the insertion of *non* not rescue the (b) examples, but it would even make them worse; cf., e.g., (i):

(i)   (*)La moglie di nessuno non è stata invitata

'The wife of no one was not invited'

If acceptable at all, (i) may only have a meaning completely different from that of (36a) and (36b): in fact the two negative elements have to be interpreted as independent of each other and instead of yielding the "simple negation" meaning of (36) (suggested in the English glosses by "not ... anyone" or "no one"), they display a "double negative" reading (as suggested by "no one ... not" in English), i.e., the essentially affirmative interpretation of ii.:

(ii)   Everyone's wife was invited

[11] For an earlier proposal about boundedness of some scope phenomena cf. Rodman (1972) and, for criticism of his approach, Chomsky (1977) and Higginbotham (1980b).

As we have said before (cf. note 6), the interpretation of English *any*, used as a negative polarity item, seems to be immune from island effects and most of the ungrammatical Italian examples of the text become relatively acceptable in English if translatable with *any*-forms. Correspondingly, and consistently, *any* does not display ECP effects either (see Kayne 1982; Hornstein 1984 a.o.).

Even Italian has a class of negative polarity items immune, like *any*, from the ECP and the island constraints, and, thus, minimally contrasting with *nessuno, niente*, etc. Its most typical representatives are items of the series *alcun-*, like *alcuno* "any" (more literarily also "anyone") and *alcunché* "anything".

The latter have essentially the same distribution and licensing conditions as postverbal *nessuno* and *niente*, but do not observe ECP and islands:

(1) a.   Non credo che alcunché possa spaventarla

          'I do not think that anything may frighten her'

    b.   Non credo alla possibilità che Maria abbia fatto alcunché di illegale

          'I do not believe the possibility that Maria did anything illegal'

    c.   *Non credo alla ragazza che ha fatto alcunché di illegale

          'I do not believe the girl who did anything illegal'

    d.   Non credo che, in realtà, che tu faccia alcunché di illegale sia necessario

          'I do not think that, actually, that you do anything illegal is necessary'

    e.   Non credo che Maria sia scappata dopo aver fatto alcunché di illegale

          'I do not think that Maria has fled after doing anything illegal'

    f.   Non credo che Maria abbia detto alcunché o chiamato aiuto

          'I do not think that Maria has said anything or called for help'

All the sentences in (1), except c., are quite acceptable: if *niente* is substituted for *alcunché*, it has narrow scope, contrary to *alcunché*, in (1a), and the acceptability of the other examples quickly decreases.

As for (1c) an additional factor must intervene to block scope assignment out of the relative clause: cf. note 15 for discussion; anyway it must be noticed that even in the paradigm with *niente* (1c) would constitute a far more severe violation than the other sentences.

[12] Given the relatively meager evidence available to a child to decide that the ECP and the island constraints do apply in LF and given the essentially negative nature of the evidence which could be required for such a task, we should expect no variation to arise across languages and speakers.

However, it is the case that a number of Italian speakers and probably the totality of the Spanish ones accept what appears to be the wide scope reading of *nessuno* and *niente* as preverbal subjects (in Spanish of the corresponding items *nadie* and *nada*).

It can be argued, though, that this need not lead us to hypothesize a variation in the level of application of the relevant condition, but rather a different classification of negative elements in the two varieties. The whole question has been addressed in a certain detail in Longobardi (1987b).

A fuller explanation for the relevant pattern of data, along with an exploration of the typological implications of Romance negation systems, will be provided in forthcoming work of ours.

[13] These cases could also involve a Superiority effect (cf. Chomsky 1973). Kayne (1983), however, has pointed out examples of unacceptable *wh-in situ* in subject position for which no Superiority account can be invoked (cf. also Chomsky 1981, 236):

(1)   *I know perfectly well who thinks that who is in love with him

Like (50b) of the text, (1) can be improved by the addition of a second *wh-in situ* in a lower governed position, but not by one itself in subject position (Kayne 1982, note 7, 1983):

(2) a.   ?I know perfectly well who thinks that who is in love with whom

    b.   *I know perfectly well who thinks that who said that who was in love with Mary

More importantly, the offending *wh-in situ* cannot be licensed by another one higher in the tree, a location which can be viewed as 'non proper' in the sense of (44c) of the text:

(3)   *I know who persuaded whom that who was in love with Mary

Therefore, the diagnostics presented in (49) suggests that we have to do with a "connectedness" phenomenon.

[14] In order for the examples containing a preverbal negative quantifier to be acceptable the latter must always be focused.

This seems independent of the parasitic strategy, since we are likely to have to do with the same requirement which imposes the focused interpretation (excluding the left-dislocated, non focused, one) to preverbal negatives also in such simple sentences as *Nessuno viene* "Noone comes".

Another similar constraint seems often to impose an intonational break between an *only*-phrase taking wide scope and the part of the sentence preceding it.

However the phenomenon cannot be generalized, since in many sentences wide scope can also be achieved without any break, as in the following examples:

(1) a.   Io pretendo che tu veda solo Mario. Quanto agli altri, decidi tu

          'I require that you see only Mario. As for the others, you decide'

    b.   Occorre premere solo questo pulsante per ottenere l'effetto voluto

          'It is necessary to press only this button to obtain the required effect'

[15] A constraint which often appears to be inviolable for negative quantifiers, even under a perasitic strategy is the "relative clause" subcase of the CNPC:

(1)   *Il medico che ha salvato nessuno dovrebbe mai essere ricompensato da niente di più che il suo orgoglio professionale

          'The doctor who has saved no one should ever be rewarded by anything more than his professional pride

Apart from the cases independently excluded by the Specifity Condition, sentences like (1) above may be ruled out because, in additon to the island constraints active in the Syntax as well, LF scope rules also obey the restriction that wide scope of a quantifier is anyway limited to the first clause containing an indicative non-future verb. (cf. note 8) In other words, wide scope is possible only out of clauses having a subjunctive, conditional, future indicative or non-finite Infl:

(2) a.
Questo non vuol dire che Maria $\left\{ \begin{array}{c} \text{ha} \\ \text{abbia} \end{array} \right\}$ fatto bene

This does not mean that Maria $\left\{ \begin{array}{c} \text{has (indic.)} \\ \text{has (subjunc.)} \end{array} \right\}$ behaved well

    b.
Questo non vuol dire che Maria $\left\{ \begin{array}{c} \text{*ha} \\ \text{abbia} \end{array} \right\}$ fatto niente di male

This does not mean that Maria $\left\{ \begin{array}{c} \text{has (indic.)} \\ \text{has (subjunc.)} \end{array} \right\}$ done anything bad

The independence of this phenomenon with respect to the other island constraints is also shown by its applicability to bare polarity items such as *alcunché*:

(3)
Questo non vuol dire che Maria $\left\{ \begin{array}{c} \text{*ha} \\ \text{abbia} \end{array} \right\}$ fatto alcunché di male

It is not theoretically obvious that the application of the condition must also be sensitive to the parastic or non parasitic status of the relevant quantifier. Anyway, if we assume it is precisely such a constraint, which we might term the Tense Indefiniteness Condition, that rules out (1), we may check whether a relative clause with subjunctive mood is less "bounding" for parasitic quantifiers. Perhaps this can be true in some cases, like the following, although the contrasts are scarce and subtle:

(4) a.   *Al giornalista che dovesse intervistare nessuno consiglierei di dire questo

          'The reporter who ought to interview noone would I advise to say this'

(4) b.   ??Al giornalista che dovesse intervistare nessuno consiglierei di dire niente di simile

'The reporter who ought to interview noone would I advise to say anything similar'

A special case to be considered is that of relative clauses with negative NPs as heads: such clauses too admit of wide scope quantifiers in many cases:

(5)   ?Non ho trovato nessuno che volesse fare niente di positivo

'I did not find anyone who wanted to do anything positive'

In (5) it is possible that a "connectedness" effect between the head and the embedded *niente* licenses the latter. However it is also conceivable that the relative clause is extraposed out of the NP and governed by the matrix verb, along lines discussed by Taraldsen (1981). In fact even simple extractions out of similar relative clauses are grammatical and may be analyzed in the way proposed in the reference cited.
[16] Essentially the same contrasts arise, as expected, in the interrogative usage of polarity *nessuno* and *niente*; cf., for instance, the following pair:

(1) a.   *Chi fa questo lavoro per aiutare nessuno, al giorno d'oggi?

'Who does this work in order to help anyone, nowadays?'

   b.   Chi fa niente per aiutare nessuno, al giorno d'oggi?

'Who does anything in order to help anyone, nowadays?'

[17] Analogous to Kayne's examples (as involving *wh-in situ*) and to ours (as involving an island violation) is the following contrast, pointed out by Pesetsky (1982):

(1) a.   *Who said that for Bill to marry who would be a surprise for me?

   b.   ?Who said that for Bill to marry who would be a surprise for whom?'

In (1a) the second *who*, embedded inside a preverbal sentential subject is hardly able to reach its scope position, marked by the first *who*, presumably because of a Sentential Subject violation. But the sentence can be improved, according to Pesetsky's judgment, by a "connectedness" effect, i.e, by the addition of a lower "licensing" wh-phrase, as in (1b).
[18] The need for an absorption process between two operators of the same type is also illustrated by the difficulty of the "connectedness" effect with negative words such as *nemmeno* "not even/neither" and *né . . . né* "(n)either . . . (n)or":

(1) a.   *Chiamare nessuno servirebbe nemmeno a Mario

'To call no one would help even Mario'

   b.   *Chiamare nessuno servirebbe né a me né a te

'To call no one would help either me or you'

This must be related to the non-existential interpretation of such negative operators, which cannot, then, be taken to be sufficiently "parallel" to *nessuno* to be absorbed with it. A condition on absorption seems thus to be that all the quantifiers involved be parallel in the sense that they contain a similar type of operator. The impossibility of (1) above, due to the failure of absorption with these negative phrases, is certainly related to the failure of the same items to occur in an interrogative polarity context:

(2) a.   ?*Hai visto nemmeno Gianni?
          'Have you seen even Gianni?'

   b.*   Hai parlato né con lui né con lei?
          'Have you talked either with him or with her?'

On the interpretation of *nemmeno* see also note 5.

[19] Under the CH (61) cannot be meant to represent the actual, linguistically relevant Logical Form of (51a); as such, it would violate the ban against P-stranding otherwise active in Italian. For a possible solution of the issue and a more plausible LF structure some conclusion can be drawn from the discussion in the following section. See Longobardi (forthcoming) for an explicit analysis.

[20] Given the possibility for negative phrases to enter parasitic strategies we may expect to find parasitic violations not only of island constraint but also of the ECP. Such cases do exist, in fact, at least for certain speakers, and have already been pointed out pretheoretically by Rizzi (1982, 175) and analyzed by Kayne (1983):

(1) a.   Non pretendo che nessuno dica questo
          'I do not require that nobody say that'

   b.   Non pretendo che nessuno dica niente
          'I do not require that anybody say anything'

the wide scope reading of *nessuno* seems easier, for several speakers, in (1b).

Notice that for the same speakers wide scope should also be marginally available in the following example, a probably correct prediction:

(2)   Non credo che invitare nessuno serva a niente
          'I do not believe that to invite anyone will do any good'

[21] In sum we can say that *only*-phrases always contain a negative operator, whereas *nessuno, niente* and the like contain a negation of their own just when they occur in preverbal position (in the sense qualified in note 7), but are interpreted as bare existentials elsewhere.

[22] The best argument which continues, to my knowledge, to support a movement (QR) analysis for these non-negative quantifiers (essentially Hornstein's 1984 Type II quantifiers) is the one traditionally derived from weak crossover (unless the latter phenomenon is analyzable as an S-structure process, as, e.g., in Reinhart (1976) or Haïk (1984)).

[23] Hornstein (1984) tries to relate the scope boundedness of the quantifiers in question to the locality conditions of the Binding theory in an even more direct way.

[24] For a detailed study of the aspect and tense value of Italian verbs in the indicative mood cf. Bertinetto (1986).

[25] In a sense the applicability of (83) is in complementary distribution with the possibility of achieving the same results by prefixation: *only* does not give rise to percolation effects but has the property of being prefixable to any kind of X max, quantifying it; words like *no one*, instead, are intrinsically NPs, but may transmit their +Q feature to larger, non-NP, phrases. As we said, exactly identical to that of *solo* is the behavior of *nemmeno, neppure* etc. both from the distributional and scopal viewpoints.

The similarity between the two strategies of prefixation or Q-feature percolation is reinforced by the fact that it is always possible to prefix *only* (and the other items of its class) to a category even letting it focus just on a proper subpart of such a category, e.g., in a sentence like the following:

(1)   Sarei disposto solo a sposare la sorella di Gianni

       'I would be ready only to marry Gianni's sister'

In (1) *only* may have at least three interpretatively distinguishable *foci*: Gianni, Gianni's sister and the event of marrying Gianni's sister. These interpretations are elucidated by making reference to the following different situations, respectively:

(2) a.   I would not be ready to marry the sister of anyone other than Gianni.

   b.   I would not be ready to marry anyone other than Gianni's sister

   c.   I would not be ready to do anything other than marrying Gianni's sister

It must be kept in mind that the category on which *only* focuses is the one which acts as the restriction of the resulting quantifier (so that the three quantifiers could roughly be represented like: (a) Only for marrying x's sister, x = Gianni; (b) Only for marrying x, x = Gianni's sister; (c) Only for x, x = marrying Gianni's sister); such a category must not be confused with the scope of the quantifier which, in (1), corresponds to the matrix sentence in all the cases. The "long distance" focusing of *only*, however, may be exploited to overcome the expressive limitations otherwise imposed by the constraints on scope assignment. In (3) below, for example, *solo* has sentential scope, being prefixed to the whole adverbial clause, but can be let to focus just on *Maria*, thus achieving an interpretation analogous to the one forbidden for (48a) of the text:

(3)   Fa il suo dovere solo per aiutare Maria (non Gianni)

       'He does his duty only to help Maria (not Gianni)'

This fact enables us to make sense of an interesting observation suggested by an anonymous reviewer, namely that if *solo* or, better, *soltanto* is suffixed instead of being prefixed in examples like (45b) or (48a), a matrix scope interpretation becomes possible:

(4) a.   Chiamare Gianni soltanto sarà possibile

       'To call Gianni only be possible'

   b.   Fa il suo dovere per aiutare Maria soltanto

       'He does his duty to help Maria only'

Such cases, in fact, will not represent surprising exceptions to general claims about boundedness of scope, if only we assume that *soltanto* is not suffixed here to the NPs *Gianni* or *Maria* but to the whole island constitutent, though focusing just on *Gianni* and *Maria*. This way (4) would be analogous in interpretation to (3) and no island would be violated. A crucial confirmation of the correctness of this analysis comes from sentences in which *soltanto* is clause-internal and cannot, then, be suffixed to the whole island constituent:

(5) a.   Presentare *Gianni soltanto* a Maria sarà possible

          'To introduce Gianni only to Maria will be possible'

    b.   Fa il suo dovere per dare *aiuto soltanto* a Maria

          'He does his duty to provide help only to Maria'

In fact, here wide scope of *soltanto*, even when it focuses on the preceding NPs, *Gianni* and *aiuto* respectively, becomes impossible again.

[26] The contrasts involving genitive arguments are often weaker than the others. Actually adnominal genitives of clause-final NPs may be either string-vacuously extraposed or directly base generated in right-dislocated position, interpreted as "topics" and then construed *ad sensum* with the relevant head noun. It is even conceivable that *all* cases of wide scope of *only* out of an NP involve right dislocation of the *only*-phrase: in fact all such cases require the intonational break mentioned in fn. 14 and it is possible that LF does not admit of the escape strategy for extraction from NP through Spec that we advocate in Longobardi (1987a) and in the text. Were this the case, it would be unnecessary to appeal to the Subject Condition in LF to exclude wide scope of *only* from a preverbal NP (right dislocation is always clause-final) and the readings of (87)—(90) could be explained on the basis of the fact that extraposition or right dislocation only involves genitive arguments and sometimes tends to have a marked status when violating the normal constraints on extraction from NP.

[27] Another proposal to treat ECP effects on quantifiers *in situ* by means of an S-structure constraint, however, was put forward by Kayne (1983), who noticed that in examples like (1a) the trace of *where*, moved in the Syntax, appears unable to parasitically license *who* (unlike *what in situ*):

(1) a.   *I'd like to know where who hid it *e*

    b.   ?I'd like to know where who hid what *e*

It is clear that after LF movement the two structures would be indistinguishable, in the sense of both containing only moved *wh*-phrases and their traces. It is at S-structure, instead, that *who* and *what in situ* can be argued to be "uniform" enough to trigger a "connectedness" effect (unlike *who* and *e*). If only S-structure, then, encodes such an information, Kayne's CC must apply at this level, undermining the probatory value of bounding effects on quantifiers *in situ* as arguments for a separate LF level. Whatever the exact relevance of such an interesting argument, it must be recalled that even assuming the existence of an LF level created by movement and constrained by ECP and island conditions it is necessary to maintain that the same conditions *also* apply to S-structure (or surface structure): this is needed in order to prevent wh-phrases *in situ* from licensing overt parasitic gaps:

(2)   *Who said that you filed *which article* before reading *e*?

At S-structure (but not al LF), in fact, the empty category inside the adverbial adjunct of (2) is ruled out since, for lack of uniformity with the coindexed *wh-in situ*, the "connectedness" effect will not take place.

REFERENCES

Aoun, J., Hornsein, N. and Sportiche, D.: 1980, 'On some aspects of wide scope quantification', *Journal of Linguistic Research* **1**, 3.

Barwise, J. and Cooper, R.: 1981, 'Generalized quantifiers and natural language', *Linguistics and Philosophy* **4**.

Bertinetto, P.: 1986, *Tempo, aspetto e azione nel verbo italiano*, Accademia della Crusca, Firenze.

Chomsky, N.: 1973, 'Conditions on transformations' in: S. Anderson and P. Kiparsky (eds.), *A Festschrift for M. Halle*, Holt Rinehart and Winston, New York.

Chomsky, N.: 1975, *Questions of Form and Interpretation*, The Peter De Ridder Press, Lisse, the Netherlands.

Chomsky, N.: 1976, 'Conditions on rules of grammar', *Linguistic Analysis* **2.4**.

Chomsky, N.: 1977, 'On Wh-movement' in: P. Culicover, T. Wasow and A. Akmajian (eds.), Academic Press, New York.

Chomsky, N.: 1982, *Some Concepts and Consequences of the Theory of Government and Binding*, MIT Press, Cambridge, MA.

Chomsky, N.: 1986a, *Knowledge of Language*, Praeger, New York.

Chomsky, N.: 1986b, *Barriers*, MIT Press, Cambridge, MA.

Cinque, G.: 1980, 'On extraction from NP in Italian', *Journal of Italian Linguistics* **5**. **1/2**.

Cushing, S.: 1978, 'Not only *only* but also *also*', *Linguistic Inquiry* **9**.

Engdahl, E.: 1981, 'Parasitic gaps', *Linguistics and Philosophy* **4**.

Fiengo, R. and Higginbotham, J.: 1981, 'Opacity in NP', *Linguistic Analysis* **7**.

Geach, P.: 1962, *Reference and Generality*, Cornell Univ. Press, Ithaca, NY.

Giorgi, A.: 1984, 'Toward a Theory of Long Distance Anaphors: A GB Approach', *The Linguistic Review* **3**.

Giorgi, A.: 1987, 'The Notion of Complete Functional Complex: Evidence from Italian', *Linguistic Inquiry* **18**.

Giorgi, A. and Longobardi, G.: 1987, *The Syntax of Noun Phrases*, CUP, Cambridge UK (to appear).

Haïk, I.: 1984, 'Indirect Binding', *Linguistic Inquiry* **15**.

Higginbothan, J.: 1980a, 'Pronouns and Bound Variables', *Linguistic Inquiry* **11**.

Higginbotham, J.: 1980b, Review of *Montague Grammar*, ed. by B. Hall Partee, Academic Press, New York 1976, *Journal of Philosophy*.

Higginbotham, J. and May, R.: 1981, 'Questions, Quantifiers, and Crossing', *The Linguistic Review* **1**.

Horn, L.: 1969, 'A Presuppositional Analysis of *only* and *even*', *Chicago Linguistic Society* **5**.

Hornstein, N.: 1984, *Logic as Grammar*, MIT Press, Cambridge, MA.

Huang, J.: 1982, *Logical Relations in Chinese and the Theory of Grammar*, Ph.D. Dissertation. MIT, Cambridge, MA.

Kayne, R.: 1982, 'Two notes on the NIC', in: A. Belletti, L. Brandi, L. Rizzi (eds.), *Theory of Markedness in Generative Grammar*, Scuola Normale Superiore, Pisa.

Kayne, R.: 1983, 'Connectedness', *Linguistic Inquiry* **14**.

Lasnik, H. and Saito, M.: 1984, 'On the nature of proper government', *Linguistic Inquiry* **15**.

Longobardi, G.: 1983, 'Connectedness, complementi circostanziali e soggiacenza', *Rivista di grammatica generativa* **5**.

Longobardi, G.: 1985a, 'Connectedness, Scope and C-command', *Linguistic Inquiry* **16**.

Longobardi, G.: 1985b, 'The theoretical status of the Adjunct Condition', ms. Scuola Normale Superiore, Pisa.

Longobardi, G.: 1986, 'Connectedness and Island Constraints', in: J. Guéron, H. G. Obenauer, J. Y. Pollock (eds.), *Grammatical Representation*, Foris, Dordrecht.

Longobardi, G.: 1987a, 'Extraction from NP and the Proper Notion of Head Government', in Giorgi and Longobardi (1987).

Longobardi, G.: 1987b, 'The negation systems of Romance', Talk given at the GLOW Workshop, Venice.

Longobardi, G.: forthcoming, *Movement, Scope and Island Constraints*, ms.

May, R.: 1977, *The Grammar of Quantification*, Ph.D. Dissertation MIT, Cambridge, MA.

May, R.: 1985, *Logical Form: Its Structure and Derivation*, MIT Press, Cambridge, MA.

Pesetsky, D.: 1982, *Paths and Categories*, Ph.D. Dissertation MIT, Cambridge, MA.

Pesetsky, D.: 1985, 'Unselective Binding and wh-*in situ*', ms. U Mass. Amherst, MA.

Pollock, J. Y.: 1988, 'V-raising, UG and the structure of IP', *Linguistic Inquiry* **20**.

Reinhart, T.: 1976, *The Syntactic Domain of Anaphora*, Ph.D. Dissertation MIT, Cambridge, MA.

Riemsdijk, H. van and Williams, E.: 1982, 'NP structure', *The Linguistic Review* **1**.

Rizzi, L.: 1982, *Issues in Italian Syntax*, Foris, Dordrecht.

Rodman, R.: 1972, 'The Proper Treatment of Relative Clauses in Montague Grammar' in: R. Rodman (ed.), *Papers in Montague Grammar*, UCLA, CA.

Ross, J. R.: 1967, *Constraints on Variables in Syntax*, Ph.D. Dissertation MIT, Cambridge, MA.

Taraldsen, K. T.: 1981, 'The Theoretical Interpretation of a Class of Marked Extractions', in: A. Belletti, L. Brandi, L. Rizzi (eds.), *Theory of Markedness in Generative Grammar*, Scuola Normale Superiore, Pisa.

Williams, E.: 1977, 'Discourse and Logical Form', *Linguistic Inquiry* **8**.

TAISUKE NISHIGAUCHI

CONSTRUING *WH*

1. 'INDETERMINATE PRONOMINALS'

1.1. *Some Taxonomy*

The purpose of the present paper is to discuss the status of WH-phrases as quantificational expressions. In particular, we will address the question of how the WH-expression should be characterized in terms of its quantificational force. We will see that the syntactic and semantic behavior of constructions in Japanese involving the class of words which Kuroda (1965) very pertinently referred to as 'indeterminate pronominals' provides an interesting insight to the issue at hand. The 'indeterminate pronominals' essentially correspond to WH-expressions.[1] Some of them are listed below:

(1)   *dare* 'who', *nani* 'what', *itu* 'when', *doko* 'where', *dore* 'which' (NP), *dono* 'which' (Det) . . .

Here, we will generally refer to these elements as WH-phrases/expressions. As the glosses suggest, these words are used as WH-(interrogative) expressions, as in the following.[2]

(2)   *Dare*-ga *nani*-o *itu doke-de* kai-masi-ta ka?
       who N what A when where-at buy   -P Q
       'Who bought what when were?'

The properties of these constructions in connection with their logical form respresentations (LF) have been discussed elsewhere (Harada 1971; Nishigauchi 1985, 1986).

The italicized elements in (2) cannot be simply identified as 'interrogative pronouns', because the use exemplified therein is not the only way they behave.[3] In this article, our attention is focused on other kinds of environment in which the indeterminate pronominals occur. Sentences like the following exemplify the kind of constructions we are interested in.

197

(3) a. *Dare-mo* ga *nani-ka*   o   tabe-te-iru.
        someone N something A eating-be

'Everyone is eating something.'

b. *Dare-ni-mo* aw-a-na-katta.
    who-D-also meet-not-P

'I did not meet anybody.'

These sentences indicate that the 'WH-expression' in Japanese behaves as (part of) the universal or the existential quantifier in combination with the quantificational (particle) elements (Q-elements) *ka* and *mo*.[4]

The quantificational expressions in (3a) might suggest that *dare-mo* 'every/anyone' and *nani-ka* 'something' are morphologically related but separate 'words'. However, we also have expressions like the one italicized in (3b), where the case-marker *ni* intervenes between the WH-expression *dare* and the quantificational particle *mo*. Since a 'word' in Japanese normally does not contain a case-marker (postposition), it is rather difficult to conceive of the expression *dare-ni-mo* as a lexical element.

The forms observed in (3c—d) suggest more clearly that the processes involved here are syntactic.[5]

(3) c. [*Dono* gakusei]-*ka*-ga rakudai-si-ta.
        which student   Q N   flunk-P

'Some student flunked.'

d. [*Dono* gakusei]-ni-*mo* A-o   age-nakat-ta.
    which student   to Q   A   gave not

'(I) did not give an A to any student.'

In (3c), the Spec *dono* 'which' and *gakusei* 'student' form a phrasal expression (NP), and the Q-element *ka* is attached to this NP, forming a larger phrasal expression, whose category I assume is PP.

The syntactic structure of the quantificational expression (QP) in (3b) might be something like this.

(3')

Here, the Q-element *mo* attaches to a phrasal expression which consists of a WH-expression and a dative case-marker, and the resulting expression has a quantificational force of *any/every* or, something that comes close to WH-*ever* in English. This type of expression may be used either in a negative or non-negative context. If it is used in a negative environment, its semantics comes close to that of the negative polarity *any*, as in (3b). If it appears in a non-negative environment, as in (4), it is associated with an interpretation close to that of *every*.[6]

(4) [*Dono* gakusei]-ni-mo A-o age-ta.
     which student to Q   A gave

'For all *x, x* a student, I gave an A to *x*.'

There is slight complication here concerning case-marking. That is, the nominative marker *ga* in the position immediately preceding *mo* is obligatorily deleted, and the accusative marker *o* is normally deleted in colloquial style — with *o* undeleted, the resulting sentence takes on an archaic, or formal flavor.

(5) a. Dare(*-ga)-mo   ko-na-katta.
         who   N ever come-not-P

     'Nobody came.'

   b. Dare(-o)-mo   ais-a-nai.
         who A   ever love-not

     '(I) don't love anybody.'

The distinction between the items in (3a) and in (3b) should then be drawn in terms of the constituent structure. The quantifier expressions in (3a) are of this structure.

(3″)

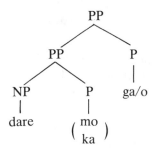

It is not our purpose here to spell out the exact mechanism for describing the syntactic contrast between the two cases. It would be sufficient to say that the resulting quantificational force is determined depending on whether the phrase governed by a Q-element is case-marked or not. With Q-element *mo*, if it governs a non-case-marked NP, the entire phrase has the quantificational force of 'every', and if it governs a case-marked NP (in fact, PP), the entire phrase comes out as an expression whose meaning is close to 'any', when it appears in a negative environment, and to 'every' in non-negative contexts. We will discuss this in more details in the next subsection.[7]

Another Q-element *ka* gives rise to a different contrast with respect to the case-marking of the NP/PP that it governs. The entire phrase that contains this element is associated more or less with the quantificational force of the existential quantifier, whether or not it governs a case-marked argument — the contrast that shows up is a more subtle one. Consider the following sentences.

(6) a. Dare-ka-kara henna   tegami-ga todoi-ta.
         who Q from   strange letter-N   arrived

         'A strange letter came from somebody.'

    b. Dare-kara-ka henna   tegami-ga todoi-ta.
        who from Q   strange letter-N   arrived

        'A strange letter came from god knows who.'

The quantifier phrase (QP) *dare-ka* in (6a), which may be paraphrased by 'someone' or an indefinite NP, is associated with the quantificational force of the existential, and may or may not be interpreted as having a specific reference in the mind of the speaker. On the other hand, sentence (6b) disallows a specific interpretation on *dare-kara-ka* — its interpretation is something like 'a letter came from someone, but I don't know who it is from.' The contrast in the following sentences, which contain a modifier expression which forces the specific interpretation, shows the point in question.[8]

(7) a. Itumo Pleasant St.-no ano kado-ni tat-te-iru
         always   gen that corner-at stands
         dare-ka-kara henna   tegami-ga todoi-ta.
         who   from   strange letter-N   arrived.

         'A strange letter came from somebody who is always stand-
         ing on that corner of Pleasant St.'

(7) b. *Itumo Pleasant St.-no ano kado-ni tat-te-iru *dare-kara-ka* henna tegami-ga todoi-ta.

The semantics of PP-*ka* is somewhere in between an indefinite NP and an embedded question. This suggests strongly that the nature of Q-element *ka* in these cases is essentially homogeneous with the interrogative marker *ka*, which further suggests that the ideas of Karttunen (1977), who argues that the quantificational force of the WH phrases in interrogative environments should be identified as the existential quantifier, are on the right track. It might be possible to assume that the particle *ka* in these constructions is really a COMP element, on a par with the question marker, which has the same phonetic form. This is reminiscent of the proposal of Riemsdijk (1978), who argues that PPs have a COMP node. We will see in Sec. 3.2 that this idea has an interesting consequence in the theory of LF-representations.[9]

Constructions involving *mo* and those involving *ka* behave differently when they occur with an NP containing a WH-Spec *dono* 'which', *donna* 'what king of'. As example (4) above shows, *mo* attaches to PP which dominates a WH-NP and a postposition which governs it. The sequence NP-*mo*-P, as in (8), is low in acceptability.

(8)   *[Dono gakusei]-mo ni A-o age-ta.
        which student   Q   to A gave

This is puzzling, in light of the fact that the sequence *dare/nani-mo*-P, as in (3a) is perfectly grammatical, although its use is restricted to non-negative environments — contrast (9) with (3b) above.

(9)   *Dare-mo-ni awa-nakar-ta.
        who-Q-with   meet-not-P

However, the Q-element *ka* behaves differently in that it is attached to WH-NP, and not to a PP which contains it.

(10)   [Dono gakusei]-ka-ni A-o age-ta.
        which student Q to   A gave

        'I gave an A to some student (though I don't remember who).'

(11)   *[Dono gakusei]-ni-ka A-o   age-ta.
        which student   to Q   A gave

There may be some diachronic explanation for this paradigm, which is beyond the scope of the present work.[10]

1.2. *Some Semantics*

Kuroda (1965, 92—94) discusses the behavior of another particle *demo* (literally, 'even') in constructions involving WH-expressions. According to Kuroda (92), when *demo* is attached to a WH-phrase, the resulting expression comes to have the meaning of *every*, while, according to him (93ff), the expression consisting of WH and *mo* closely corresponds to the negative polarity *any*.[11] The following is one of the examples provided by Kuroda.[12]

(12)   Dare-demo hon-o   kat-ta.
        who even   book-A bought

        'Everyone bought books.'

However, the sequence WH-*demo* corresponds more closely to the 'free choice' *any*, viz. the non-negative use WH-*mo*, being the Japanese counterpart of *every*. This is based on the following observations.

As Vendler (1967) observes, the following two sentences are clearly distinct orders.

(13) a.   Take every apple.

     b.   Take any apple.

Order (13a) can be fulfilled only when the addressee takes all the apples that there are, while the speaker of (13b) will be satisfied if the addressee takes one among the available apples — the choice with respect to which apple he should take is up to the addressee. In this sense, (13b) is a more 'general' order than (13a).

The same contrast is observed in the following pair of Japanese sentences.

(14) a.   *Dono isu-ni-mo*   suwar-te mi-te kudasai.
         which chair on-Q   sit   try   please

         'Try sitting on every chair, please.'

(14) b. *Dono isu-ni-demon*   suwar-te mi-te kudasai.
     which chair on-even sit   try   please

     'Try sitting on any chair (you like), please.'

The request (14b), which involves WH plus *demo*, is a 'general' request, in that the speaker of this sentence can be satisfied if the addressee tries sitting on any one chair (or more) that he likes, and it is up to the addressee which of the available chairs in the situation he might sit on. On the other hand, the request (14a) cannot be fulfilled unless the addressee tries sitting on all the chairs that are present in the situation. This is parallel with the contrast in (13) with respect to *every* vs. *any*.

Our second point has to do with pronominal binding across sentence-boundaries. Hornstein (1984) observes that the 'free choice' *any* can be coindexed with a pronoun that occurs across a sentence boundary, while this is impossible with *every*.

(15) a. Take *any number$_i$*. I will divide *it$_i$* by three.

   b. Take *every number$_i$*. *I will divide *it$_i$* by three.

The same contrast can be observed in Japanese using the pronominal *sore* 'it'.

(16) a. *Dono sakana$_i$-demo* mot-te ki-te kudasai.
     which fish   even carry   come please
     Sore$_i$-o   ryoori-si-te agemasu kara.
     it   -A   cook-for-you   because

     'Bring in any fish$_i$ (you like): I will cook it$_i$ for you.'

   b. *Dono sakana$_i$-mo* mot-te ki-te kudasai.
     which fish   Q   carry come please

     Sore$_i$-o   ryoori-si-te agemasu kara.
     it   -A   cook-for-you   because

     'Bring in every fish$_i$: I will cook it$_i$ for you.'

These observations suggest that the semantics of WH plus Q-element *mo* in the non-negative context is close to that of English *every* while the behavior of WH plus *demo* is parallel with the 'free choice' *any*. Although the point that we are going to make will apply to these two constructions equally well, our discussion in what follows will be on the WH . . . *mo* constructions.

1.3. *Non-Adjacent Cases*

The examples (17a—b) suggest that the quantificational particle *mo* may be attached, not only to a WH-expression directly, but to a clause or a complex NP that contains a WH-expression.

(17) a. *Dare* ga ki-te   *mo*, boku wa aw-a-nai.
       who N come Q   I   T   meet-not

   'For all x, if x comes, I would not meet (x),' or
   'Whoever may come, I will not meet (him).'

   b. [$_{NP}$ [$_{\overline{S}}$ *dare* ga kai-ta] tegami] ni *mo* onazi koto ga
              who N wrote letter   in Q same thing N
      kai-te-at-ta.
      written-be-P

   'For all x y, x a person, y a letter x wrote, the same thing was written in y.'

What distinguishes these cases from those that we observed in the previous section is that in (17), the WH-expression *dare* is not adjacent to the quantificational particle *mo* — and yet, the semantic properties of the WHs appear to be the same: they essentially behave as *every* or *wh . . . ever*.[13]

   Kuroda (1965) argues that the form as seen in (17a), where the morpheme *(te)mo* is attached to a clause which contains a WH-expression, derives from a clausal counterpart of a sequence WH-P-*demo*, as in (14b), which we repeat here.

(14) a. *Dono isu-ni-demo*   suwar-te mi-te kudasai.
       which chair on-even sit   try   please

   'Try sitting on any chair (you like), please.'

That is, Kuroda argues that the concessive clause in (17a) in fact derives from an underlying structure like (18):

(18)   [$_S$ dare-ga ki]-*demo* . . .

If this is correct, we should expect that the WH-expression in (17a) will have the quantificational force of the 'free choice' *any*. However, the semantics of the WH-expression in the concessive clause in (17a) is closer to that of the WH-P-*mo* sequence, which we argued above shares the semantics of *every*.

Firstly, consider the following sentence.

(19) [Dare-ga ki-te-mo] hookoku-si-te-kudasai.
      who-N come Q report-do   please

'For all x, x a person, report to me if x comes.'

This request asks the addressee to report every visitor to the speaker of (19). The speaker would be dissatisfied if the addressee fails to report any single visitor, which would be permissible if the WH here were the Japanese counterpart of the 'free choice' *any*. This shows that the semantics of the WH-phrase in constructions exemplified by (19) involves universal quantification and has the semantics that corresponds to that of *every* in English.

Secondly, we observed above that WH-P-*demo* may be coindexed with a pronoun that appears across a sentence boundary. Recall (16a) above. However, as the following shows, this type of pronominal coindexing is impossible with the concessive clause with (*te*)*mo*.[14]

(20) [*Dono ronbun*$_i$-o yon-demo] taikutu-datta.
      which paper   A read Q   boring was
      *Sikasi, Yamada-*san-*wa sore*$_i$-o nessin-ni yon-da.
      but   T it   A seriously read

'For all x, x a book if I read x, x was boring. However, Yamada read x seriously.'

Thus, in what follows, we will assume that the concessive clause in (17a) derives from a structure where the Q-element *mo* is attached to the clause which contains a WH.[15]

To recapitulate, the examples that we have considered so far suggest that the function of each WH-phrase is not identifiable until we look at the larger syntactic environment in which it finds itself — it may be a WH-interrogative expression, or (part of) a quantificational expression. If you find a quantificational particle (Q-element) *mo* somewhere in a position that c-commands a WH, its function is (part of) *wh . . . ever* — a quantificational expression that may be identifiable as the universal quantifier. If the WH occurs in an $\overline{S}$ whose COMP contains [+wh] *ka* (and if there is no Q-element more immediately c-commanding it), the WH is an interrogative expression.

In this paper, we will explore the possibility thast the essential properties of WH-expressions can be characterized in terms of the the notion of *unselective binding*, discussed in important work by Heim

(1982), who attributes the original idea to the work of David Lewis (Lewis 1976). In the next section, we will present a brief outline of this crucial notion.

2. UNSELECTIVE BINDING

2.1. *Indefinite NPs*

According to Heim, indefinite NPs are not equipped with any quantificational force by themselves, and essentially serve as free variables in the logical representation. The quantificational force of the indefinite NPs is rather determined by an expression that c-commands it in a larger domain (which can possibly extend to discourse and is not restricted to a sentence,) such as adverbs of some sort which involves quantification, designating frequency, like *always, in most cases, sometimes, rarely*, etc. Thus, consider the following sentences.

(21) a. If a man owns a donkey, he always beats it.

b. In most cases, if a table has lasted for 50 years, it will last for another 50 years.

c. Sometimes, if a cat falls from the fifth floor, it survives.

d. If a person falls from the fifth floor, he very rarely survives.

Heim observes that the indefinite NPs that appear in these examples can not simply be characterized as existentials but act as all sorts of different quantifiers depending on their environments. This point can be made clear if we notice that sentences (21a—d) can be paraphrased by (22a—d) respectively.

(22) a. For every man and every donkey such that the former owns the latter, he beats it.

b. Most tables that have lasted for 50 years last for another 50 years.

c. Some cats that fall from the fifth floor survive.

d. Very few people that fall from the fifth floor survive.

Heim captures this intriguing property of indefinite NPs by assuming that they have basically the meaning of variables which are ultimately bound by an element in a larger domain, like adverbs of quantification, which she characterizes as having the characteristics of 'unselective binders', which bind not just one particular variable, but an unlimited number of them simultaneously (Heim 1982; 124ff.) Thus, in her theory, Heim represents (23) first as something like (24) in the logical representation.[16]

(23) If a man owns a donkey he beats it.

(24) [man(x) & donkey (y) & own(x, y)] → [beat (x, y)]

If there is an adverb of quantification, such as *always*, somewhere higher in the domain, it unselectively binds the variables x and y in (24), so that the logical representation for (21a) would be something like (25).[17]

(21) a. If a man owns a donkey, he always beats it.

(25) Always$_{x, y}$ [[man(x) & donkey(y) & own(x, y)] → [beat(x, y)]]

On the assumption that the semantics of *always* is associated with universal quantification (cf. Heim's rule of interpretation (i) (p. 25)), it turns out that the logical representation (25) is identical in truth conditions to (26), which, Heim claims, is the logical representation of (22a).

(22) a. For every man and every donkey such that the former owns the latter, he beats it.

(26) $\forall xy$ [[man(x) & donkey(y) & own(x, y)] → [beat(x, y)]]

This straightforwardly accounts for the fact that sentences (21a) and (22a) are equivalent, or, at least, close in meaning.

2.2. *Unselective Binding in Japanese*

Let us now return to our problem cases in Japanese. The point that I am going to make in this section is that the behavior of Q-element *mo/ka* and *Comp ka* is parallel to that of *always*: WHs such as *dare* 'who' do not have their own quantificational force at all — it is only when they find *mo/ka* somewhere higher in the domain at S-structure can they be identified as expressions associated with a certain quantificational force.

That the process under consideration works in unselective fashion is shown by examples like the following.

(27)   *Dare*-ga *doko*-de *nani*-o kaw-te-*mo*, boku-wa
       who -N where-at what-A buy -Q I   -T
       kamawa-nai
       care-not

'For all *x, y, z, x* a person, *y* a thing, *z* a place, I don't care if *x* buys *y* at *z*.'

In (27), which contains three occurrences of WH-expressions, the quantificational force of these three WH-expressions is determined uniformly by the single Q-element *mo* which occurs in COMP of their clause, in such a way that all of them function as (part of) universal quantification. This illustrates the way in which *mo* plays a role parallel to that of *always* in (21a) above, where we observed that this adverb of quantification determined the quantificational force of the two indefinite NP's, *a man* and *a donkey*, in unselective fashion.

Heim's insight would be incorporated into the present context if we treat WHs as variables which get bound by a Q-element that appears in COMP. There are at least two ways of executing this idea. One is to treat WHs as variables directly at the logical representation — the binding relations would be effected by coindexing the WHs and their respective unselective binders. Another way is to assume that WHs are subject to Move α — binding relation here would be established between a WH and the variable created by movement of WH. On this latter analysis, the relation between the WH and its unselective binder will be dictated by the relation of government in some fashion at the level of logical representation. I assume that the first alternative is closer to Heim's analysis of cases involving indefinite NPs and adverbs of quantification.[18] Also cf. Haïk (1984) and Williams (1986). The second is essentially in the spirit of Huang (1982), May (1985), Nishigauchi (1985, 1986), Pesetsky (1987).

In the present paper I assume that all non-D-linked WHs are subject to WH-Movement at LF.[19] This is based on the observation that the behavior of construal processes involving WHs in this type of construction in fact shows the properties of WH-Movement.

First, the construal of WHs in this type of construction is in principle unbounded — the position of the WH in question may be separated by more than one clause from the position of Q-element.

(28) Kimi-ga [ₛ *nani*-0 kureru to] iw-te-*mo*, boku-wa
      you N   what-A give   that say -Q I   -T
      ik-a-nai.
      go not

      'Whatever you might say you would give me, I would not
      go.'

Second, this type of construal is subject to the locality condition of
the sort noted by Harada (1971) and Nishigauchi (1985, 1986) — a
WH must be construed within the minimal domain defined by the
binder — in other words, with the closest unselective binder available:
essentially (a rather strong form of) the WH-island effect. Thus, observe these examples.

(29) Kimi-wa [ₛ *dare*-ga ki-te-*mo*] ik-a-nai *no*?
      you T   who-N   come   Q go-not Q

      'Are you not going, whoever may come?'
      NOT 'For which *x, x* a person, are you not going if you
      know whether *x* is coming?'

(30) John-wa [ₛ *dare*-ga ku-ru *ka*] sir-te-ite-*mo* ik-a-nai.
          T   who-N   come Q   know be Q   go-not

      'John will not go *even if* he knows *who* will come.'
      NOT 'For all *x, x* a person, John will not go if he knows
      whether *x* is coming.'

The point here is that (29) can be interpreted only in such a way that
dare is associated with Q-element *mo*, yielding the *wh . . . ever* interpretation: *no*, an interrogative COMP, simply indicates that the entire
sentence has the function of a *yes/no* question. This is because the
unselective binder *mo*, more immediately c-commanding *dare* than *ka*,
defines the minimal domain in which the WH may be construed.
Sentence (30), on the other hand, can be interpreted only in such a way
that *dare* is construed with *ka*, yielding an embedded question. *Mo*
here, thus, is unable to bind anything, and can only be interpreted as
heading an adjunct clause which can be translated as *even if . . .* as in.[20]

(31) John-ga ki-te-*mo*, . . .
          N come

      'Even if John comes, . . .'

This is due to the effect of the locality principle, or the WH-Island Condition effect of Subjacency: *ka* c-commands the WH more immediately than *mo*.

It may be possible to interpret (29) as a WH-question, given some marked intonation (perhaps a heavy stress on *dare*). However, this interpretation appears to be acceptable only when the entire sentence is interpreted as an echo-question — an extreme form of D-linking in the sense of Pesetsky (1987). In Japanese, this type of question appears to require that the interrogative be headed by (that is, end in) *no ka/no* in COMP, and this is difficult to obtain when the interrogative is headed by *ka*, which is a marker for a genuine question. Cf. Kuno (1981) for subtle observations that hinge on this distinction.[21] Thus, (32) can be interpreted only as a *yes/no* question, where the WH is construed only with the Q-element *mo*, subject to the WH-Island effect.

(32)   Kimi-wa [$_{\bar{S}}$ dare-ga ki-te mo] iki-taku-nai   desu-ka?
        you -T   who-N come Q   come-want-not be- Q

        'Do you not want to go, whoever may come?'

This might bear an important consequence for the theory of binding in LF — if we assume a theory of LF-derivation such that D- and non-D-linking are distinguished in such a way that the latter is represented in terms of movement while the former is represented by coindexing without movement (notice that this is a rather strong position — in fact, Pesetsky allows ambiguity in both cases — see, however, his fn.32.), we obtain the following generalization: movement is subject to the WH-Island effect, while coindexing is not.[22]

Third, sentences involving apparent violation of Subjacency (the Complex NP Constraint effect) exhibit properties which confirm the observations and the analysis presented in Nishigauchi (1985, 1986), in an illuminating way.

As example (33) shows, it is possible (superficially, I claim) for a WH that appears within a complex NP at S-structure to be construed with Q-element *mo* that appears outside of it.

(33)   [$_{\bar{S}}$[$_{NP*}$[$_{\bar{S}}$ *dare*-ga kai-ta] hon]-o yon-de *mo*],
                who-N   wrote book-A read   Q
        omosiro-katta.
        interesting was

        'For all *x*, *y*, *x* a person, *y* a book *x* wrote, *y* was interesting.'

What must be noted about this example is that, while the WH *dare* appears within a complex NP, the sentence is grammatical, with *dare* construed with *mo* that c-commands it. So, it appears to involve violation of Subjacency. However, it must also be noted that this binding relation is not the only construal relation that is in effect here. There is another construal relation between the Q-element *mo* and the complex NP containing the WH *dare*, giving rise to the interpretation 'every book such that . . .' That is, the quantificational force of the complex NP — not just the WH contained in it — is unselectively determined by Q-element *mo*. Thus, consider the following sentence.

(34)   [[Dare-ga kai-ta] ronbun]-o yonde-mo, *hitotu*
         who -N wrote paper -A read -Q   one
         hihyoo-o kai-te kudasai.
         review -A write please

         'For all x, y, x a person, y a paper that x wrote, please write one review if you read y.'

In (34), there is a scope interaction not only between authors and 'one review' but also between 'papers' written by those authors and 'one review' — the addressee is asked to write a review per author/paper pair.[23] This is because the quantificational force of the complex NP containing the WH has been determined by the Q-element *mo* in such a way it carries the meaning of the universal quantifier.

The construal of the WH with *mo*, furthermore, is possible only when the complex NP containing the WH is construed with *mo*. Thus, if the (head of the) complex NP is associated with its own referential force by means of a definite (or deictic) determiner, the construal of the WH with *mo* is blocked.

(35)   *[$_{\bar{S}}$[$_{NP^*}$[$_{\bar{S}}$ *dare*-ga kai-ta] *sono* hon]-o yon-de-*mo*],
               who-N wrote that book-A read   Q
         omosiro-kata.
         interesting was

This is essentially the 'Specificity Condition' effect (Fiengo and Higginbotham 1981). In the following section, I will show how these characteristics follow from the analysis that assumes Move α in the derivation of LF-representations.

3. THE MOVEMENT ANALYSIS

3.1. *Movement and Unselective Binding*

Following the analysis of WH-interrogative constructions that I presented in Nishigauchi (1985), let us assume that all (non-D-linked)
WHs undergo Move α at LF. This type of movement, I assume, has
these two essential properties: (i) it is successive cyclic; and (ii) it obeys
Subjacency. Further, there is a well-formedness condition on LF, which
requires that the WH, which has been moved, be governed by a certain
class of element — in the present context, this requirement must be
somewhat generalized in such a way that the possible governors for the
WH in LF must comprise all unselective binders — not only the
interrogative *comp ka*, but also Q-elements such as *mo* and *ka*. Here,
we assume that all these elements appear in COMP, so that they govern
a WH which gets moved to SPEC of CP (=$\overline{\text{S}}$) by WH-Movement,
following Chomsky (1986).

(36)

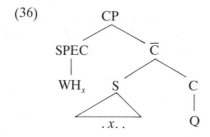

(Where Q stands for the unselective binder.) There is a further possibility that the Q-element is the head of PP which dominates $\overline{\text{S}}$. In
section 3.2, we present some evidence that a Q-element should occupy
a COMP node. Once this representation is obtained, the Q-element in
COMP governs the WH-phrase which occupies SPEC of CP — this is
the structural realization of unselective binding in our terms: the
quantificational force of the WH-phrase is thus determined by Q-element under government. If the Q-element is *mo*, the WH-phrase that it
governs is given the quantificational force of the universal quantifier. If
there is more than one WH phrase, the other WH phrase(s) will be
adjoined to the Spec node which is occupied by a previously moved
WH-phrase, where order of application is irrelevant, and they will be
governed by the same Q-element, which in turn determines their
quantificational force in unselective fashion.

This analysis extends to cases involving apparent violation of Subjacency, such as (33), which we repeat here, along the lines of analysis suggested in Nishigauchi (1985, 1986).

(33) $[_{\bar S}[_{NP}[_{\bar S}$ *dare*-ga kai-ta] hon]-o   yon-de-*mo*], boku-wa
who-N   wrote   book-A   read Q   I-T
manzoku-deki-nai.
satisfied-can-not-be

'For all *x, y, x* a person, *y* a book *x* wrote, I can not be satisfied reading *y*.'

The observation above was that the Q-element *mo* determines not only the quantificational force of the WH *dare*, but also that of the complex NP that contains it, so that both the WH and the complex NP containing it are associated with the quantificational force of *every*.

I am going to show here that this fact follows from the lines of analysis suggested in Nishigauchi (1985, 1986) for cases of WH-interrogative constructions exhibiting apparent violation of Subjacency, such as this:

(37) $[_{NP}[_{\bar S}$ *dare*-ga kai-ta] hon]-ga omosiroi-desu-*ka*?
who-N   wrote   book-N interesting-be-Q

'(A) book that who wrote is interesting?'

In the analysis that I presented in the aforementioned work, the WH *dare* that appears within the complex NP in S-structure does not move outside of that NP, for, on our assumption, WH-Movement is subject to Subjacency. The WH, instead, moves only within the relative clause. Once the WH occupies the operator position within the relative clause, the feature [wh] associated with the WH gets percolated up to the dominating S.

(38)

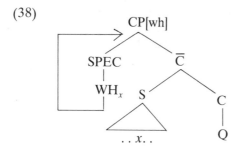

This has the effect of having $\overline{S}$ identified as [+wh]. On the assumption that a relative clause in Japanese is a Spec(ifier), the quantificational feature associated with the Spec gets percolated to the NP immediately dominating it, on condition that the head of NP is not specified with respect to referentiality. This idea would be motivated by the movement of *whose mother* as in *Whose mother do you like t?* Cf. The Condition on Analyzability due to May (1977) for a different, but perhaps more standard approach.

(39)   NP[+wh]

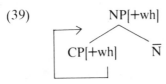

CP[+wh] $\overline{N}$

This permits the entire NP to be affected by WH-Movement. Thus, our LF-representation for (37) is something like (40).

(40) $[_{NP}[_{\overline{S}}\, dare_x[x\text{-ga kai-ta}]\, hon]_y\, y\text{-ga omosiroi-desu-}ka?$

This representation (or its derivation) involves no violation of Subjacency: movement within the complex NP does not, nor does movement of the entire complex NP. Notice that Q-element *ka* governs the complex NP that occupies the SPEC position of CP and the WH-phrase contained within it — the WH-phrase, not itself configurationally governed by Q-element, is related with the latter via percolation chain. Cf. section 1, chapter 3 of Nishigauchi (1986) for more on this notion.

We assume that the same feature, [+wh], is assigned to any occurrence of WH. So, one does not 'know' what kind of function a given WH may perform in the given environment. Further, the instance of Move α involved in the derivation of LF is the same whether it is for WH-interrogative constructions or for the type of quantificational construction we have been discussing here — it is successive cyclic, and has the effect of moving a WH to SPEC of CP. Thus, the derivation of LF for sentences like (33a) proceeds exactly the same way — the representation would look like this:

(41) $[_{NP}[[dare_x][x\text{-ga kai-ta}]]\, hon]_y\, y\text{-o yon-de}\, [_{comp}\, mo]\dots$

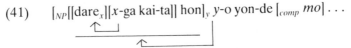

The Q-element *mo*, in this representation, governs both the complex NP and the WH-phrase contained in it — the latter, by percolation chain. If we suppose that this government relation determines the quantificational force of the WH-phrase, the fact naturally follows that the quantificational force of the WH *dare* and that of the complex NP containing it are the same — they are governed by the same Q-element and thus are assigned the same quantificational force. In what follows, I will assume this line of approach, which is essentially the same idea that I put forth in Nishigauchi (1985, 1986) for WH-questions.

In chapter 3 of Nishigauchi (1986), I argue that the Specificity Condition effect simply follows from the condition on percolation of the feature [+wh] from within the relative clause to the entire complex NP, which identifies it as [+wh] and licenses movement of the entire NP by WH-Movement. Our assumption here is that the feature associated with the head and that assigned to its Spec are both percolated up. If the head is marked as definite by means of a determiner, e.g. *sono*, as in (35), which we repeat here, the percolation procedure results in ungrammaticality.

(35) $*[_{\bar{S}}[_{NP^*}[_{\bar{S}}$ *dare*-ga kai-ta] *sono* hon]-o   yon-de *mo*],
           who-N   wrote that   book-A read   Q
       boku-wa   manzoku-deki-nai.
       I -T   satisfied-can-not

This is because, if the head of NP is marked for referentiality, the feature associated with the head is automatically percolated. In the case of (35), the feature [+def(inite)] associated with the head $\bar{N}$, due to the presence of *sono*, will be percolated to the immediately dominating NP. If the feature [+wh] associated with the Spec (=$\bar{S}$) gets also percolated, the dominating NP will end up receiving contradictory features with respect to referentiality/quantification.

(42)

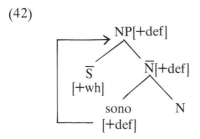

Therefore, only one of the two must climb up. One reasonable possibility is that, given a situation like this, it is only the feature assigned to the head that gets percolated up to the dominating node, following the familiar idea of the Head Feature Percolation (cf., e.g., Selkirk 1981), which insures that percolation of the feature associated with the head takes priority over percolation of the feature of a non-head. Given this, since the complex NP, NP* in (35) is now identified as definite, it cannot move by WH-Movement. The only way, then, the WH can move and get governed by the Q-element *mo* in COMP is to move out of the complex NP, which is in violation of Subjacency, and hence blocked. Thus, given the lines of analysis being developed here, there is no way (35) can be mapped to a well-formed LF-representation, which accounts for its ungrammaticality.

If a quantifier expression associated with the head of the complex NP is not incompatible with [+wh], a sentence which exhibits apparent violation of Subjacency does not result in ungrammaticality.

(43)   [*$_{NP}$[$_{\bar{S}}$ *dare*-ga eran-da] *hutatu-no* suu]-o   tasi-te-*mo*,
              who-N   chose   two   number-A added Q
        guu-suu-ni nar-a-na-katta.
        even   -D become-not-past

        'For all *x, y, x* a person, *y* a pair of numbers *x* chose, *y* did not add up to an even number.'

In (43), the head of the complex NP containing the WH *dare* contains the quantifier *hutatu-no* 'two', which is inderminate with respect to definiteness. In this case, both the [+wh] feature associated with the Spec (=$\bar{S}$) and the quantifier expression of the head jointly determine the quantificational force of the entire NP.[24] The point to be noticed about the interpretation of (43) is that the semantics of the complex NP can be characterized not as just *two numbers*, but as *every pair of numbers chosen by an individual that belongs to the relevant set*. This fact, again, would follow if we assume an LF-representation for (43), where the variable left behind by the pied-piping of the complex NP is bound by NP*, which is governed by Q-element *mo*, and also does have its own quantificational force, due to the presence of the quantifier in the determiner position, *hutatu-no* 'two'.

To recapitulate, we have shown in this section how the properties of unselective binders which show up in a certain class of Japanese quantificational expressions can be captured in the LF-representation. We have argued that all non-D-linked WHs undergo WH-Movement at LF. These elements are subject to the requirement that they must be governed by an unselective binder in LF. The unselective binders, viz. quantificational and interrogative particles, govern WH-phrases which have undergone movement to SPEC of CP at LF, thus determining the quantificational force of the given WH-variable construal relation. Further, we have seen that sentences showing apparent violations of Subjacency in this construction provide further evidence for the analysis that I presented in chapter 3 of Nishigauchi (1986) where the island which contains a given WH itself undergoes WH-Movement — a pied-piping operation. The quantificational force of both the WH-phrase and the complex NP containing it is determined by the same Q-element under government at LF.

3.2. *More Movement*

We have as yet to discuss the properties of constructions exemplified by (17b), which we repeat below.

(17) b. [$_{NP}$[$_{\bar{S}}$ *dare*-ga kai-ta] tegami] ni *mo* onazi koto ga
who N wrote letter in same thing N
kai-te-at-ta.
written be-P

'For all *x, y x* a person, *y* a letter *x* wrote, the same thing was written in *y*.'

This sentence is more or less parallel, syntactically and semantically, with sentences like the following, where one has a simple WH-expression in stead of a complex NP containing a WH-expression.

(44) [$_{NP}$ *Dono* tegami]-ni *mo* onazi koto-ga kai-te -at-ta.
which letter in Q same thing-N written-be P

'For all *x, x* a letter, the same thing was written in *x*.'

One important difference between (17b) and (44), of course, is that, in (44), the Q-element *mo* has the function of determining the quantificational force of the expression associated with the set of letters, while in (17b), *mo* determines both the set of letters and the set of people who wrote them. The parallelism between these sentences will be explored in detail later on.

Our assumption here is that the function of the Q-element *mo* in both sentences is the same. The particle *mo* in these examples, further, is playing the same semantic role as in the constructions we have observed thus far, where, syntactically, *mo* was assumed to be an element of COMP which governs S which, somewhere down below, contains a WH at S-structure. Yet, in (17), *mo* is not a COMP element in the conventional sense, for it is not in a position that governs a clausal expression. Its syntactic function, rather, is to govern a PP, *NP-ni*, forming, presumably, a larger PP. For convenience, in the discussion below, we will refer to the type of *mo* exemplified in examples like (17b) and (44) as PP-*mo*, and the kind of *mo* discussed in the previous sections as $\overline{\text{S}}$-*mo*, although our belief here is that they are seemingly distinct instantiations of the same entity.

A possible problem that arises here is, if we pursue the line of analysis that we have been developing thus far, how can we maintain the well-formedness condition on LF, which says that a [+wh] element that has been moved must end up being governed by an unselective binder, which, in all the cases considered so far, has been a COMP element immediately dominated by $\overline{\text{S}}$?

One possibility is to allow COMP to govern PP as well as S, where the Q-element occupies a position under COMP — a possibility briefly touched on in section 1. The resulting structure then would be something like this:

(45)

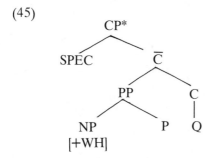

We maintain that this CP is functionally or behaviorally identical with PP in several respects. This will not be unnatural, on the assumption that COMP is a category-neutral node, in the sense that it is 'transparent' with respect to the category of the element that it immediately dominates. Thus, the lexical features of CP may be determined, not by its own head C, which is devoid of lexical features, but rather by whatever maximal projection is governed by C. In the usual case, C governs IP(=S), so that the categorial status of the entire CP is determined by the categorial properties of IP, or its head, Infl — exactly the point which is to be captured by the notion 'head-head agreement', in the sense of Chomsky (1986). In this particular case, which is perhaps a marked option permitted in Japanese, the lexical properties of CP are determined by P, so that it behaves as though it were a PP.

Given this much, we can argue that WH-Movement applies within CP in such a way that WH[+wh] is moved to SPEC of CP, as usual, so that (part of) the resulting LF-representation would look like this:

(46)

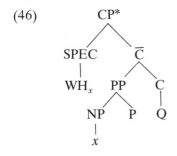

Sentence (44), along this line, would be mapped to a representation like the following in the process of LF-derivation.

(47) $[_{CP}[\text{dono tegami}]_x \; x \; \text{ni} \; [_{comp} \; mo]] \ldots$

One might wonder whether this type of WH-Movement really has theoretical motivation. Does it share the properties of other instantiations of WH-Movement, which, in all the cases we have considered so far, have had $\overline{\text{S}}$ as their domain of application? Examples like (48) indicate that it does, with respect to the locality principle.

(48)   [Dono tegami]-ni-*mo* onazi koto-ga kai-te-
          which letter   in Q   same thing-N written
          ari-masi-ta-*ka*?
          be   -P Q

          a. 'Is it the case that the same thing was written in which-
          ever letter there was?'
          b. NOT *'For which x, x a letter, the same thing was written
          also in x.'

The point here is that the construal of the WH-phrase with *mo*, the most immediate binder, is obligatory, which yields the quantifier reading as in (a), and the presence of the latter precludes the construal of the WH-phrase with the clause-final COMP *ka*, which, if possible, would result in an unacceptable reading shown in (b).[25] This would be an unexpected situation if we do not assume that the same type of movement is operative within a domain which has a structure distinct from what has been traditionally assumed, and that it is subject to the same locality condition as in more familiar cases of WH-Movement.

The analysis of sentences like the following should proceed the same way as the cases of complex QP headed by PP-*mo*, and with no additional theoretical apparatus.

(17) b. $[_{NP}[_{\bar{S}}$ *dare* ga kai-ta] tegami] ni *mo* onazi koto ga
           who N wrote letter   in Q   same thing N
      kai-te-at-ta.
      written-be-P

      'For all *x, y, x* a person, *y* a letter *x* wrote, the same thing was written in *y*.'

The only difference between this and cases like (44) (*dono tegami ni mo* . . .) is that in (17b), we have a relative clause containing a WH-expression in the position of Spec for the head N *tegami*, while in (44) there is a simple WH-Spec *dono* in the corresponding position. Thus, the LF-structure of (17b) must be parallel with sentences like (33), which we discussed in the previous section.

(33) $[_{\bar{S}}[_{NP*}[_{\bar{S}}$ *dare*-ga kai-ta] hon]-o yon-de-*mo*], boku-wa
              who-N wrote book-A read Q   I   -T
        manzoku-deki-nai.
        satisfied-can-not-be

        'For all *x, y, x* a person, *y* a book *x* wrote, I can not be satisfied reading *y*.'

The only difference here is that in (17b) we have PP-*mo*, while in (33), there is $\bar{S}$-*mo*, in the head-position of the complex QP. This parallelism is captured in the present analysis by means, again, of pied-piping and percolation at LF. That is, WH-Movement takes place so that the WH *dare* is moved only within the relative clause, in keeping with our assumption that this type of LF-movement is subject to Subjacency.

The feature [+wh] will be percolated up onto the dominating NP, which identifies the entire complex NP as [+wh], which permits it to move by WH-Movement, so that it gets adjoined to COMP governing PP. The resulting LF for (17b) would be (49).

(49) $[_{CP}[_{NP}[dare]_x[y$ ga kai-ta] tegami]$_x$ x ni $[_{comp}$ *mo*] ...

Given this representation, the Q-element *mo* governs both the complex NP and the WH contained in it. Since *mo* is, on our assumption, an unselective binder, it determines the quantificational force associated with the WH-phrase and the variable that it binds — thus, the LF (49) can be 'interpreted' as follows.

(50) For all *x, y, x* a person, *y* a letter, *x* wrote *y*, the same thing was written in *y*.

The function of *mo*, thus, corresponds to that of the operator *for all x,y* in (50), determining the quantificational force of the two variables in unselective fashion.

LF-movement that occurs within the relative clause in (17b), again, has the properties of WH-Movement. First, it is in principle unbounded.[26]

(51) $[_{NP}[_{\bar{S}}[_{\bar{S}}$ *Doko*-de kaw-ta to] Mary-ga iw-te-i-ta]
        where-at bought that   N saying-was
      omiyage]-ni-*mo* 'Made in Japan' to kai-te-ar-ta.
      gift   -on-Q   that written-was

      'For all *x, y, x* a place, *y* a souvenir-gift, Mary said she bought *y* in *x*, *y* was marked "Made in Japan".'

Second, this type of construal is subject to the locality condition. So, if there is an interrogative COMP-element intervening between a WH-expression and *mo*, the construal must hold between the WH-expression and the intervening COMP, so that it can never be construed with *mo*.

(52) $[_{NP}[_{\bar{S}}[_{\bar{S}}$ *dare*-ga kai-ta *ka*] Mary-ga siri-tagar-te-
        who-N wrote Q   N   know-want
      iru] tegami]-ni-*mo* John-ga henzi-o kai-ta.
      be letter -to-Q   N   answer-A wrote

a. 'Also to the letter such that Mary wants to know who
wrote it, John wrote a reply.'
b. NOT *'For all x, x a letter, Mary wants to know for y, y
a person, y wrote x, John wrote a reply to x.'

In (52), the WH *dare* can only be construed with the interrogative
COMP *ka*, which yields the embedded question interpretation within
the relative clause — *mo* cannot be construed with anything, since *ka*
more immediately c-commands the position of WH at S-structure, and
thus it can only be interpreted as an adverbial particle meaning 'also/
even'.

Further, we observe the same Specificity Condition effect in examples like (53) as in (35).

(53)   *[$_{PP}$[$_{NP}$[$_{\overline{S}}$ *dare*-ga kai-ta] *sono* hon]-ni-*mo* onazi-koto-
                      who-N   wrote   that   book-in-Q   same thing
        ga kai-te-ar-ta.
        N   written-was

The badness of this example, again, follows from the condition on
percolation of the feature [+wh] and pied-piping of the complex NP
containing the WH — the WH-phrase *dare* can move only within the
relative clause, and the feature [+wh] cannot climb up to the topmost
NP node, since the head of the complex NP is preceded by a definite
marker *sono*. Because of this, the entire complex NP is identified as a
definite NP, and hence the pied-piping of this NP is impossible.

4. MORE PROBLEMS

So far, we have been arguing that the Q-elements *mo* and *ka* play the
role of *unselective binders* in the sense of Heim (1982) in that they
determine the quantificational force WH-expressions which they govern
at LF.

In the following subsections, we will point out, without going into
details, further problems associated with the kinds of construction
considered in this article.

4.1. *Adverbs of Quantification*

In addition to the Q-elements in COMP, there is another class of elements which appear to share the property of unselective binders with respect to WH-expressions. These are adverbs of quantification, which designate frequency, on a par with their English counterparts, such as *seldom, usually,* which we observed in section 2.1, where we discussed Heim's analysis, in connection with their properties as unselective binders with respect to indefinite NPs.

Adverbs of quantification appear to behave in a way parallel to Q-elements in the construction involving the Q-element *mo,* as in the following.[27]

(54)　*Dare*-ga ki-te-*mo*, boku-wa *taitei*　aw-u.
　　　who-N　come -Q　I-T　　　usually　meet

This sentence can be ambiguous with respect to the interpretation of the WH-expression, which is indicated by the following translations.

(55) a.　For all *x, x* a person, if *x* comes over, I *usually* meet *x*.

　　b.　I meet *most people* who come over.

The interpretation indicated by (55a) simply derives from the properties of *mo*, a Q-element which determines the quantificational force of the WH-expression under government at LF. The adverb of quantification *taitei* designates the frequency at which I meet each guest. What is novel to us is the interpretation (55b). Here, the quantificational meaning of the WH-expression appears to be determined not so much by the Q-element *mo* but by the adverb *taitei*, so that the resulting semantics of the sentence is such that its WH-phrase consitutes (part of) the quantifier expression *most*.

The picture that emerges from the observations is that the properties of the Q-element *mo* is parallel with those of *if* in Heim's analysis of indefinite NPs — they both have the ability to determine the quantificational force of the indefinite NPs/WH-expressions under certain structural relations,[28] but if there is another element which has the ability as unselective binder in the same domain, the latter is allowed to 'override' the effect of the binding force of *mo/if*. That is, unselective binding by *mo/if* is a 'default' case of the process under consideration. More detailed discussion of this phenomenon is found in chapter 4, section 4 of Nishigauchi (1986).

4.2. *Donkey Sentences in Japanese?*

Given our understnading of Weak Crossover (WCO) phenomena (cf. Saito and Hoji 1983), which states roughly that the trace of the operator expression must c-command the pronominal that purports to be coindexed with it, the high acceptability of the binding relation in sentences like the following is in striking contrast to the status of (57).

(56) [*Dono* hon$_i$-o kaw-te-*mo*] Mary-wa kanarazu e$_i$ yon-da.
      wh   book A buy   -Q   T   w/o fail   read-P

'For all *x, y, x* a book, when Mary bought *x*, Mary read *x* without fail.'

(57) ??[Dono hon$_i$-o   moraw-ta toki-ni] Mary-wa e$_i$ yom-i-
      which book A received   time-at   T   read-
      masi-ta-ka?
      past   Q

'When receiving which book$_i$ did Mary read it$_i$?'

If it is the structural relation between the positions of the variable bound by WH at LF and pro that is relevant, there is no difference in this respect between (56) and (57) — in neither of these examples does the former c-command the latter. Thus, Ban on WCO predicts that both (56)–(57) must disallow the binding of pro. Why, then, is the binding in (56) good?

We argue, in chapter 6 of Nishigauchi (1986), that the pronominal in (56) has the properties of *Donkey*-pronouns, exemplified by the occurrence of pronoun *it* as in the following.

(58) Every man who owns [a donkey]$_i$ likes it$_i$.

This type of binding relation requires that the pronoun must appear within the scope of the quantifier phrase which contains its antecedent indefinite NP. Thus, we cannot have a *donkey*-pronoun in sentences like (59), because the scope of the quantifier *everyone* does not extend across a sentence-boundary.

(59) *Everyone who owns a donkey$_i$ came, and Mary bought it$_i$.
      [= Haïk's (56).]

Haïk (1984) captures this by invoking the notion *indirect binding*: if the value of an indefinite NP is dependent on a quantifier, a pronoun bound by that indefinite NP is *indirectly bound* by that wide-scope quantifier. Indirect binding requires that the wide-scope quantifier c-command the pronoun to be bound by the indefinite NP. Thus, the absence of the binding relation in (59) is attributed to the failure of the wide-scope quantifier to c-command the pronoun.

In chapter 6 of Nishigauchi (1986), we discuss the problems raised by sentences like (56) in terms of the mechanism of Indirect Binding and the restrictions that must be imposed on it. The idea is that the domain that is headed by the Q-element indirectly binds both the WH phrase governed by that Q-element and the pronominal. Since the coindexing relation in (56) is mediated by the relation of indirect binding, it is a natural consequence that the c-command relation between the WH phrase itself and the pronominal in (56) is not of material relevance — it is rather the c-command relation between the domain that contains the WH-phrase and the pronominal that really matters.

5. CONCLUDING REMARKS

As early as 1965, S.-Y. Kuroda expounded the following statement in reference to the nature of WH-expressions.

It can be said that the role of the indeterminate pronouns [is] very much like that of yet unbound logical variables. (1965, 101)

The present paper has been an attempt to incorporate this remarkable insight into the theory of LF-representations. Kuroda's claim is justified in light of our observations (which confirm Kuroda's, though in a slightly different way) that WH-expressions are not to be simply identified as 'interrogative pronouns' — WH-phrases in interrogative sentences have been shown to have the quantificational force of the existential quantifier (cf. Karttunen 1977). We have seen here that the quantificational force of a WH-expression is not identifiable until we look at a larger syntactic domain where we find some quantificational element which has the property of determining the quantificational force of that WH-expression. In this sense, WH-phrases are free variables in the logical representation. In particular, we have observed here that a class of items which we refer to as Q-elements, such as *mo* and *ka*, exhibit the important property in question. These elements show the behavior of *unselective binders* in Heim's (1982) sense. The restrictions on this type of binding are stated in terms of the syntactic notion of government — a Q-element must govern a WH-phrase in order for the former to dictate the latter's quantificational meaning — and locality principles, which would be subsumed under Subjacency. The level of representations where the relevant restrictions on the process in question are stated is the syntactic level of LF. Further consequences of this line of approach are discussed in Nishigauchi (1986).

ACKNOWLEDGMENTS

This paper derives from chapter 4 and part of chapter 6 of Nishigauchi (1986). I would like to thank Emmon Bach, Roger Higgins, Hajime Hoji, Kiyoshi Kurata, Yukinori Takubo, and especially Nobuko Hasegawa, Susumu Kuno, Barbara Partee, David Pesetsky, and Edwin Williams for comments and discussion.

NOTES

[1] The attitude represented by Kuroda's terminology, which carefully avoids identifying WH's as 'interrogative pronominals' appears to be widespread among the traditional Japanese grammarians. Cf. Onoe (1983), for example.

[2] The following abbreviations will be employed in the glosses: A: accusative; D: dative; G: genitive; N: nominative; P: past; Q: 'Q-element'; T: topic.

[3] See Kuroda (1965, 91—102) for this insight. We will turn to this in the final section.

[4] The particle *ka* has at least two other, obviously related uses: (i) as an interrogative marker, which, categorically, has been standardly identified as a Comp element in such work as Nishigauchi (1986), though Fukui (1986) has an alternative view; and (ii) as a disjunctive connective: *A ka B (ka)* '(either) A or B'. The other Q-element *mo* has also at least two other important uses: first, it may be used as a conjunctive connective: *A mo B mo* '(both) A and B', from which, presumably, derives the adverbial use which may be associated with *also*:

(i)   John *mo*   ki-ta.
                 also   came

          '(In addition to other persons,) John also came.'

The other use of *mo* is as a clause-connective element which heads a concessive clause 'even if . . .'.

(ii)   John ga ki-te-mo, . . .
                 N   come even-if

          'Even if John comes, . . .'

[5] Previous work that discusses constructions exemplified by (3a—d) includes Kuroda (1965), Ohno (1984), Hoji (1985).

[6] Throughout this paper, I use the quantifier *all* in the gloss of a sentence involving WH . . . *mo*. The idea is simply that the quantificational force carried by this type of construction is that of a universal quantifier. In section 1.2, we will present some arguments that the quantificational force of the non-negative WH . . . *mo* should be characterized as being the Japanese counterpart of *every* in English.

[7] In addition to case-marking, it has been noticed, by Kato (1985) among others, that the negative and non-negative uses of WH . . . *mo* differ with respect to accent: with the non-negative use, an accent or pitch contour falls on the first mora of the WH-expression, while with the negative use there is no accent on the WH, so that it is pronounced flat high.

(i)   D̅a̅r̅e̅-ni-mo awa-nakat-ta. 'I didn't see anybody.'

(ii)   D̅are-mo-ni at-ta. 'I met everybody.'

[8] Sentence (7b) may be all right if the speaker has a specific set of people in mind who are always standing on Pleasant St., but he does not know who, among those people, wrote to him. In this latter sense, the reference here is still strongly non-specific.

[9] Again there is complication connected with case-marking. The nominative form, in which, again, the case-marker *ga* does not show up on surface, and the accusative form, where the case-marker *o* does appear, are almost extinct in present-day colloquial Japanese. These did (and still do?) exist in archaic style.

(i)   Tare(=dare)-φ-ka kokyoo-o   omow-a-zaru.
           who (nom)   home-land-acc love   not

           'Who should not miss his homeland?' =
           'Anybody should miss his homeland.'

[10] The form exemplified by (11) can be found in the classical literature: the opening chapter of *The Tales of Genji*, the novel of the eleventh century starts as follows:

(i)   Idure-no o-on-toki-ni-ka, . . .
           which's   time-in-Q

           'Lit. In some emperor's time (but I don't remember which emperor), . . .'

[11] Kuroda considers the non-negative use of the latter sequence as in (4) as being derived from a structure which involves *demo*. Given the body of discussion in this section, his factual judgments on this matter must be refuted.

[12] This, in fact, involves the nominative case marker in the position between the WH and *demo*, which is unrealized on the surface: *dare-o-demo. This is essentially the same process as that touched on in note 9.

[13] In fact, the concessive clause headed by *no matter*, as in (i), would be the real English counterpart of the concessive clause in (17a).

(i)   No matter who$_i$ comes in, I will kiss him$_i$.

Detailed discussion of this type of sentence will be found in chapter 5 of Nishigauchi (1986).

[14] This type of pronominal coindexing appears to be possible intrasententially, as in:

(i)   [*Dono sakana$_i$-o* kaw-te-mo] *sore$_i$-o* mise-te kudasai.
        which fish   -A buy   Q   it   -A show   please

        'For all x, x a fish, if you buy x, please show x to me.'

We will have more to say on this problem in section 4, and, at greater length, in chapter 6 of Nishigauchi (1986).

[15] The pronominal coindexing in the following discourse, suggested to me by Susumu Kuno appears to be relatively acceptable.

(i)   [Dono ronbun$_i$-ga erab-are te mo] manzoku-desu.
        which paper -N chosen   Q   satisfied -be
        Boku-wa, *sore$_i$-o* boku-ga hensyuu-si-te-iru zassi-   ni
        I   -T it   -A I   -N edit   do be   journal in
        nose-ru tumori-desu.
        put   intend -be

        'For all x, x a paper, I will be satisfied if x is accepted. I will put *it* in the journal for which I am an editor.'

This will be due to at least two reasons: one is that some kind of modal force of the concessive clause in the first conjunct extends across the sentence boundary, a process analogous to 'modal subordination', discussed by Jackendoff (1972) and Roberts (1985). The other reason has to do with the semantic nature of the main clause predicate. With a predicate which suggests arbitrariness in the main clause, such as *manzoku-desu* 'I'm satisfied', *kamai-masen* 'I don't care', the WH phrase in the concessive clause appears to be interpretable as free choice *any*. If this second point is correct, the claim in the text may have to be a little weakened, so that we must allow for structural ambiguity for constructions under consideration — one possible source structure for concessive clauses with WH phrases might involve *demo* attached to a clause, as in (18). This latter possibility has been suggested to me by Susumu Kuno and Nobuko Hasegawa, independently.

[16] In fact, Heim argues that *if* induces the necessity operator, which has the characteristics of the unselective binder, which determines the quantificational force of indefinite NPs as the universal quantifier. Therefore, even without the adverb of quantification *always*, the representation (24) is mapped to the representation (26), indicated below.

[17] Heim assumes an operation that has the property of raising a quantificational expression in such a way that it c-commands everything that it has in its scope, in the process of deriving a logical representation. Adverbs of quantification, such as *always*, are also subject to this rule, and are allowed to take maximal scope, as in (25).

[18] Notice that Heim does assume an operation which is essentially analogous to OR for quantificational expressions other than indefinites.

[19] Pesetsky (1987) draws an important distinction for the functions of WH-expressions with respect to whether they are D (discourse)-linked, that is, their value is restricted in the discourse-domain, or non-D-linked, that is, there is no such discourse-oriented restriction with respect to the possible value for the WH-operator.

[20] See note 4.

[21] This distinction in terms of the interrogative marker, though, appears to be independent of the D-/non-D-linked interpretation. That is to say, there WH questions ending in *no ka* which are not D-linked. Cf. Kuno and Masunaga (1985).

[22] In English, the construal of WH-in-situ, viz. WH-Movement or WH-indexing at LF, is generally supposed to be free from Subjacency, in particular, the WH-Island effects (cf. Chomsky (1981) etc.). Thus, examples (i)—(ii) below, originally due to Baker (1970), are assumed to be ambiguous with respect to the scope of *what/which book* in the embedded clause — they could either be construed as having the complement clause or the entire clause in their respective scope. However, Pesetsky (p.c.; also Pesetsky (1987, note 12)) observes that many speakers of English find it easier to perceive the ambiguity in (i) than in (ii).

(i)   Who remembers where Mary bought which book?

(ii)   Who remembers where Mary bought what?

This is because *which book* tends to be more easily interpreted as a D-linked expression, which presumably is a factor that allows it to take scope over the entire clause, in violation of the WH-Island effect. If this is correct, we may be able to make a rather strong claim here, on the assumption that non-D-linking is effected by Move α while D-linking is yielded by coindexing without movement at LF — WH-Movement, whether at Syntax or at LF, is subject to Subjacency (the WH-Island effect), while coindexing without movement is not. This, again, points at the same direction as the status of the WH-Island effect in Japanese.

[23] N. Hasegawa (p.c.) observes that the latter scope interaction is more prevalent.

[24] In Nishigauchi (1985) I claimed that the [+wh] feature of Spec may be percolated only when the head is unspecified with respect to reference/quantification. This gives rise to a wrong result in cases like (43), for, here we would predict that only the feature of the head can percolate up, the [+wh] feature of Spec playing no role.

[25] Recall that *mo*, when it governs a non-WH-expression, serves as an adverbial particle, meaning *also* — *John-ni-mo* 'also to John'. Cf. note 4.

[26] Word order may be playing a role here: this type of constructions sounds a little awkward if the WH-expression does not appear in the initial position within the relative clause: thus (i) sounds a little worse than (51).

(i)   ?[[Mary-ga [doko-de kaw-ta to] iw-ta] omiyage]-ni-mo . . .

This does not seem to be restricted to complex NPs involving complement clauses — in complex NPs with a simplex clause, there appears to be a hierarchy of acceptability having to do with word order: if the WH-phrase is a non-subject, it still opts for the initial position in the relative clause, so that (iii) is a little better than (ii):

(ii)   [[Mary-ga doko-de kaw-ta] omiyage]-ni-mo . . .
        N   where-at bought gift   on-Q

        'For all x, y, x a place, y a gift, Mary bought y in x, . . .'

(iii)   [[Doko-de Mary-ga kaw-ta] omiyage]-ni-mo, . . .

The sentence is further improved if the subject of the relative clause is 'deleted' — or, is replaced with a pragmatically controlled *pro*. Thus, (iv) is even better than (iii).

(iv)   [[Doko-de kaw-ta] omiyage]-ni-mo, . . .

For more discussion on this, cf. Hoji (1985).
[27] I am much indebted to David Pesetsky for 'soliciting' examples like (54) and the line of consideration represented here.
[28] See note 16.

REFERENCES

Baker, C.L.: 1970, 'Notes on the description of English Questions: The Role of an Abstract Question Morpheme', *Foundations of Language* **6**, 197—219.

Chomsky, N.: 1981, *Lectures on Government and Binding*. Foris, Dordrecht.

Chomsky, N.: 1986, *Barriers*. Linguistic Inquiry Monograph. MIT Press, Cambridge, MA.

Fiengo, R. and Higginbotham, J.: 1981, 'Opacity in NP', *Linguistic Analyisis* **7**, 395—421.

Fukui, N.: 1986, *A Theory of Category Projection and its Applications*. Doctoral dissertation, MIT, Cambridge, MA.

Haïk, I.: 1984, 'Indirect Binding', *Linguistic Inquiry* **15**, 185—223.

Harada, K.: 1971, 'Constraints on WH-Q Binding', *Descriptive and Applied Linguistics* **5**, 180—206, ICU, Tokyo.

Hasegawa, N.: 1986, 'More Arguments for the Pied-Piping Analysis of WH-Questions in Japanese', *University of Massachusetts Occasional Papers in Linguistics* **11**.

Heim, I.: 1982, *The Semantics of Definite and Indefinite Noun Phrases*. Doctoral dissertation. University of Massachusetts, Amherst.

Hoji, H.: 1985, *Logical Form Constraints and Configurational Structures in Japanese*. Doctoral dissertation, University of Washington.

Hornstein, N.: 1984, *Logic as Grammar*. MIT Press, Cambridge, MA.

Huang, C.-T. J.: 1982, *Logical Relations in Chinese and the Theory of Grammar*. Doctoral dissertation, MIT, Cambridge, MA.

Jackendoff, R.: 1972, *Semantic Interpretation in Generative Grammar*. MIT Press, Cambridge, MA.

Karttunen, L.: 1977, 'Syntax and Semantics of Questions', *Linguistics and Philosophy* **1**, 3—44.

Kato, Y.: 1985, *Negative Sentences in Japanese*. Doctoral dissertation. Sophia University, Tokyo.

Kuno, S.: 1982, 'The Focus of the Question and the Focus of the Answer.' *CLS: Papers from the Parasession on Nondeclaratives*. University of Chicago, Chicago.

Kuno, S. and Masunaga, K.: 1986, 'Questions with WH-phrases in Islands,' *University of Massachusetts Occasional Papers in Linguistics* **11**.

Kuroda, S.-Y.: 1965, *Generative Grammatical Studies in the Japanese Language*. Doctoral dissertation, MIT, Cambridge, MA.

Lewis, D.: 1976, 'Adverbs of Quantification', in: E. Keenan (ed.), *Formal Semantics of Natural Language*. Cambridge University Press.

May, R.: 1977, *The Grammar of Quantification*. Doctoral dissertation, MIT, Cambridge, MA.

May, R.: 1985, *Logical Form: Its Structure and Derivation*. The MIT Press, Cambridge, MA.

Nishigauchi, T.: 1985, Japanese LF: Subjacency vs. ECP', *Seoul Papers in Formal Grammar Theory*, 71—105. Hanshin, Seoul.

Nishigauchi, T.: 1986, *Quantification in Syntax*. Doctoral dissertation, University of Massachusetts, Amherst.

Ohno, Y.: 1984, *On the Form and Function of the Quantifier Rule*. B.A. thesis, Sophia University. Tokyo.

Onoe, K.: 1983, 'Futeigo no gosei to yoohoo. [The nature and use of the indeterminate.]' *Fukuyoo-go no Kenkyuu. [Studies on Adverbials.]* in: M. Watanabe (ed.,) Meiji Shoin, Tokyo.

Pesetsky, D.: 1987, 'WH-in-situ: Movement and Unselective Binding ', *The Representation of (In)definiteness*, in: EJ. Reuland and A. ter Meulen (eds.), MIT Press, Cambridge, MA.

Riemsdijk, H.: 1978, *A Case Study in Syntactic Markedness*. Foris, Dordrecht.

Roberts, C.: 1985, 'Modal Subordination and Pronominal Anaphora', Ms. University of Massachusetts.

Saito, M. and Hoji, H.: 1983, 'Weak Crossover and Move α in Japanese', *Natural Language and Linguistic Theory* **1.2**.

Selkirk, E.: 1981, *The Syntac of Words*. The MIT Press, Cambridge, MA.

Vendler, Z.: 1967, *Linguistics in Philosophy*. Cornell University Press, Ithaca.

Williams, E.: 1984, 'A Reassignment of the Functions of LF', *Linguistic Inquiry* **17.2**.

MARGARITA SUÑER

TWO PROPERTIES OF CLITICS IN CLITIC-DOUBLED CONSTRUCTIONS[1]

One of the well-known facts about Spanish is that it permits object clitic-doubling (CL-D). CL-D is the process by which an object clitic (CL) enters into a chain with a lexical constituent in argument position, thus forming a discontinuous element (Borer 1984). Both parts of the CL-chain must match in the relevant features (Suñer 1986a). Spanish CLs may double indirect objects (IOs) and direct objects (DOs). In all dialects, IO-D is quite free in the sense that the features of the doubled constituent do not appear to interact crucially with the doubling process; consequently, doubling takes places irrespective of the features for animacy, specificity and/or definiteness of the IO phrase (1).

(1) a.   *Le* di agua . . .
       lsg to-3sg gave water . . .
       (i)   . . . a un/al vagabundo.   [+spec +anim ± def]
            to a/to the bum
       (ii)   . . . a una/a la planta.   [+spec −anim ± def]
            to a/to the plant

    b.   No *le* hablé a nadie.   [−spec +anim −def]
        lsg no to-3sg talked to nobody 'I didn't speak with anybody.'

    c.   *Les* dejaré todo mi dinero a los pobres.   [−spec +anim +def]
        I to-them will-leave all my money to the poor

In contrast, DO-D is far more restricted. Although no dialect seems to be completely free of DO CL-D, the process is widespread in a few. The main data from this study comes from Porteñro Spanish, the dialect spoken in the city of Buenos Aires and surrounding area. In this region, the DO CL-chain must obey a specificity requirement; thus, the doubled argument must be positively marked as specific in addition to animate (2).[2]

(2) a.   *La* vi a . . .
      lsg her saw . . .
      (i)   . . . la niña/la gata.   [+spec +anim +def]
         . . . the girl/the cat(f).
      (ii) . . . una mujer que vendía cobras.   [+spec +anim −def]
         . . . a woman who was-selling (indicative) copperheads.

    b.   Nunca (**lo*) conocí a alguien que fuera domador de fieras.
        [−spec +anim −def][3]

       'I never him met anybody who was (subjunctive) a wild-animal trainer.'

    c.   (**La*) buscaban (a) una mujer que vendiera cobras.
        [−spec +anim −def]

       'They her were-looking for a woman who sold (subjunctive) copperheads.'

The objective of this essay is to argue that clitics (CLs) in clitic-doubled (CL-D) constructions serve to circumvent effects which would other-wise render sentences ungrammatical. They achieve this end in two slightly different ways. On the one hand, Spanish CLs have the property of serving as antecedent-governors, which means that CLs save struc-tures that would be in violation of the Empty Category Principle (ECP) in the syntax proper (section 1.1). This behavior is in contrast to what happens at the level of Logical Form (LF) where CLs appear to be irrelevant to the well-formedness of the sentences where Quantifier Raising has applied (section 1.2). Nevertheless, CLs interact with LF phenomena in another way. By forming a pronominal chain with the element in argument position they are coindexed with, CLs help surmount Weak Crossover effects (section 2.1) and Principle C type violations (section 2.2). Crucially, the evidence about CL-D in (1) and (2) argues against analyzing these properties of CLs as a consequence of the resumptive pronoun strategy.

1. CLS AS ANTECEDENT-GOVERNORS

1.1. *Syntax*

It has been widely noticed that short (3a) and long (3b) extraction of CL-D IOs renders sentences grammatical (Jaeggli 1982, among others).

(3) a. ¿A quién$_3$ le^3 dieron *los jueces* el premio e_3?[4]

    'To whom did the judges to-him/her give the prize?'

  b. ¿A quién$_3$ te dijeron *pro* que le^3 habían dado *los jueces* el premio e_3?

    'To whom did they tell you that the judges to-him/her had given the prize *e*?'

Taking into account the fact that WH-movement leaves an empty category (*ec*) in argument position, and that this *ec* forms a chain with a CL, it must be established what features e_3 has. Is e_3 a [−pronominal, −anaphoric] trace, or is it a [+pronominal, −anaphoric] one? Note that this decision impinges on what principle of Binding Theory interacts with the *ec*, and on whether the ECP is relevant in instances of extraction from CL-D constructions. Considering that non-reflexive CL-chains are pronominal in Spanish (cf., Suñer 1986a), I will assume that a CL always licenses a pronominal *ec*; this pronominal is bound by the quantifier-like expression in pre-IP position in examples like (3). Consequently, e_3 falls under Principle B of BT, which is trivially satisfied since the *ec* is argument free in its governing category.

The derivation of (3) proceeds as follows. The WH-phrase first adjoins to VP (to void the VP barrier), to then land in the Spec of Comp. WH-movement causes the verb as well as any CLs which appear with it, to front in main and embedded clauses,[5] (Torrego 1984) as demonstrated by the postverbal positioning of the subjects (in italics). Moreover, the CL antecedent-governs e_3 by governing the trace of the WH-phrase adjoined to VP which in turn governs the *ec* left in argument position.[6] Schematically, the indexing of the links of the chain are as in (4).

(4) $[_{CP}$ WH$_3$ CL$_3^3$ + V $[_{IP}$ subject $[_{I'}$ t$'_V$ [VP e_3 $[_{VP}$ t$_V$ DO $e_3^3]]]]]$

What is crucial to our aim, though, is that IOs can be long WH-moved out of indirect questions (i.e. out of a WH-island) where V-fronting has applied, despite the claim that once V-fronting has operated, the V no longer governs a VP-internal trace (Torrego 1984).

(5)   ¿A quién$_3$ no sabías pro [qué diccionario$_2$ le^3 había devuelto $[_S$ Celia $[_{VP}$ t$_V$ e_2 e_3?]]]

    'To whom didn't you know which dictionary Celia to-her had returned?'

In (5) the DO e_2 is antecedent-governed by the WH-phrase in the internal COMP (henceforth, I omit reference to VP-adjoined traces unless it becomes crucial to the argumentation); however, the IO e_3 cannot be properly governed by its antecedent since this antecedent is in the matrix COMP and separated from its trace by a filled lower COMP. Nevertheless, the sentence is grammatical because the IO-CL *le* forms a chain with e_3. In other words, the presence of the CL serves to anchor the IO trace.[7] Note that when the IO-CL is omitted, the sentence is ill-formed for most speakers (6).

(6)   ?*¿A quién no sabías qué diccionario había devuelto Celia?

This is because in the absence of a corresponding CL, the *ec* left by WH-movement of the indirect object is [−pronominal]. Hence, the ECP, which requires that all nonpronominal traces be properly governed, is violated because neither antecedent government, nor lexical government obtains in (6).

Parallel evidence with DOs can be tested only in those dialects where DO CL-D is common. Contrary to what has been claimed (Jaeggli 1982; Aoun 1981; Borer 1984), WH-extraction of the doubled element is permitted if the CL and the doubled phrase match in features (cf. Suñer 1986a); that is, if they coincide in the features [+spec +anim], the same features needed for plain doubling to take place, cf. (2). The examples in (7) are grammatical because of the specificity given to the WH-phrase by the lexical partitives (in bold), which cause the quantifier to range over a definite set/group.

(7) a.   ¿A cuántos de **los generales** *los* condecoraron?

'How many of the generals did they them (m) decorate?'

b.   ¿A cuáles de **ellas** *las* reconocieron?

'Which of them did they them (f) recognize?'

On the assumption that (8) (=Torrego's (47b)) is ungrammatical because the trace of the long-extracted DO is not properly governed, the prediction is that a CL-D dialect should be able to rescue the same type of structure provided the matching of features is complied with. This is exactly what happens in (9).

(8)   *¿Qué diccionario no sabías a quién había devuelto Celia?

Which dictionary didn't you know to whom Celia had returned?'

(9)   ¿[A cuántos de los niños]$_2$ no sabían [a qué familia]$_3$ (se^3) los^2 había encomendado el director del orfanato t_V t_2 t_3?

'How many of the children didn't they know to what family the director of the orphanage had entrusted?'

This rescuing trait that CLs have becomes more interesting when one notices that even speakers of non-DO-D dialects (such as Caribbean and Madridian) may resort to this strategy to surmount the effects of what would otherwise be an illegal trace. Some of the tested examples are found in (10).

(10) a. ¿Qué libro$_2$ me dijiste que quién lo^2 había escrito?
        what book to-me told (you) that who it (acc) had written?

        'What book did you tell me (that) who had written?'

   b. ¿Qué libro$_2$ no recuerdas (tú) dónde lo^2 había puesto Ana?

      'What book don't you remember where Ana had put (it)?'

   c. ¿Qué libro$_2$ no sabías a quién (se) lo^2 había regalado Bri el sábado?

      'What book didn't you know to whom Bri had given (it to-him/her) on Saturday?'

Worthy of note is that the DO-phrase *qué libro* 'which book' does not fulfill the Porteño dialect specificity requirement for DO-D. Nevertheless, Porteño speakers judged the sentences as grammatical. What this seems to indicate is that the anchoring properties of CLs extend beyond the confines of the dialects where DO-D is widely accepted. Critically, if resumptive elements are strictly defined as those which materialize in cases in which no movement can occur (because of syntactic islands, for example), then the DO-CLs in (10) cannot be claimed to be resumptive. Note that the positioning of the WH-phrases and V-fronting strongly argue for movement in (10), that is to say, the sentences illustrate instances of syntactic binding (Zaenen *et al.* 1981).

In sum, CLs provide Spanish with a device to rescue structures that would otherwise be in violation of the ECP. This happens as a consequence of the CLs entering into a relation of proper government with the other subpart (the element in argument position) of the CL-chain, relationship which is mediated through the intermediate VP-adjoined trace. Therefore, in the context of syntactic WH-movement, CLs provide an example where proper government is reduced to antecedent government.

1.2. *LF*

In contrast to the anchoring properties of CLs in the syntax proper, CLs do not appear to interact in any major way with scope facts and that instance of Move-α known as Quantifier Raising (QR).

The dissimilar scope patterns exhibited by direct and indirect CL-chains are exemplified in (11) and (12) respectively. To be noted is that while CL-D DOs receive only a wide scope reading (11), CL-D IOs are ambiguous between wide and narrow scope (12).[8]

(11) a. Todos los electores *los* eligieron a [algunos de los candidatos].
       Every voter them voted for some of the candidates.

   b. $\exists y, y$ a candidate, $\forall x, x$ a voter (x voted for y)

(12) a. Todos los candidatos *les* han dicho la verdad a [algunos electores].
       Every candidate to-them had told the truth to some voters.

   b. $\forall x, x$ a candidate, $\exists y, y$ a voter (x has told the truth to y)

   c. $\exists y, y$ a voter, $\forall x, x$ a candidate (x has told the truth to y)

According to the wide scope interpretation of the indefinite quantifier, (11) means that every voter voted for the same set of candidates and (12) means that every candidate told the truth to the same set of voters. In other words, the non-subject quantifier in each instance is interpreted as specific. This agrees with the dictum that specificity entails wide scope interpretation. But why is it that only CL-D IOs are ambiguous? The answer is straightforward; it directly correlates with the doubling peculiarites of each type of CL (cf. (1) and (2)). Since

DO-D is successful only when the CL and the doubled phrase match with respect to specificity and animacy, it follows that the quantified DO in (11) can only be interpreted has having scope over the quantified subject. Crucially, if the DO is not CL-D, then a quantified phrase in this position is ambiguous (13).

(13) a. Todos los electores eligieron a [algunos de los candidatos].
Every voter voted for some of the candidates.

b. $\forall x$, x a voter, $\exists y$, y a candidate (x voted for y) (=narrow scope)

c. $\exists y$, y a candidate, $\forall x$, x a voter (x voted for y) (=wide scope)

On the other hand, since IO-D takes place irrespective of the features [± animate, ± specific] of the IO phrase, specificity is not a condition on IO-D, therefore, the IO CL-chain is free to receive both types of scope interpretations.

Now that the semantics of the sentences in (11) and (12) is clear, one can look at the syntax of this type of sentences to establish whether their constituent structure after QR has operated helps in explaining the disparate CL patterning. In order to do this, I assume the treatment of QR as found in May (1985) and in Chomsky (1986) in which quantifiers are adjoined to the S (=IP) node. The scope of any quantifier coincides with its LF c-command domain.

Let us start with the LF syntax of CL-D IOs. The LF-representation should give us the solution to the problem of ambiguities due to multiple quantification. Working still with the sentence in (12), the wide scope interpretation is captured by the LF representation in (14).

(14) $[_{IP}$ a algunos electores$_3$ $[_{IP}$ todos los candidatos$_1$ $[_{IP}$ e_1 $[_{VP}$
             to some voters   every candidate e
        les^3 han dicho la verdad $e_3]]]]]$
        to-them has told the truth e

In (14) both QPs have been adjoined to IP. The subject *todos los candidatos* properly governs the subject trace e_1. The IO quantified phrase adjoins to IP over the already adjoined subject. But is e_3 a licit trace? On the assumption that an object is always lexically governed by its head (theta-governed in Chomsky's 1986 terms), the IO trace is legitimate from the start. Recall that the CL provides the *ec* with pronominal features, therefore, the pronominal trace only needs to be argument free, which it is. Hence, (14) is a well-formed structure.

An important difference between (14) and the example in (5) with WH-movement, is that in the latter V-fronting precludes theta-government; therefore, antecedent government must obtain. This last observation results in an interesting prediction. Since a verb which remains in place always theta-governs its complements, one should be able to interpret the IO as having wider scope than the subject QP even when it is not CL-D. This prediction is borne out. Example (15) without the *les* 'to-them' may still be understood as meaning that every candidate told the truth to the same set of voters.

(15)   Todos los candidatos han dicho la verdad a algunos electores.

       Every candidate has told the truth to some voters.

However, if proper government were to be equated with antecedent government, then the IO QP in both (14) and (15) would first need to adjoin to VP (to overcome VP barrierhood) before adjoining to IP, as illustrated in (16) for (15).[9]

(16) $[_{IP}$ a algunos electores$_3$ $[_{IP}$ todos los candidatos$_1$ $[_{IP}$ e_1 $[_{VP}$ e_3
         to some voters   every candidate   *e*   *e*
      $[_{VP}$ han dicho la verdad $e_3]]]]]]$
        has told   the truth$_e$

How is the narrow scope interpretation of (14) represented at LF? In this instance, there are two possibilities. By the Scope Principle (May 1985 34), (14) would yield this interpretation also. The Scope Principle maintains that whenever two quantifiers c-command each other (note that in (14) no X^{max} intervenes between two), they have the same absolute c-command domain and hence the same absolute scope. Consequently, they are free to take on any type of relative scope in relation to one another (or be independent of each other). The second possibility for the narrow scope reading is VP-adjunction of the IO QP, as in (17).

(17) $[_{IP}$ todos los candidatos$_1$ $[_{IP}$ e_1 $[_{VP}$ a algunos electores$_3$ $[_{VP}$
        every candidate   *e* to some voters
      les^3 han dicho la verdad $e_3]]]]$
      to-them has told   the truth e

Worth noticing is that the scope of a phrase in this position is that of the minimal maximal projection that dominates it — IP (=S) for Chomsky (1986), S' for May (1985) — because the VP-adjoined QP is dominated by just one segment of VP.[10] In this way, its scope is narrower than that of a phrase adjoined to IP or to CP, exactly the result desired for (17).

At this time, I see no principled way to decide whether the narrow scope interpretation should be represented as in (14) with the indefinite QP adjoined to IP, or as in (17) with the QP adjoined to VP.

Let us now move on to DOs. The LF structure for (11) with wide scope reading of the DO is found in (18).

(18) $[_{IP}$ algunos de los candidatos$_2$ $[_{IP}$ todos los electores$_1$
            some of the candidates   every voter
        $[_{IP}$ e_1 los^2 eligieron $e_2]]]$
            e them   voted for e

The reasoning for the well-formedness of (18) is parallel to the one in (14). The subject e_1 is antecedent governed by the subject QP, and the DO trace is theta-governed by the verb. Could this structure also represent narrow scope interpretation? The answer is negative. Even though both QPs are in a relationship that satisfies the Scope Principle, another factor comes into play in this case: DO chains are [+specific] by nature. This condition, which requires that the DO QP take the broader scope, effectively constrains the possibility of interpreting the quantifiers as if they were in the reverse order. As a matter of fact, since DO CL-D bars a narrow scope interpretation of a DO QP, for a narrow scope reading to obtain the CL must not be present. One way to capture this narrow scope interpretation is by VP-adjoining the DO QP as in (19).

(19) $[_{IP}$ todos los electores$_1$ $[_{IP}$ e_1 $[_{VP}$ algunos de los candidatos$_2$
            every voter   e   some of the candidates
        $[_{VP}$ eligieron $e_2]]]]$
            voted for e

This representation unambiguously indicates that the scope of the DO QP is narrower than that of the subject QP. Note that the same specificity requirement on DO CL-D which prevents the Scope Principle to assign narrow scope to *algunos de los candidatos* in (18), precludes a representation with *los eligieron* instead of *eligieron* in (19).

A second possibility is to have the exact parallel of (18) *minus* the clitic. This structure would meet the conditions for the Scope Principle to apply and the QPs would be able to commute; consequently, one of the readings will be the one in which the DO has narrow scope.

Given the assumption that the verb stays in place when Move-α adjoins QPs to IP, the objects are always lexically governed by their head. This is the crucial difference between Move-α applying by S-structure with its concomitant Verb fronting consequence (section 1.1), and Move-α operating at LF. Only in the former are the anchoring properties of CLs appealed to because antecedent government must obtain for the structure to be grammatical. Furthermore, even if proper government were reduced to antecedent government, intermediate VP-adjunction of the relevant QP would be needed irrespective of the presence or absence of the CL, fact which further confirms the disparate behavior of CLs in the syntax proper as opposed to LF.

2. CL-CHAINS AS OPERATOR BINDEES

Despiste the conclusion arrived at in section 1.2, CLs in CL-D constructions play a role at LF in Weak Crossover and Focus phenomena.

2.1. *Weak Crossover Effects*

The classical English subject/object asymmetry typical of WCO effects (20) is replicated in Spanish (21). WCO occurs when a quantifier moved to A-bar position leaves behind a variable which is in turn coindexed with a pronoun to its left.[11]

(20) a.   Everybody$_2$ likes his$_2$ mother.
           Everybody$_2$ [x$_2$ likes his$_2$ mother]

b.   ??His$_2$ mother likes everybody$_2$.
      Everybody$_2$ [his$_2$ mother likes x$_2$]

(21) a.   Todos$_2$ quieren a su$_2$ madre.

b. ? *Su$_2$ madre quiere a todos$_2$.

It is clear that the contrast between the (a) and the (b) versions above is due to the position of the pronoun with respect to the variable in (20b) and (21b); only in (20a) and (21a) does the variable c-command the pronoun at LF. This situation leads Chomsky (1976) to posit the descriptive statement known as the Leftness Condition (22):

(22)   A variable cannot be an antecedent for a pronoun to its left.

Since then many other hypotheses have been advanced to account for WCO phenomena (Higginbotham 1980a, b; Koopman and Sportiche 1982, 1983; Safir 1984, among others). In what follows, I concentrate on data from Spanish to show that CLs, once more, can save structures of the type in (21b) by circumventing WCO effects. Consider the sentence in (23a) with its LF-representation in (23b); it shows that the mere addition of a CL to (21b) converts it into a perfectly grammatical sentence.

(23) a. Su_2 madre los_2 quiere a $todos_2$.

   'Their mother them likes everybody.'

    b. A $todos_2$ [su_2 madre los_2 quiere x_2]

The disparity between (21b) and (23a) has parallels in other instances of extraction. Examine (24) and (25) which are extractions of WH-elements with DOs and IO CLs, respectively.

(24)   ¿[A cuáles de ellos]$_2$ no *(los^2) aguanta ni su_2 madre e_2?
        Which ones of them not them can stand even their mother?

   'Which one of them can't even their mother stand?'

(25)   ¿[A quiénes]$_2$ no *(les^2) dejó su_2 madre ningún dinero e_2?
        To whom no to-them left their mother any money?

   'To whom didn't their mother leave any money?'

What (24) and (25) suggest is that the presence of the CL makes all the difference between grammaticality and ungrammaticality. Furthermore, the examples in (26) demonstrate that the phenomenon is not peculiar to situations where the pronominal *su(s)* forms part of the subject; it also holds between two arguments of VP.

(26) a.   (Les_2) mostré a [todos mis amigos]$_2$ sus_2 fotos.
        1sg to-them showed all my friends their pictures

(26) b.   ?*(Les$_2$) mostré sus$_2$ fotos a [todos mis amigos]$_2$
           lsg to-them showed their pictures to all my friends

The CL is optional in (26a) where *sus* 'their' is in the structural domain of the variable, but is obligatory in (26b) where *sus* is to the left of the variable (cf. Barss and Lasnik 1986, for English). Notice that the Leftness Condition can account for (24)—(26) but not for (23). The reason is that in the former set the CL, which forms a discontinuous element with the phrase in argument position, is to the left of the pronoun, thus the CL+V complex c-commands *su(s)*. However, in (23) the CL is to the right of the pronoun. This situation in (23) can also be illustrated by sentence (27) which contains an IO CL (instead of a DO one).

(27)   Su$_2$ madre *(les^2) dejó dinero a todos$_2$.

'Their mother to-them left money to everybody.'

In essence, given these examples the Leftness Condition is not observationally adequate.

One way to encompass all of the above data is to assume that the CL+V complex moves to INFL (to merge with the inflectional features of mood, tense and agreement; cf. Chomsky 1986), from where the CL+V c-commands the *su(s)* in subject position.[12] Hence, the generalization for Porteño Spanish could be stated as in (28).

(28)   A variable cannot be an antecedent for a pronoun to its left *unless* the latter is c-commanded by a CL coindexed with the variable.

The problem with (28) is that, just as with the Leftness Condition, it is merely a descriptive statement with little explanatory power. Furthermore, although it can accommodate all the examples dealt with so far, it falls short in contexts in which the CL does not c-command the pronoun as is the case when the relevant elements are in different IPs (29).[13]

(29) a. ¿[A cuáles de ellos]$_2$ dijo su$_2$ madre que no *(los) aguanta e_2?

'Which one of them did their mother say that she can't stand (them)?'

    b. ¿[A quiénes]$_2$ dijo su$_2$ madre que no *(les) dejaría ningún dinero e_2?

'To whom did their mother say that she would not leave any money (to them)?'

Another possibility would be to assume that WCO effects fall out of the Bijection Principle (Koopman and Sportiche 1982, 1983), which requires a one-to-one correspondence between operators and A-bar bound phrases. The Bijection Principle explains the less than perfect status of (20b) and (21b) because the quantifier directly binds both its own trace (the variable) and the pronoun. This principle likewise accounts for the ill-formedness of (24) and (25) without the CL because the WH-phrase behaves in all relevant aspects as an operator. Nevertheless, the Bijection Principle does not establish the necessary distinctions between the ungrammaticality of the sentences without a CL and the grammaticality of those with the CL; that is, it fails to acknowledge the fact that CLs can rescue the ungrammatical sentences.

A more promising alternative is to claim that since the CL and the empty category that appears in the LF-representation form a pro-nominal chain, this chain is what antecedes the *su(s)* and not the variable by itself. Under this conception, the Leftness Condition as well as (28) become irrelevant. Considerations of this kind but from the vantage point of English, are what led Safir (1984) to venture that a single operator can A-bar bind multiple variables provided these variables are of the same type (i.e., either all emply categories or all pronouns). The implication of his Parallelism Constraint on Operator Binding (PCOB) (30) is that WCO examples violate the constraint because the operator binds an empty category and a pronoun (i.e., one non-lexical category and another lexical one).

(30)   PCOB: If O is an operator and **x** is a variable bound by *O*, then for any *y*, *y* a variable bound by *O*, **x** and **y** are [α lexical]

Confirmation that the PCOB provides a viable way of accounting for WCO effects in Spanish emerges from parasitic gap data. Note that since in a parasitic gap construction the CL must obligatorily be absent, the result is that the WH-phrase binds two non-lexical categories (31).

(31) a. ¿A cuál de tus futuros colegas (*lo) invitaste *t* sin conocer *e*?

'Which of your future colleagues CL did you invite without knowing (him)?'

(31) b. ¿A cuántos candidatos (*les) mandarás dinero *t* sin avisar *e*?

'To how many candidates CL will you send money without warning (them)?'

Furthermore, if one devises a context in which the CL must be present, such as extraction from a WH-island (cf. section 1.1), it is possible to test further the adequacy of the PCOB. In (32) the obligatoriness of the CL prevents the appearance of a parasitic gap, with the consequence that the operator binds two lexical categories as predicted by the PCOB.[14]

(32) a. ¿A cuál de tus futuros colegas no sabías quién . . .

Which of your future colleagues didn't you know who . . .

   (i)   *lo* invitó sin conocer*lo*?

       him invited without having-met him?

   (ii) *lo* invitó sin conocer *e*?

  b. ¿A cuántos candidatos no sabías quién . . .

    To how many candidates didn't you know who . . .

   (i)   *les* mandaría dinero sin avisar*les*?

       to-them would send money without warning them?

   (ii) *les* mandaría dinero sin avisar *e*?

Of importance to our discussion of CLs is that the PCOB supplies us with a principled explanation for the peculiar "saving" properties of the CLs in instances of WCO (as well as for their peculiar distribution with parasitic gap type data). By entering into a chain with the empty category, the pronominal character of the chain is what counts for the PCOB. In other words, the operator in all of the CL-D examples binds two variables of the same type: two pronominal categories (i.e., *su(s)* and the CL-chain).

2.2. *Focus*

The examples in (33) show that CLs enter into chains with focussed constituents. Moreover, since the contrastive element (in capitals) is a pronoun, the CLs are obligatory in all dialects of Spanish.

(33) a.   Mara$_2$ quería que la^2 eligieran a ELLA$_2$.

        Mara wanted that they her elected HER

(33) b. Mara$_2$ quería que le^2 dieran el premio a ELLA$_2$.
Mara wanted that they to-her gave the prize to HER

Assuming that focal elements receive their interpretation by means of the rule of Focus which in effect preposes (and identifies) the stressed constituent leaving a variable in its original position (Chomsky 1976 and elsewhere), the LF-representations for (33) are those in (34).

(34) a. for x = she, Mara wanted that they her elected x

b. for x = she, Mara wanted that they to-her give the prize to x

This analysis entails that the rule of Focus Raising is in all respects similar to that of QR, that is, another instance of Move-α operating at LF. Now notice that there arises a potential problem with the representations in (34). These configurations violate Principle C of Binding Theory which maintains that referring expressions (variables and names) must be A-free. This is because in the intended reading the variable in (34) is bound by the matrix subject argument *Mara*. Granting without discussion that B.T. is operative at LF, the Spanish examples are amenable to a solution along the lines of the one resorted to for WCO effects. The CLs in (33) provide the variable left behind by Focus Raising with pronominal features, effectively nullifying Principle C violations. If what counts for the focus operator is the pronominal features of the chain, then the empty category falls under Principle B of B.T. (a pronominal must be A-free in its governing/binding category), and the focused structures in (33) present no problem for the grammar.[15] In short, CLs once more intervene to rescue ill-formed sentences.

3. CONCLUSION

After examining the interaction of CLs in CL-chain with severals processes, once and again we have concluded that the CL forms a pronominal chain with the empty category left behind after syntactic or LF movement. This outcome makes one wonder why the pronominal *ec* cannot be lexical; in other words, what prevents the occurrence of (35) (compare it with (3a)).

(35) *¿A quién le dieron los jueces el premio *a él*?
'To whom did the judges to-him give the prize to him?'

The answer is to be found in Montalbetti's (1984) Overt Pronoun Constraint which essentially specifies that an overt pronoun cannot be locally bound by an operator iff the alternation overt/empty obtains. Since *a él* in (35) is bound by *a quién*, the result is an ungrammatical sentence.[16]

Despite the fact that the CL always licenses a pronominal, it is obvious that the contribution of these morphemes to S-structure phenomena is different from their contribution to LF operations. In the former, the CLs serve to anchor the traces left by syntactic WH-extractions by acting as antecedent governors. That this is not their mission at LF was seen by examining scope interpretations and the rule of QR. However, CLs do interplay with LF processes to save structures which would otherwise be ill-formed. This was shown by examining their role with WCO and focus data. That CLs behave this way should not come as a surprise, given an analysis which considers them to form one part of a discontinuous element with the phrase in argument position as the other part (Borer 1984). In Suñer (1986a), CLs are analized as object agreement morphemes. Given the role that agreement in general plays in determining the content of empty categories, it is no wonder that CLs help identify empty categories either in the syntax proper or at LF.

NOTES

[1] Earlier versions of this paper have benefited from comments and suggestions made by Jim Huang, by the participants in the Cornell Tuesday Colloquium, and by two anonymous reviewers. To all my sincere thanks.

[2] In Porteño some inanimate DOs may also double provided they are plus specific. I disregard this fact because they are irrelevant to the discussion at hand. For a detailed discussion of CL-D and justification of the specificity requirement that DO CL-chains must adhere to, I direct the reader to Suñer (1986a).

[3] That accusative or "personal" *a* — the marker that appears before DOs under certain conditions — is not a sign of specificity in the case of quantified DOs (cf. Bello 1970; Suñer 1986a) is shown by the fact that the DO in (2b), where this *a* is obligatory, is modified by a relative clause in the subjunctive. These clauses serve to indicate non-specific antecedents (Rivero 1977).

[4] I follow the convention of using subscripts to indicate relationships relevant for Binding Theory, and superscripts for irrelevant ones.

[5] For most dialects it appears that V-fronting is obligatory only in the clause in which the WH-phrase appears with lexical content. However, like in the embedded clause of (3b) the V may front optionally when there is no overt WH in the Spec of CP. In a pre-Barriers theoretical framework, S′ being the relevant bounding node for Spanish, the WH-phrase could skip the lower COMP and move directly to the upper one without causing V-attraction.

[6] The CL plus the argument position are superscripted because the chain they form before movement takes place is an instance of agreement, the mirror image of subject-verb agreement (cf. Suñer 1986a, for justification).

[7] Torrego (1984, ftn, 39) remarks "It must be explained why indirect objects may move from within a question whose verb is preposed. It is clear that in Spanish the presence or absence of V in VP does not affect the proper government of an indirect object phrase." It must be kept in mind that in all examples she uses to illustrate this point the IO is CL-D.

[8] To my knowledge, Hurtado (1984) was the first to point out these scope facts and the weak crossover effects discussed in the following section. He offers a very different explanation from the one in this article. My examples are coined after his as a token to his memory.

[9] This last assumption rests on Chomsky's (1986) definition of government in terms of exclusion (**A** governs **B** iff a m-commands **B** and there is no **C**, **C** a barrier for **B**, such that **C** excludes **A**). In May's (1985) treatment only lexical government sanctions (14) as grammatical because he maintains that the adjoined subject QP blocks government between the IP adjoined IO QP and the VP adjoined e_3.

[10] This is the segment-theory of domination. It claims that **A** dominates **B** iff **B** is dominated by every segment of **A**. (It is due to May 1985, and adopted in Chomsky 1986).

[11] To be noted is that the unacceptability of (20b) and (21b) cannot be ascribed to an ECP violation since the traces left behind by QR are properly governed.

[12] See Koopman and Sportiche (1982, 1983, and references therein) for an appraisal of the differences and similarities between the c-command vs. the scope approach to pronominal binding by a quantifier.

[13] I am grateful to a reviewer for bringing the examples in (29) to my attention. Higginbotham's 1980 condition on binding, "If **A** is a quantifier and **B** a pronoun, then **A** can bind **B** only if **A** is coindexed with something **C** that c-commands **B** at S-structure", also runs into problems with (29).

[14] The inverse correlation between DO CL-D and parasitic gaps is also mentioned in Jaeggli 1986. However, his treatment predicts that IOs should be able to license pg's contrary to what actually happens.

[15] Taking into account that the focused element might be a subject (i), it could be argued that the expletive *pro* does what CLs do in (33).

(i)   Mara$_1$ prometió que pro$_1$ ganaría ELLA$_1$.
         Mara promised that pro would-win SHE

However, in (ii) the contrastive subject remains in its basic position, thus there is no obvious pronominal element to void a Principle C violation.

(ii)   Mara$_1$ prometió que ELLA$_1$ ganaría.
         'Mara promised that SHE would-win.'

This situation suggests that the pronominal nature of AGR in INFL (to my knowledge, first suggested in Rizzi 1982) might be strong enough to cancel the violation. If correct, this conclusion provides further support for the hypothesis advanced in Suñer (1986a) that Spanish CLs are instances of agreement morphemes.

[16] Further support for the pronominal status of the *ec* comes from examples like (i) where the existence of the empty bound pronominal serves as a link which sanctions the presence of a coreferent overt pronoun.

(i)   ¿A cuál de ellos lo convencieron e que *él* tenía que matricularse?

            'Which one of them did they convince that he had to register?'

      b. ¿A cuántos les dijeron e que *ellos* podrían reintegrarse al trabajo el lunes?

            'To how many of them did they tell that they could return to work on Monday?'

If the *ec* were a true variable, the overt pronoun could not be interpreted as coreferential with the CL-chain.

REFERENCES

Aoun, J.: 1981, *The Formal Nature of Anaphoric Relations*, MIT doctoral dissertation, Cambridge, MA.

Aoun, J. and Sportiche, D.: 1982, 'On the Formal Theory of Government', *The Linguistic Review* **2**, 211–236.

Barss, A. and Lasnik, H.: 1986, 'A Note on Anaphora and Double Objects'. *L.I.* **17**, 347–354.

Barwise, J. and Cooper, R.: 1981, 'Generalized Quantifiers and Natural Language', *Linguistics and Philosophy* **4**, 159–219.

Bello, A.: 1970, *Gramática de la lengua castellana*, Rev. by R. J. Cuervo and N. Alcalá-Zamora y Torres, Sopena, Buenos Aires.

Borer, H.: 1984, *Parametric Syntax*, Foris, Dordrecht.

Chomsky, N.: 1976, 'Conditions on Rules of Grammar', *Linguistic Analysis* **2**.

Chomsky, N.: 1981, *Lectures on Government and Binding*, Foris, Dordrecht.

Chomsky, N.: 1982, *Some Concepts and Consequences of the Theory of Government and Binding*, MIT Press, Cambridge, MA.

Chomsky, N.: 1986, *Barriers*, MIT Press, Cambridge, MA.

Higginbotham, J.: 1980a, 'Pronouns and Bound Variables', *L.I.* **11**, 679–708.

Higginbotham, J.: 1980b, 'Anaphora and GB: Some Preliminary Remarks', NELS X. *Cahiers Linguistiques d'Ottawa*. Dept. of Linguistics: Univ. of Ottawa.

Higginbotham, J. and May, R.: 1981, 'Questions, Quantifiers and Crossing', *The Linguistic Review* **1**, 41–80.

Hurtado, A: 1984, 'On the Properties of LF' ', *Cornell Working Papers in Linguistics* **5**.

Jaeggli, O.: 1982, *Topics in Romance Syntax*, Foris, Dordrecht.

Jaeggli, O.: 1985, 'On Certain ECP Effects in Spanish', Univ. of Southern California unpublished paper.

Koopman, H. and Sportiche, D.: 1982/83, 'Variables and the Bijection Principle', *The Linguistic Review* **2**, 139–160.

Lasnik, H. and Saito, M.: 1984, 'On the Nature of Proper Government', *L.I.* **15**, 235–289.

May, R.: 1985, *Logical Form: Its Structure and Derivation*, L.I. Monograph 12. MIT Press, Cambridge, MA.

Montalbetti, M.: 1984, *After Binding: On the Interpretation of Pronouns*, MIT doctoral dissertation, Cambridge, MA.

Rivero, M.: 1977, 'Specificity and Existence: A Reply', *Language* **53**, 70—85.

Rizzi, L.: 1982, *Issues in Italian Syntax*, Foris, Dordrecht.

Safir, K.: 1984, 'Multiple Variable Binding', *L.I.* **14**, 603—638.

Suñer, M.: 1986a. 'The Role of Agreement in Clitic-Doubled Constructions', *Natural Language and Linguistic Theory* **6**, 391—434.

Suñer, M.: 1986b, 'On the Structure of the Spanish CP', Cornell Univ., unpublished paper.

Torrego, E.: 1984, 'On Inversion in Spanish and Some of its Effects', *L.I.* **15**, 103—129.

Wahl, A.: 1985, 'Two Types of Locality', Univ. of Maryland, unpublished paper.

Zaenen, A., Engdah, E., and Maling, J.: 1981, 'Resumptive Pronouns Can Be Syntactically Bound', *L.I.* **12**, 679—682.

WAFAA ABDEL-FAHEEM BATRAN WAHBA

LF MOVEMENT IN IRAQI ARABIC

0. INTRODUCTION

Wh-operators in Iraqi Arabic (IA) have the option of appearing in the Comp node or in their base position (*in-situ*). Like English, the wh-operator appears in Comp and the questioned site is marked by a gap:

(1) a. meno$_i$ Mona shaafat e_i?
Who   Mona saw

'Who did Mona see?'

  b. weyya meno$_i$ Mona xarjat e_i?
with   whom Mona left   ?

'With whom did Mona leave?'

Like Turkish (Hankamer 1975), Imbabura Quechua (Cole 1981), and Chinese (Huang 1982), wh-operators may optionally occur in their base position:

(2) a. Mona$_i$ shaafat meno$_i$?
Mona   saw   whom?

  b. Mona xarjat weyya meno?
Mona left   with   whom?

'With whom did Mona leave?'

  c. memo ishtara sheno min ?ajl meno?
who   bought what   for   whom

'Who bought what for whom?'

The fact that the grammar of IA allows wh-movement both in the Syntax and in the LF provides us with the opportunity to contrast the syntax of SS (i.e., Surafce Structure) with the Syntax of LF, as manifested in the same construction, in the same grammar. This paper is divided into two main parts. The first part addresses the question as to

253

what extent the properties of the LF rule and the syntactic rule of wh-movement are the same. The second part investigates some locality restrictions observed by the LF rule *Move wh* in IA. The data examined in the first part provide strong support for the existence of an abstract wh-movement rule in LF and, hence, for the level itself. This rule affords a uniform account for the numerous significant generalizations that hold between the two levels of reperesentations of SS and LF, which might otherwise be describable via a conjunction of unrelated properties. Section 1 deals with some scope as well as distributional properties of wh-in-situ. Section 2 discusses the weak crossover phenomenon which holds of both levels in IA. Section 3 provides empirical evidence that LF Comp to Comp movement exists. As a consequence, the wh-in-situ may surface in any Comp node intervening between its base position and the controlling Comp.

The second part of the paper deals with several locality requirements observed by LF movement in IA. Section 4 analyzes the behaviour of wh-in-situ with respect to some island constraints. Section 4.1 shows that LF movement observes some island conditions that could be subsumed under the *Subjacency* principle. Section 5 discusses another locality requirement on *Move wh* in LF, in which *tense* defines an opaque domain with respect to LF movement. This restriction is observed by both arguments such as *who, whom* and *which*, and adjuncts, such as *where, when* and *why*. Section 6 tackles the role of an overt scope definer of wh-in-situ that could partially nullify the tense locality requirement. Section 7 shows that an analysis along the lines of the *Empty Category Principle (ECP)* cannot account for the above-mentioned tense locality requirement. Section 8 discusses some *Superiority* effects in IA. Section 9 demonstrates that an analysis along the lines of the *Subjacency Principle* can account for both the tense locality requirement and the island violations in LF. As a result, *Subjacency* has to be parameterized at LF in *Universal Grammar* so as to account for such langauge differences with respect to its application as part of the grammar of LF.

1. SCOPE PROPERTIES OF WH-IN-SITU

This section argues in favor of a movement rule in LF to account for the fact that syntactically unmoved wh-operators exhibit properties similar to syntactically moved ones. This abstract rule, which raises the wh-in-situ in LF to a position that c-commands its domain (cf. Aoun *et al.* 1981), also helps to account for scope ambiguities excercised by wh-in-situ in IA.

I assume, following Chomsky (1973), that the Comp node is marked [+wh] to mark its complement as interrogative, and as [−wh] to mark it as indicative. In the light of this assumption, consider the following paradigm where the wh-phrase appears in the complement clause of a verb that subcategorizes only for indicative complements as in (3a), for both [+wh] and [−wh] Comp's as in (3b), and, finally, for [+wh] Comp only as in (3c):

(3) a.   Mona itmannat tishtiri *sheno*?
        Mona hoped   to-buy what?

        'What$_i$ did Mona hope to buy e_i?'

    b.   Mona nasat tishtiri *sheno*?
        Mona forgot to-buy what

        'Mona forgot what$_i$ to buy e_i?'
        'What$_i$ did Mona forget to buy e_i?'

    c.   Mona se?lat Ali Ro?a ishtarat *sheno*?
        Mona asked Ali Ro?a bought   what?

        'Mona asked Ali what$_i$ Ro?a bought e_i?

In (3a), *sheno* may only have wide scope since the lower Comp is marked [−wh]. In (3b), it may have narrow scope resulting, thus, in an indirect question reading, or wide scope over the entire sentence, which, in turn, provides a direct question interpretation. In (3c), *sheno* must have narrow scope since the matrix verb, *se?al* 'to ask', obligatorily takes an interrogative complement. The scope proprties exhibited by the wh-in-situ *sheno* in (3a—c) above mirror those of syntactically moved wh-operators. The paradigm in (4) below illustrates this point with respect to *Move wh* in the Syntax, while the paradigm in (5) shows that the same facts obtain with respect to syntactic wh-movement in English:

(4) a.   [sheno$_i$ [Mona itmannat[e_i[tishtiri e_i]]]]
        what   Mona hoped   to-buy

        'What did Mona hope to buy?'

(4) b.   [Mona nasat [sheno$_i$ [tishtiri e_i]]]
         Mona forgot what   to-buy.

         'Mona forgot what to buy.'

    b'.   [sheno$_i$ [Mona nasat [e_i [tishtiri e_i]]]]?
         what   Mona forgot   to-buy?

         'What did Mona forget to buy?'

    c.   [Mona se?lat Ali [sheno$_i$ [Ro?a ishtarat e_i]]]
         Mona asked Ali what   Ro?a bought.

         'Mona asked Ali what Ro?a bought.'

(5) a.   what did Mona hope to buy e_i?

    b.   John forgot [what$_i$ [to buy e_i]].

    b'.   What$_i$ did John forget to buy e_i?

    c.   John asked Mary [what$_i$ [Tim bought e_i]].

If we assume that wh-in-situ undergoes movement in LF in a way
similar to wh-movement in the syntax, we could capture the fact that
they excercise the same scope properties excercised by syntactically
moved wh-operators as in (4) and their English counterparts in (5).
Positing such an abstract rule of wh-movement in LF accounts also for
the scope ambiguities in (3b) by allowing the wh-phrase to move to
where it can c-command its scope at LF. Hence, (3c) can have two LF
structures as in (6) below:

(6) a.   [sheno$_i$ [Mona nasat [e_i [tishtiri e_i]]]]

    b.   Mona nasat [sheno$_i$ [tishtiri e_i]]

In (6a), *sheno* moves to the matrix Comp, which results in a direct
question reading. An indirect question interpretation is provided in (6b)
via moving *sheno* to the embedded Comp.

2. WH-MOVEMENT AND THE WEAK CROSSOVER

The second argument which strongly supports the existence of an
abstract movement rule at LF has to do with the weak crossover
phenomenon. The general property of this phenomenon is that a
variable cannot be preceded by a coindexed pronoun (Chomsky 1976).

Thus, (7) is excluded on the grounds that *e* is preceded by the coreferential pronoun *his*:

(7)   *Who$_i$ did his$_i$ mother see e_i?

The weak crossover phenomenon has received several treatments in the literature (cf. Chomsky 1976; Koopman and Sportiche 1982; Safir 1984; Reinhart 1983). One way to exclude (7) is to assume that a moved element should not cross a coindexed pronoun in its path to Comp. The weak crossover phenomenon holds in the Syntax as well as the LF components in the grammar of IA. Thus, a syntactically moved wh-phrase cannot cross a coindexed pronoun as in (8a), whereas a wh-in-situ cannot be preceded by a coindexed pronoun in its domain as in (8b):

(8) a.   meno$_i$?uxta-ha$_{*i/j}$ darabat e_i?
            who   sister-her   hit   *e*?

         "*Who did her$_i$ sister hit$_i$?'

    b.   ?uxt-ha$_i$ darabat   meno$_{*i/j}$?
            sister-her   hit   who?

         "*Who$_i$ did her$_i$ sister hit e_i?'

(8a) is ruled out because the moved wh-operator crosses the coindexed pronoun *-ha* resulting, thus, in a crossover violation. In (8b), there is no visual movement, but the sentence is ruled out due to the presence of a coindexed *pronoun* that precedes the wh-in-situ. This predicts that (8b) can receive a reading if the pronoun *her* and the wh-in-situ are disjoint in reference, which is indeed the case. The similarity between (8a) and (8b) can be captured if we make the assumption that *meno* in (8b) undergoes movement in LF in a way that mimics wh-movement in the Syntax. Accordingly, (8b) has the LF structure in (9):

(9)   [meno$_i$ [?uxt-ha$_i$ darbat e_i]]

In (9), we have a crossover violation since *meno*, in its path to Comp, crosses a coindexd pronoun. Thus, (8b) is ruled out on the same grounds as (8a) and (7), the latter involve syntactic wh-movement in IA and English respectively.

3. MOVE ALPHA AND THE SUCCESSIVE CYCLICITY IN
SS AND LF

The grammar of IA provides empirical evidence that *Move Alpha* applies in a successive cyclic mode. This section presents independent evidence that LF Comp-to-Comp movement exists.

In addition to the fact that wh-operators in IA appear in argument (*in-situ*) as well as non-argument (*Comp*) positions, wh-phrases-in-situ have the option of appearing in any intermediate Comp that intervenes between their base position and the controlling Comp. In (10a) below, *meno* appears in base position in the most embedded clause. In (10b), it appears in the next high Comp ($Comp_3$). In (10c) it appears in $Comp_2$. In (10d), it appears in the matrix Comp ($Comp_1$):

(10) a. $[_{COMP_1}$[Mona raadat$[_{COMP_2}$[tijbir   Su'ad$[_{COMP_3}$
            Mona wanted   to-force Su'ad
         [tisa'ad *meno*]]]]]]?
         to-help who?

   b. [Mona raadat [tijbir Su'ad [*meno*$_i$[tisa'ad e_i]]]]]?

   c. [Mona raadat [*meno*$_i$[tijbir S. [e_i [tisa'ad e_i]]]]]]?

   d. [*meno*$_i$ [Mona raadat [e_i [tijbir S. [e_i [tisa'ad e_i]]]]]]]?
       'Who did Mona want to force Su'ad to help?'

The four sentences in (10) share a direct question reading in which *meno* assumes wide scope over the entire sentence regardless its locus at SS. As a result, (10a—d) have a single LF structure, (11) below, where *meno* moves to the matrix Comp, which more or less, looks like (10d) in the Syntax:

(11)   [meno$_i$ [Mona raadat [e_i[tijbir Su'ad [e_i [tisa'ad e_i]]]]]]]

The paradigm in (10) has a number of significant consequences with respect to the rule *Move Alpha* in general and the LF movement rule in particular. The first has to do with the mode of application of Move Alpha, i.e., whether it moves in successive cyclic steps or in a single step from its base position to the controlling Comp. In order to capture the fact that *meno* in (10a—c) above exhibits wide scope over the entire sentence, we may assume that Move Alpha applies in successive steps. Thus, we could account for the fact that *meno* surfaces in the intermediate Comp's excercising wide scope over the entire sentence and *not over the domain it c-commands at SS*.

A second observation based on the paradigm in (10) is that LF movement exhibits identical behaviour to SS movement in that *extraction at LF takes place from argument as well as nonargument positions*. In (10b—c), LF movement obligatorily moves *meno* from Comp$_1$ and Comp$_2$, respectively, to the matrix Comp where it c-commands the entire domain (contra Aoun *et al.* 1981). This also indicates that *a wh-operator at S-structure may occupy a [−wh] Comp node at SS*. Hence, principle (19) in Lasnik and Saito (1984), repeated below as (12), does not hold of the grammar of IA:

(12)   **Comp, if it contains a [+wh] element.*
     [−wh]

Principle (12) holds universally of LF. Lasnik and Saito (L&S) claim that (12) holds in LF for languages that have syntactic movement like English, and vacuously for languages that lack syntactic movement such as Chinese. (12), however, does not hold of the Syntax of IA since wh-operators may optionally appear in [−wh] Comp as SS (cf. 10b—c). Thus, whereas (12) is universal in LF, it has to be parameterized with respect to SS to explain why there are languages that have syntactic movement and still violate the SS contraint in (12). Finally, the paradigm in (10) provides more compelling evidence for the presence of a non-overt wh-movement rule at LF, and hence, for the level itself. This rule, which is assumed to be an instance of Move Alpha, captures striking similarities that hold between *wh-in-Comp* and *wh-in-situ* questions in IA. So far, both constructions are shown to behave the same with respect to: (1) *Scope Properties*, (2) *The weak crossover phenomenon*, (3) *Extraction from argument as well as non argument positions*. In sum, from the data examined above, we may conclude that LF Comp to Comp movement exists.

PART II

This part analyzes several locality restrictions on LF movement in IA. Section 4 discusses the behaviour of wh-in-situ with respect to the island constraints. Section 5 tackles another locality restriction on LF movement in which tense defines an opaque domain with respect to LF movement in IA. Section 6 deals with the role of a syntactic device employed by the grammar of IA to overtly define the scope of wh-in-situ. Section 7 provides an *Empty Category Principle* analysis in an attempt to account for all types of locality restrictions observed by LF movement. Section 8 tackles some Superiority effects that hold in the grammar of IA. Section 9 attempts another alternative in terms of *Subjacency*.

4. LF MOVEMENT AND THE ISLAND CONSTRAINTS

It has been assumed so far that LF movement freely violates the various island conditions subsumed under the Subjacency Principle. As a result, in such languages as Chinese, Turkish, Japanese, English etc., a wh-in-situ can exercise wide scope if it originates inside a syntactic island. In IA, however, both argument and adjunct wh-in-situ phrases are barred from occuring inside a wh-island (13a), a complex NP (13b), and finally a coordinate structure (13c):

(13) a. *Mona nasat   [li-meno$_i$ [tinti sheno e_i]]?
      Mona forgot   to-whom   to-give what

    '*What did Mona forget to whom to give'
    'Mona forgot [for which x, for which y [to give x to y]]'

b. *Mona 'urfit   [il-bint$_i$ [illi [e_i ishtarat   sheno]]]?
   Mona knew   the-girl   who   bought   what

   '*What$_i$ did Mona know the girl who bought e_i?'

c. *Mona gablat Ro?a wi-ishtarat sheno?
   Mona met   Ro?a and-bought what ?

   '*What did Mona meet Ro?a and bought?'

The ungrammaticality of the sentences in (13) presents compelling evidence that LF movement has to be constrained. This goes against the widely held assumption that LF movement is free in the sense that a wh-in-situ may freely occur inside syntactic islands. (cf. Huang 1982, among others). The fact that the syntactic islands are observed by wh-in-situ questions suggests that we treat them the same way we treat violations caused by syntactic movement. In other words, if we assume that the above constructions in (13) are derived via a movement rule that mimics the one we have in the syntax, only then, can we account for the ungrammaticality of the constructions in question. In the next section, another constraint on LF movement is investigated, one in which *tense* plays a crucial role

5. TENSE AND LF EXTRACTION IN IA

In this section, I discuss another locality restriction on LF movement in IA. According to this restriction, *tense* defines an opaque domain with respect to both adjunct and argument wh-in-situs. This tense locality restriction (TLR) can be defined as follows:

(14)   *A wh-phrase-in-situ may not cross more than one tensed clause in its path to Comp.*

The fact that the wh-in-situ may not be separated from its controlling Comp with more than one tensed clause can be seen in the following contrasts:

(15) a. [+wh [Mona$_i$ hawlat [PRO$_i$ *tishtiri* sheno]]]]
          Mona   tried   to-buy   what

         'What did Mona try to buy?'

    b. *[+wh [Mona tsawwarat [−wh [Ali *ishtara* sheno]]]]]?
          Mona thought   Ali bought   what

         'What did Mona think Ali bought?'

(16) a. [+wh [Mona raadat   Ali$_i$ [PRO$_i$ *yruuh* weyn]]]]?
          Mona wanted   Ali   to-go   where

         'Where did Mona want Ali to go?'

    b. *[+wh [Mona tsawwarit [Ali *raah* weyn]]]]?
          Mona thought   Ali went   where

         'Where did Mona think Ali went?'

In examples (15) and (16), the TLR applies equally to both arguments and adjuncts. The (a) sentences are possible grammatical structures because there is a single tensed clause which intervenes between the matrix [+wh] Comp and the wh-in-situ in the embedded clause. The (b) examples are ruled out because there is more than one tensed clause that intervenes between the locus of the wh-in-situ and the matrix

Comp. The TLR holds even if the wh-in-situ optionally moves at SS to the next higher Comp, a possibility permitted by the grammar of IA which allows the surface appearance of wh-in-situ in any intermediate Comp. Consider the case in which *sheno* in (15b) above, for example, moves to the next higher Comp:

(15) c. *[Mona tsawwarit [sheno$_i$ [Ali ishtara e_i]]]

(15c) is ungrammatical despite the fact that there is a single tensed clause which intervenes between the wh-operator and the matrix Comp at SS. This indicates that the TLR looks at the original locus of the wh-in-situ, i.e., its base position, and not at its SS position. Notice that the matrix verb in (15c) does not subcategorize for [+wh] Comp. Consider the case where *tsawwar*, in (15c), is replaced by *'uruf* 'to-know', which allows both [+wh] and [−wh] Comp's. Assuming the TLR, we predict that such a sentence would have a single reading of an indirect question. Such a prediction is born out as (17) below indicates:

(17)   Mona *'urfut* [sheno$_i$ [Ali ishtara e_i]]
         Mona knew what   Ali bought

         'Mona knew what Ali bought.'
         '*What did Mona know that Ali bought?'

sheno in (17) cannot have wide scope since there are two tensed clauses between its base position and the matrix Comp. As a consequence, (17) cannot receive a direct question reading. Contrast, further, (17) with (18), below, where the lower clause is untensed. Our theory predicts that both direct and indirect question readings obtain. This is indeed the case:

(18)   Mona *'urfut* [sheno$_i$ [tinti e_i li-Ali]] ./?
         Mona knew what$_i$ to-give e_i to-Ali./?

         'Mona knew what to give to Ali.'
         'What did Mona know to give to Ali?'

sheno in (18) may have narrow scope, resulting in an indirect question, or wide scope, resulting in a direct question.

To sum up this section, LF movement in IA is constrained by a tense locality requirement, according to which a wh-in-situ cannot cross more than one tensed clause in its path to the controlling [+wh] Comp in LF. This TLR looks at the base position of the wh-in-situ, and not at its SS position, bearing in mind that wh-in-situ in IA may appear in any intermediate Comp at SS.

The question that immediately poses itself is whether the TLR holds of syntactic wh-movement as well. The answer is yes, with one basic difference. At SS, the locality requirement in (20) holds only of adjunct wh-operators such as *leesh* 'why', but not of argument wh-operators such as *meno* 'who' and *sheno* 'what'. The following contrast illustrates the effects of the TLR at SS:

(19)   *[leesh$_i$ [tsawwarit Mona [e$_i$ [Ali   masha e$_i$]]]]
         Why   thought   Mona   Ali   left

       'Why did Mona think Ali left?'

(19)' [sheno$_i$ [tsawwarit Mona [e$_i$ [Ali   ishtara e$_i$]]]]
        what   thought   Mona   Ali   bought

       'What did Mona think Ali bought?'

(19) is ungrammatical because the wh-operator is an adjunct. Thus, it cannot cross more than one tensed clause in its path to the matrix Comp at SS. (19') is grammatical because the wh-operator is an argument. I do not have any explanation as to why the TLR in (14) applies to adjunct wh-operators at SS, while it applies to all wh-operators, both adjuncts and arguments, at LF. There is, however, a tentative universal that adjuncts observe stricter locality requirements than their argument counterparts. This has been shown to be the case with respect to several languages (cf. Huang 1982). Before seeking an analysis that could help to account for the TLR and the island conditions as restrictions on LF movement in IA, I will, in the following section, consider a syntactic device employed by the grammar of IA to overtly define the scope of other wh-in-situ's. One of the immediate effects of this device, which we shall call a question particle (QP), is that it partially overcomes some effects of the TLR. The following section discusses ther syntactic properties of the QP with respect to LF movement in IA.

6. THE QP AND LF MOVEMENT IN IA

In this section, I discuss a syntactic device used by the grammar of IA to define the scope of wh-in-situ. This syntactic device takes the form of the word *sheno* 'what' when preceding the subject, or the contracted form *sh-* when preceding the verb.

6.1. SYNTACTIC FACTS

The QP as a wh-operator has the following characteristics: (a) The QP occurs always at the beginning of the sentence; (b) it does not co-occur with other wh-in-situ's in the matrix clause; (c) it cannot occur in embedded Comp nodes, i.e., it is barred from occurring in embedded clauses; (d) it is optional when the TLR is satisfied and obligatory when the TLR is not observed. The following examples help to illustrate the above facts:

(20) a. sh-tsawwarit Mona [Ali raah weyn]?
          QP-thought Mona Ali went where?

   'Where did Mona think Ali went?'

   b. sh-tsawwarit Mona [weyn$_i$ [Ali raah e_i]]
       QP-thought Mona where Ali went

   'Where did Mona think Ali went?'

(21) a. (sh-)raadat   Mona Ali ygaabal meno?
          (QP)wanted Mona Ali to-meet whom?

   'Whom did Mona want Ali to meet?'

   b. (sh-)raadat   Mona [meno$_i$ [Ali ygabal e_i]]
       (QP)wanted Mona whom Ali to-meet

   'Whom did Mona want Ali to meet?'

In (20a), *weyn* is separated from the matrix Comp by two tensed clauses. Hence, the presence of the QP is obligatory to define the scope of the wh-in-situ *weyn* 'where'. In (20b), the presence of the QP is obligatory, despite the presence of *weyn* in the intermediate Comp, i.e., it is separated from the matrix Comp by a single tensed clause. This, further corroborates our claim that the TLR looks at the base position of the wh-in-situ in question and not at its SS locus. The pair in (21), on the other hand, demonstrate the optionality of the QP when the TLR is satisfied. As a result, *meno* may appear in-situ, (21a), or in the lower Comp, (21b), assuming wide scope over the entire sentence. To account for the role played by the QP with respect to wh-in-situ questions, the following assumption is made:

(22)   *The QP occurs in the matrix Comp and marks it as [+wh].*

The assumption in (22) enables us to account for the scope properties excercised by the QP with respect to other wh-operators. Accordingly, (20a, b) have a single LF structure in which *weyn* obligatorily moves to the matrix Comp:

(20) c.   [QP weyn$_i$ [Mona tsawwarit [e$_i$ [Ali raah e$_i$]]]]

I further assume *The wh-criterion*, a well-formedness condition at LF (May 1985):

(23)   *The wh-criterion*:
         a. *Every [+wh] Comp must contain a wh-operator.*
         b. *Every wh-operator must occur in Comp.*

The assumption made in (22) coupled with the wh-criterion in (23) can account for the scope characteristics of the QP in IA. Consider the following paradigm where the matrix verb takes [−wh] Comp in (24a), allows [+/−wh] Comp in (24b), and permits only a [+wh] Comp in (24c):

(24) a.   sh-tsawwarit Mona [−*wh* [Ali gabal meno]]
                            [meno$_i$ [Ali gabal e$_i$]]
          QP-thought Mona [−*wh* [Ali met who]]
                            [who$_i$ [Ali met e$_i$]]

     'Who did Mona think Ali met?'

     b.   sh-'urfut Mona [−/+*wh* [Ali gabal meno]]
                            [meno$_i$ [Ali gabal e$_i$]]
          QP-knew Mona [−/+*wh* [Ali met who]]
                            [who$_i$ [Ali met e$_i$]]

     'Who did Mona know that Ali met?'
     '*Mona knew who Ali met.'

(24) c. *sh-se?lat   Mǫna   [+*wh*   [Ali gabal meno]]
                            [meno$_i$ [Ali gabal e$_i$]]
        QP-asked Mona   [+*wh* [Ali met who]]
                            [who$_i$ [Ali met e$_i$]]

   '*Who did Mona ask Ali met?'
   '*Mona asked who Ali met?'

The sentence in (24a) causes no problems since the lower Comp can only be marked [−wh]. Hence, *meno* may only exercise wide scope. In (24b), *meno* must move to the matrix Comp in LF. If *meno* chooses to land in the lower Comp, a possibility allowed by the fact that the verb *'uruf* 'to know', may allow both [+wh] and [−wh] Comp's, we will be left with an unfilled [+wh] Comp in LF, namely, the matrix one. This, in turn, results in a violation of the wh-criterion in (23) above. Therefore, an indirect question reading is not possible. Sentence (24c) receives no interpretation at all. It has either structure in (25) below where the matrix and embedded Comp's are marked [+wh], the first by virtue of the presence of the QP, and the second due to the matrix verb *se?al*, 'to ask', which obligatorily subcategorizes for [+wh] Comp:

(25) a. [+*wh* [[*meno$_i$* [e$_i$]]]]
     b. [*meno$_i$* [[e$_i$ +*wh* [e$_i$]]]]

LF movement in (25a, b) results in an unfilled [+wh] Comp, violating, thus, the *wh-criterion* which universally holds of LF movement. The paradigm in (24) indicates that the QP must have a wh-operator *in its domain*. Hence, (24b) has a single reading of an indirect question, despite the fact that the verb *'uruf* allows interrogative complements.

   We need to pause here and consider the phrase *in its domain*. By this, I mean a single tensed clause. In other words, a *tensed clause* constitutes a single *domain* with respect to LF movement. Suppose, now, we have more than one wh-in-situ in more than one domain. A question that could be raised here would be: Will the QP be able to nullify the TLR effects in both domains? The answer is *no*. The QP may only define the scope of the wh-operator(s) in the *domain* closest to it. The following contrast confirms this:

(26) a. sh-tsawwarit Mona [meno rada   [Ali ysa'ad
         QP-thought Mona who   wanted Ali to-help
         meno]]?
         who

         'Who$_i$ did Mona think Ali wanted e_i to help who?'
         'For which x, for which y, M. thought x wanted A. to help
         y)

    b. *sh-i'tiqdit   Mona [meno tsawwar [Ali sa'ad
       QP-believed Mona who   thought Ali helped
       meno]]?
       who

       'Who$_i$ did Mona believe e_i thought Ali helped who?'

In (26a), we have two tense domains, the matrix clause, and the rest of
the sentence which includes another tensed verb. The two wh-in-situ
occur within the same tense domain, that of the middle clause and its
untensed complement. Hence, the QP can define the scope of any
number of wh-in-situ's that occur in the same *tense* domain. (26b), on
the other hand, has two wh-in-situ's that occur in different tensed
clauses, i.e., in two *domains*. To account for the inability of QP to
define the scope of wh-in-situ's in different tense domains as in (26b)
above, we are driven to make the assumption that the QP defines the
scope of the wh-in-situ that occurs in the closest domain to its right,
and that other wh-in-situs in farther tense domains have to make it on
their own with respect to LF movement. As a result, (26b) is ruled out
because the most embedded wh-in-situ will be crossing more than one
tensed clause in its path to the matrix Comp, hence, violating the TLR.
The wh-in-situ in the middle clause raises no problems since it is
'rescued' by the QP.

To sum up, this section discusses one restriction on the QP as a
scope definer with respect to LF movement, namely, that it may only
define the scope of any number of wh-in-situs in the domain closest to
it. It cannot define the scope of wh-in-situs that exist in different
domains.

Another restriction on the QP as a scope definer prohibits it from
co-occurring with another wh-operator in the matrix clause, whether
the latter is in-situ or in Comp. In the light of this restriction, consider

the following contrast, which involves the TLR and scope properties
with respect to both SS and LF movements:

(27) a. *meno tsawwar [Ali xaraj weyya meno]
       who   thought Ali   left   with   whom?

      'For which x, for which y, x thought Ali left with y'

    b. [sheno$_i$[ishtara Ali e_i [minshaan [yenti li-meno]]]]
       what   bought Ali   in-order-to give to-whom

      'What did Ali buy to give to whom?'

In (27a), we have a wh-operator in the matrix Comp and a wh-in-situ in
the embedded tensed clause. Questions like (27a) are possible in
English since LF movement is free. The QP cannot be used with
respect to (27a) since it cannot cooccur with other wh-operators in the
matrix clause. Thus, (27a) is ruled out because the lower wh-in-situ
crosses more than one tense domain in its path to the matrix Comp in
LF, violating, thus, the TLR. (27b), on the other hand, is grammatical
since the LF movement of the wh-in-sistu, *meno*, in the embedded
tensed clause crosses a single domain in accordance with the TLR.

To recaptulate so far, we have seen two restrictions on the QP with
respect to LF movement:

1. *It cannot define the scope of wh-in-situs in different tense daomains.*

2. *It cannot nullify the TLR effects when syntactic movement is involved, i.e., where the QP cannot occur.*

Another very significant restriction on the QP with respect to LF
movement is that it cannot define the scope of wh-in-situs inside
syntactic islands, whether or not the TLR is satisfied, as manifested by
the following paradigm:

(28) a. *[sh   [-nasat Mona [li-meno$_i$ [tinti   sheno e_i]]]]?
       QP   forgot   Mona   to-whom   to-give what

      '*What did Mona forget to whom to give?'

    b. *[sh[-'urfut Mona [il-bint$_i$ [illi[e_i ishtarat sheno]]]]]]
      QP knew Mona   the-girl   who   bought   what

      '*What did Mona know the girl who bought?'

(28) c. *[sh [ishtarat Mona li-ktaab] [wi-nasat sheno]]
      QP bought Mona the-book and-forgot what

'*What did Mona buy the-book and forgot?'

The sentences in (28a—c) show that the QP cannot define the scope of a wh-in-situ when it occurs inside a wh-island (28a), a Complex NP (28b), and a coordinate structure (28c).

In sum, the QP, as a scope definer, may nullify some of the effects of the TLR. It, however, remains ineffective when island violations occur, i.e., it cannot define the scope of wh-in-situs inside syntactic islands.

The question to be posed now is how to account for the various restrictions on LF movement in IA. So far, LF movement is constrained by:

   a. *The Tense Locality Requirement (TLR)*
   b. *Subjacency*

These two restrictions apply equally to arguments and adjuncts. In the following section, I try to account for the above-mentioned restrictions in terms of an *Empty Category Principle* (ECP) analysis.

7. AN ECP ANALYSIS

This section attempts to examine the first locality restriction, i.e, the TLR, in terms of an ECP analysis in which empty categories are required to be properly governed, either lexically, or via antecedent-government. The basic difference between the indicative and subjunctive clauses in the paradigms discused above with respect to the TLR is that the former are tensed. Hence, one might say that *tense*, which, in this case, defines an opaque domain with respect to LF extraction, is an operator that moves to its Comp (Stowell 1981). According to this hypothesis, (29a), for example, has its corresponding LF structure in (29b):

(29) a. *Mona tsawwarit Ali masha leesh?
         Mona thought   Ali left   why?

      'Why did Mona think Ali left?'

   b. $[leesh_i [[e_i \, T \, [e_i]]]]$

The operator T in the lower Comp node in (29b) stands for tense. An

ECP analysis would require the *e* of an adjunct to be properly governed by a coindexed antecedent (cf. Huang 1982; Lasnik and Saito 1984). Hence, the embedded *e* in (29b) must be properly bound, i.e., c-commanded by its antecedent in the embedded Comp. This cannot obtain, however, due to the presence of the tense operator (T), a situation which results in a branching Comp. As a result, The ECP rules out (29b) since the embedded *e* is not antecedent-governed. The ECP analysis, however, cannot be extended to LF where the TLR applies to all operators, both adjuncts and arguments. Consider (30a) below where the argument *sheno* is separated from its controlling Comp with two tensed clauses. (30a) has the LF structure (30b) after the application of LF movement:

(30) a. *Mona tsawwarit Ali ishtara sheno?
       Mona thought   Ali bought what?

   '*What did Mona think Ali bought?'

   b. [sheno$_i$ [Mona tsawwarit [e_i T [Ali ishtara e_i]]]]

The embedded *e* does not violate the ECP since it is lexically governed by the preceding verb *ishtara*. Thus, an ECP analysis cannot be extended to account for all TLR violations in LF in IA. It only accounts for the behaviour of adjuncts which are required to be antecedent-governed. It fails, however, to account for the behaviour of arguments, which, in turn, satisfies the ECP since lexical government holds. One could extend a recently modified version of the ECP as developed by Lasnik and Saito (1984) in which a distinction is made between antecedent-government and government where maximal projections are barriers to the latter. In fact, their reformulation of antecedent-government looks rather similar to Subjacency. Antecedent-government, along these terms, is defined as in (31):

(31)   A antecedent-governs B iff
        a. *A and B are coindexed*
        b. *A c-commands B*
        c. *There is no y (y an NP or S) such that A c-commands y
           and y dominates B, unless B is the head of y*
                                              (1984:248 (55))

In L&S, the ECP applies to intermediate Comp's for adjunct traces. It does not apply to argument traces because lexical government holds.

As a consequence, adjuncts observe island conditions in LF, while arguments do not. The ECP as stated in (31) straightforwardly accounts for this distinction between arguments and adjuncts in LF. In IA, on the other hand, both the TLR and the island conditions apply equally to both adjuncts and arguments. Let us assume, for a moment, that (31) can be extended to the LF of IA to account for the two restrictions mentioned above. In such a case, we have to make the ad hoc and, as I show below, completely untenable assumption that lexical government does not hold in the LF of IA, and that all variables which result from LF movement must abide by (31). This restriction as ad hoc as it seems, accounts for the two restrictions observed by LF movement in IA. An immediate problem not accounted for by this assumption, however, is that lexical government is needed at the LF level of representation in IA because the *Superiority condition* (Chomsky 1976) holds in IA as will be demonstrated in the following section.

8. SUPERIORITY CONDITIONS IN IA

This section examines a further restriction on LF movement in IA that can be manifested in the following paradigm:

(32) a. Mona natat sheno li-meno?
      Mona gave what to-whom?

      'Mona gave what to whom?'

   b. $sheno_i$ Mona natat e_i li-meno?
      what Mona gave e to-whom?

      'What did Mona give to whom?'

   c. $li\text{-}meno_i$ Mona natat sheno e_i?
      to-whom Mona gave what?

      'To whom did Mona give what?'

(33) a. meno nata sheno li-meno?
      who gave what to-whom?

      'Who gave what to whom?'

   b. *$sheno_i$ meno nata e_i li-Mona?
      what who gave to-Mona?

      '*What who gave to Mona?'

(33) c. sheno$_i$ nata meno e_i li-Mona?
      what gave who   to-Mona?

'*What who gave to Mona?'

To account for the contrast between (32) and (33) above, we are driven to assume that lexical government obtains in IA as far as LF is concerned. If we assume the *Comp Indexing rule* (Aoun *et al.* 1981), according to which the [+wh] Comp acquires the index of its syntactically moved wh-operator at SS, (32a—c) do not violate the ECP since the *e's* that result from LF movement will be lexically governed (32a), for example, has (34) as its LF structure:

(34)   [sheno$_i$ meno$_j$ [Mona natat e_i li-$_j$]]

In (34), both *e*'s are lexically governed by the verb and the preposition respectively. Consider, now, (33b) which has the structure (35a) after the application of the *Comp Indexing rule*, and the LF structure in (35b):

(35) a.   [sheno$_i$ [meno nata e_i li-Mona]] Comp$_i$

     b.   [sheno$_i$ meno$_j$ [e_j nata e_i li-Mona]] Comp$_i$

(35b) is ruled out because the subject trace *e* is not antecedent-governed by the Comp node since the latter has a different index, namely, that of *sheno*. As a result, (35b) violates the ECP. Consider, now, (33c) where the subject wh-in-situ *meno* obligatorily undergoes subject/verb inversion. (33c) has the LF structure in (36):

(36)   [sheno$_i$ meno$_j$ [nata e_j e_i li-Mona]]

In (36), *meno* is extracted from a post verbal position, i.e., a position that is lexically governed. Hence, (33c) satisfies the ECP where the *e's* are lexically governed, and as a consequence, the sentence is grammatical.

To summarize, this section tackles another restriction on LF movement in IA, namely, the *Superiority Condition*. The behaviour of multiple wh-questions in (32) and (33) above provide independent evidence that lexical government is needed in the grammar of LF in IA to account for the contrast between (33a) and (33b). In addition, the recent modification of the ECP, as posited by Lasnik and Saito (1984), cannot provide a unified account for the several restrictions discussed above on LF movement in IA. In the next section, I propose a Subjacency analysis which I show to be able to provide an explanation for the various locality restrictions observed by LF movement in IA.

9. A SUBJACENCY ANALYSIS

To account for the fact that LF movement observes the island conditions as well as the *Tense Locality Requirement*, I claim that Subjacency holds as a well-formedness condition at LF in IA. To account for the TLR in terms of a *Subjacency* analysis, I assume that *tense* is a feature of both S and S' nodes, which, in addition, act as bounding nodes in the grammar of IA. The correlation between S and S' or rather Comp and its complement can be seen in the fact that certain complementizers are used with tensed clauses, such as *that* in English, while others can be used in untensed clauses such as *for* in English. Similar facts hold in Classical Arabic as well, where *?ann:* 'to' occurs with subjunctive complements, and *?anna:* 'that' which occurs only with indicatives.

Assuming that *tense* is a feature on S and S', (37) below will have the LF structure in (38) (the relevant bounding nodes are underlined):

(37) *Mona tsawwarit Ali ishtara sheno?
      Mona thought   Ali bought what?

      'What did Mona think Ali bought?'

(38) $[_{S'_1}$ sheno$_i$ $[_{S_1}$ ... $[_{S'_2}$ e_i $[_{S_2}$ ... $e_i]]]]$
         $+T$ $+T$ $+T$ $+T$

On the lower cycle, *sheno* crosses one bounding node, S_2. On the upper cycle, however, it crosses two bounding nodes, S'_2 and S_1. Thus, (37) violates Subjacency. Contrast (37) with (39) where the wh-in-situ is separated from the controlling Comp with one tensed clause:

(39) Mona radat   Ali yishtri sheno?
      Mona wanted Ali to-buy what?

      'What did Mona want Ali to buy?'

Example (39) has the LF structure in (40):

(40) $[_{S'_1}$ sheno$_i$ $[_{S_1}$ ... $[_{S'_2}$ e_i $[_{S_2}$ ... $e_i]]]]$
         $+T$ $+T$ $-T$ $-T$

The structure in (40) does not violate Subjacency since *sheno* crosses one bounding node only on the upper cycle, S_1. Subjacency also accounts for the fact that LF movement is constrained by the various island conditions.

To conclude this section, I assume that Subjacency holds as a well-formedness condition at LF in the grammar of IA. It accounts for the behaviour of wh-in-situ's with respect to the TLR and the island constraints, which apply equally to arguments as well as adjuncts. Also, it has been clearly shown that the ECP is independently needed in the grammar of IA to account for a further restriction on LF movement, namely, the Superiority Condition (Chomsky 1973).

10. CONCLUSION

In this paper, I have investigated some aspects of the Synatx of LF in IA as expounded by the behaviour of wh-in-situ questions. What is particularly interesting about this dialect of colloquial Arabic is that it possesses two strategies that are interchangeably used by its speakers to form wh-questions: the *wh-in-situ* strategy, in which the wh-operator remains in its base position, and the *movement* strategy in which the wh-operator is preposed to an initial position leaving behind a gap that marks the questioned site. In fact, IA is the second language investigated in the literature that exhibits and employs both strategies in an equal manner. The first language of this type is Imbabura Quechua (Hermon 1984). It is the first, however, to manifest that LF movement is constrained by several locality requirements. The various languages examined so far with respect to their LF syntax have clearly demonstrated that movement at the LF linguistic level of representation observes no constraints whatsoever. This has been the case with Chinese, Turkish, Japanese, etc.

The data examined in the first part (sections 1—3) provide strong evidence that LF movement in IA shares several characteristics with syntactic wh-movement. Both rules exhibit the same scope properties. Both observe the weak crossover phenomenon. Section (3) provides independent evidence that Comp-to-Comp movement exists. This, in turn, has two implications with respect to LF movement. First, LF movement can extract out of Comp position, i.e., it affects both argument and non-argument positions. Second, a wh-in-situ may surface in any Comp node that intervenes between its deep structure position and the Controlling Comp. As a consequence, a wh-operator may appear in a [−wh] Comp at SS in IA. Based on this fact, Universal (178) in Lasnik and Saito (1984, 285) is no longer a Universal. According to this Universal, a language that has SS movement cannot have a [+wh] Comp that is not headed by a wh-element. In IA, a wh-element may optionally appear in [−wh] Comp as SS assuming wide scope over the entire sentence. Hence, principle (178) has to be parameterized to account for the differences among languages in this respect.

The second part (sections 4—9) investigates several locality restrictions oberved by LF movement in IA. These include the TLR, the island conditions, and the Superiority Condition. To account for the first two, which both apply equally to adjunct as well as argument wh-operators, I claim that a new parameter is needed at LF to account for the presence of Subjacency as a well-formedness condition at the linguistic level of representations of LF in such languages as IA as opposed to its absence in other languages such as English and Ancash Quechua.

REFERENCES

Aoun, J., Hornstein, N., and Sportiche, D.: 1981, 'Some Aspects of Wide Scope Quantification', *Journal of Linguistic Research* **1**, 69—95.
Chomsky, N.: 1973, 'Conditions on Transformations', in: S. Anderson and P. Kiparsky (eds.), *A Festschrift for Morris Halle*, Holt, Rinehart and Winston, New York.
Chomsky, N.: 1976, 'Conditions on Rules of Grammar', *Linguistics Analysis* **2**, 303—351.
Chomsky, N.: 1981, *Lectures on Government and Binding*, Foris Publications, Dordrecht.
Cole, P.: 1982, 'Subjacency and Successive Cyclicity: Evidence from Ancash Quechua', *Journal of Linguistic Research* **2**, 35—38.
Hankamer, J.: 1975, 'On Wh Indexing', in: E. Kaisse and J. Hankamer (eds.), *Papers from the Fifth Annual Meeting of the North Eastern Linguistics Society*, Harvard University, Cambridge, MA.
Hermon, G.: 1984, *Syntactic Modularity*, Foris Publications, Dordrecht.
Huang, C.-T. J.: 1982, *Logical Relations in Chinese and the Theory of Grammar*, Doctoral dissertation, MIT, Cambridge, MA.
Koopman, H. and Sportiche, D.: 1982, 'Variables and the Bijection Principle', *The Linguistic Review* **2**, 139—161.
Lasnik, H. and Saito, M.: 1984, 'On the Nature of Proper Government', *Linguistics Inquiry* **15**, 235—289.

May, R.: 1985, *Logical Form: Its Structure and Derivation*, MIT Press, Cambridge, MA.

Reinhart, T.: 1983, *Anaphora and Semantic Interpretation*, Croon Helm, London.

Safir, K.: 1984, 'Multiple Variable Binding', *Linguistic Inquiry* **15**, 603—638.

Stowell, T.: 1981, *Origins of Phrase Structure*, Doctoral dissertation, MIT, Cambridge, MA.

LIST OF CONTRIBUTORS

Yoseph Aoun
University of Southern California

Adnrew Barss
University of Arizona

Robin Clark
Universite Geneve

Kenneth Hale
Massachusetts Institute of Technology

Norbert Hornstein
University of Maryland

C.-T. James Huang
University of California at Irvine and
Cornell University

Osvaldo Jaeggli
University of Southern California

Katalin É. Kiss
Hungarian Academy of Sciences

Giuseppe Longobardi
Universita di Vernezia

Robert May
University of California at Irvine

Taisuke Nishigauchi
Osaka University

Ellavina Tsosie Perkins
Ganado, Arizona

Margaret Speas
University of Massachusetts at Amherst

Margarita Suñer
Cornell University

Wafaa Abdel-Faheem Batran Wahba
King Abdul Aziz University

277

INDEX

Studies in Linguistics and Philosophy

1. H. Hiż (ed.): *Questions*. 1978   ISBN 90-277-0813-4; Pb: 90-277-1035-X
2. W. S. Cooper: *Foundations of Logico-Linguistics*. A Unified Theory of Information, Language, and Logic. 1978
   ISBN 90-277-0864-9; Pb: 90-277-0876-2
3. A. Margalit (ed.): *Meaning and Use*. 1979   ISBN 90-277-0888-6
4. F. Guenthner and S.J. Schmidt (eds.): *Formal Semantics and Pragmatics for Natural Languages*. 1979   ISBN 90-277-0778-2; Pb: 90-277-0930-0
5. E. Saarinen (ed.): *Game-Theoretical Semantics*. Essays on Semantics by Hintikka, Carlson, Peacocke, Rantala, and Saarinen. 1979   ISBN 90-277-0918-1
6. F.J. Pelletier (ed.): *Mass Terms: Some Philosophical Problems*. 1979
   ISBN 90-277-0931-9
7. D. R. Dowty: *Word Meaning and Montague Grammar*. The Semantics of Verbs and Times in Generative Semantics and in Montague's PTQ. 1979
   ISBN 90-277-1008-2; Pb: 90-277-1009-0
8. A. F. Freed: *The Semantics of English Aspectual Complementation*. 1979
   ISBN 90-277-1010-4; Pb: 90-277-1011-2
9. J. McCloskey: *Transformational Syntax and Model Theoretic Semantics*. A Case Study in Modern Irish. 1979   ISBN 90-277-1025-2; Pb: 90-277-1026-0
10. J. R. Searle, F. Kiefer and M. Bierwisch (eds.): *Speech Act Theory and Pragmatics*. 1980   ISBN 90-277-1043-0; Pb: 90-277-1045-7
11. D. R. Dowty, R. E. Wall and S. Peters: *Introduction to Montague Semantics*. 1981; 5th printing 1987   ISBN 90-277-1141-0; Pb: 90-277-1142-9
12. F. Heny (ed.): *Ambiguities in Intensional Contexts*. 1981
    ISBN 90-277-1167-4; Pb: 90-277-1168-2
13. W. Klein and W. Levelt (eds.): *Crossing the Boundaries in Linguistics*. Studies Presented to Manfred Bierwisch. 1981   ISBN 90-277-1259-X
14. Z. S. Harris: *Papers on Syntax*. Edited by H. Hiż. 1981
    ISBN 90-277-1266-0; Pb: 90-277-1267-0
15. P. Jacobson and G. K. Pullum (eds.): *The Nature of Syntactic Representation*. 1982   ISBN 90-277-1289-1; Pb: 90-277-1290-5
16. S. Peters and E. Saarinen (eds.): *Processes, Beliefs, and Questions*. Essays on Formal Semantics of Natural Language and Natural Language Processing. 1982
    ISBN 90-277-1314-6
17. L. Carlson: *Dialogue Games*. An Approach to Discourse Analysis. 1983; 2nd printing 1985   ISBN 90-277-1455-X; Pb: 90-277-1951-9
18. L. Vaina and J. Hintikka (eds.): *Cognitive Constraints on Communication*. Representation and Processes. 1984; 2nd printing 1985
    ISBN 90-277-1456-8; Pb: 90-277-1949-7

Volumes 1–26 formerly published under the Series Title: Synthese Language Library.

Studies in Linguistics and Philosophy

19. F. Heny and B. Richards (eds.): *Linguistic Categories: Auxiliaries and Related Puzzles*. Volume I: Categories. 1983   ISBN 90-277-1478-9
20. F. Heny and B. Richards (eds.): *Linguistic Categories: Auxiliaries and Related Puzzles*. Volume II: The Scope, Order, and Distribution of English Auxiliary Verbs. 1983
      ISBN 90-277-1479-7
21. R. Cooper: *Quantification and Syntactic Theory*. 1983   ISBN 90-277-1484-3
22. J. Hintikka (in collaboration with J. Kulas): *The Game of Language*. Studies in Game-Theoretical Semantics and Its Applications. 1983; 2nd printing 1985
      ISBN 90-277-1687-0; Pb: 90-277-1950-0
23. E. L. Keenan and L. M. Faltz: *Boolean Semantics for Natural Language*. 1985
      ISBN 90-277-1768-0; Pb: 90-277-1842-3
24. V. Raskin: *Semantic Mechanisms of Humor*. 1985
      ISBN 90-277-1821-0; Pb: 90-277-1891-1
25. G. T. Stump: *The Semantic Variability of Absolute Constructions*. 1985
      ISBN 90-277-1895-4; Pb: 90-277-1896-2
26. J. Hintikka and J. Kulas: *Anaphora and Definite Descriptions*. Two Applications of Game-Theoretical Semantics. 1985
      ISBN 90-277-2055-X; Pb: 90-277-2056-8
27. E. Engdahl: *Constituent Questions*. The Syntax and Semantics of Questions with Special Reference to Swedish. 1986   ISBN 90-277-1954-3; Pb: 90-277-1955-1
28. M. J. Cresswell: *Adverbial Modification*. Interval Semantics and Its Rivals. 1985
      ISBN 90-277-2059-2; Pb: 90-277-2060-6
29. J. van Benthem: *Essays in Logical Semantics* 1986
      ISBN 90-277-2091-6; Pb: 90-277-2092-4
30. B. H. Partee, A. ter Meulen and R. E. Wall: *Mathematical Methods in Linguistics*. 1990
      ISBN 90-277-2244-7; Pb: 90-277-2245-5
31. P. Gärdenfors (ed.): *Generalized Quantifiers*. Linguistic and Logical Approaches. 1987   ISBN 1-55608-017-4
32. R. T. Oehrle, E. Bach and D. Wheeler (eds.): *Categorial Grammars and Natural Language Structures*. 1988   ISBN 1-55608-030-1; Pb: 1-55608-031-X
33. W. J. Savitch, E. Bach, W. Marsh and G. Safran-Naveh (eds.): *The Formal Complexity of Natural Language*. 1987 ISBN 1-55608-046-8; Pb: 1-55608-047-6
34. J. E. Fenstad, P.-K. Halvorsen, T. Langholm and J. van Benthem: *Situations, Language and Logic*. 1987   ISBN 1-55608-048-4; Pb: 1-55608-049-2
35. U. Reyle and C. Rohrer (eds.): *Natural Language Parsing and Linguistic Theories*. 1988   ISBN 1-55608-055-7; Pb: 1-55608-056-5
36. M. J. Cresswell: *Semantical Essays*. Possible Worlds and Their Rivals. 1988
      ISBN 1-55608-061-1

Studies in Linguistics and Philosophy

Further information about our publications on *Linguistics* are available on request.
Kluwer Academic Publishers – Dordrecht / Boston / London